To Make the
Earth Whole

To Make the Earth Whole

The Art of Citizen Diplomacy in an Age of Religious Militancy

Marc Gopin

ROWMAN & LITTLEFIELD PUBLISHERS, INC.
Lanham • *Boulder* • *New York* • *Toronto* • *Plymouth, UK*

ROWMAN & LITTLEFIELD PUBLISHERS, INC.

Published in the United States of America
by Rowman & Littlefield Publishers, Inc.
A wholly owned subsidiary of The Rowman & Littlefield Publishing Group, Inc.
4501 Forbes Boulevard, Suite 200, Lanham, Maryland 20706
www.rowmanlittlefield.com

Estover Road
Plymouth PL6 7PY
United Kingdom

Copyright © 2009 Marc Gopin

British Library Cataloguing in Publication Information Available

Library of Congress Cataloging-in-Publication Data

Gopin, Marc.
  To make the earth whole : the art of citizen diplomacy in an age of religious
militancy / Marc Gopin.
      p. cm.
  Includes bibliographical references (p. 233) and index.
   ISBN 978-0-7425-5862-5 (cloth : alk. paper) — ISBN 978-0-7425-5863-2 (pbk. :
alk. paper) — ISBN 978-0-7425-6631-6 (electronic)
   1. Violence—Religious aspects. 2. Conflict management—Religious aspects. 3.
Interpersonal relations—Religious aspects. 4. Religion and international affairs. 5.
Conflict management—Syria—Case studies. 6. Interpersonal relations—Syria—Case
studies. 7. Religion and international affairs—Case studies. I. Title.
   BL65.V55G68 2009
      201'.72—dc22   2008055475

Printed in the United States of America

 ∞™ The paper used in this publication meets the minimum requirements of
American National Standard for Information Sciences—Permanence of Paper
for Printed Library Materials, ANSI/NISO Z39.48-1992.

For my five-year-old, my son, my only son, whom I have loved,

Isaac

Mischievous smile of sunlight
Eyes that mirror mine,
Is it me or is it him?
Am I five or fifty?
I cannot know.
Endless trains, cars, airplanes,
Anything that travels.
Life begins with Thomas.
Joy, fascination, endless inquiry,
A face of happy wonder.
My tiny train traveler
Who watches me travel the world,
Always loving and always loved,
Always hugging and always hugged,
Luminescent in love, affection, and connection.
Live forever my son,
Live only passionately
As lover
And as beloved.
And please allow me
To be a loving memory
As you advance to an old age
As joyful as your youth.

May 8, 2008

Table of Contents

Section IV: Conclusions about Our Future

Acknowledgments

I want to thank my family, first and foremost Robyn, as well as Ruthie, Lexi, and Isaac, for respecting my passion for writing, and giving me so much space to pursue this most difficult, time-consuming, and exhilarating work of citizen diplomacy. I know that my many trips overseas can feel nerve-wracking and I am deeply grateful for their patience and forbearance.

I want to thank Samuel Rizk, my graduate research assistant at the Institute for Conflict Analysis and Resolution (ICAR). Sam is an important pioneer himself of Middle Eastern interfaith work who helped me enormously with proper documentation of this book, as well as helping to straighten out repetitive sections. He was a pleasure to work with at every moment, and I treasure his friendship. I also want to thank Scott Cooper, also at ICAR, for volunteering to help at my center in ways that allowed me to persist in my writing and in the work overseas on which the writing is based.

I want to thank all of my colleagues at ICAR for an interesting ride as we all try to navigate the fantastic growth of our program. They are such an impressive group of accomplished intellectuals and teachers that I am privileged to join them. I want to thank especially Kevin Avruch and Richard Rubenstein for helping me with much advice on many levels. I want to thank Joe Montville for continuing to support me and believe in me through thick and thin. I am privileged to continue to be a part of his wonderful projects.

I want to thank David Cobin of Hamline University Law School, whose program in Jerusalem I have taught at in the last few years. His support for me in bringing me to Jerusalem enabled me to quietly travel more affordably to Syria for all the trips that form the basis of this book's research. His faith in me and patience with me was so helpful in my diplomacy work. In that regard I need to mention also Haynes Mahoney of the U.S. Foreign Service who was so helpful to my work. In addition, I have benefited from the counsel of Ambassador Daniel Kurtzer, as well as Ambassador Jacques de Watteville of Switzerland. Ambassador Abdul Wahab Belouki of Morocco has been such an excellent friend and supporter in Damascus. Former Minister of Information Muhdi Dakhlala was critical to our first major event and my first trip to Syria. I am forever grateful to him. I am grateful to Former U.S. Ambassador to Syria Margaret Scobie. I also acknowledge Steve Seche, DCM in the American Embassy in Syria, for his wisdom and hospitality. In Syria I must make special mention of Nizar Mayhoub whose dedication to positive social change and the future of Syria has made him a wonderful partner. I must also mention Samer Kabawat, Nousha Kabawat, John Kabawat, Jessica Radin, and Abu Ali, all of whom made me feel so welcome and safe in Syria. Mention should also be made of course of the Grand Mufti of Syria, Sheikh Hassoun, as well as Sheikh Shehadeh, Hind Obeiden, and Lina Sinjab, all of whom have been an inspiration in their dedication to peace and justice and such good friends in my home away from home. I am so grateful for their sincere friendship and partnership. I want to thank Sami Moubayed for being such a wonderful debating partner on major issues. Above all, I must acknowledge the friendship and guidance of Ambassador Imad Moustapha whose intelligence and depth, whose sincere vision of enlightenment and peace, has been an inspiration. He embodies the best future of Syria.

My sister Reissah Leigh has been a constant force of optimism and encouragement, extremely dedicated to my welfare and to my mission in life. Her ex-husband Jack Lewis, who passed away recently, joined her in encouraging me over twenty-five years ago to persist in a visionary, and risky, approach to life in which I would feel that my writing belonged to the world, that I had to see my work as one of commitment to all of humanity. That vision has formed the underlying theme of all of my books, but especially this one. I thank both of them for encouraging a lost, budding writer to persist.

My mother continues at a ripe age to persist in supporting and encouraging my family, and periodically joining in the process of raising and educating the children. Her compliments of and pride in my work, despite political differences, is a model of generous tolerance.

Robert Eisen has become the backbone of my life, my counselor, my best friend, my intellectual and activist partner. He is the foundation of my reason when my mind possesses none. I would not have rediscovered my capacity to be productive were it not for his counsel in extricating me from so many problems. Success is wonderful, except it brings so many complications and dangers, and thus true friends become essential to survival. A man could have no better friend.

Then, of course, there is the inspiration for the entire book, Hind Kabawat, my Syrian partner. Her native genius as a peacemaker is the foundation of all my intellectual curiosity in this book, and the basis for why I have tried to pioneer a new way of positive social change. We collaborate, we protect each other, we encourage each other, we plan on the spot, and then we stop planning when it is not safe. We fight like crazy, and then we forgive in an instant. What a ride! I am so deeply grateful for her friendship, for her being a role model of how to persist in life and how to mature, despite all of my desire to never mature and to remain twenty. She is a social genius, and she embodies the future of a liberated Middle East that will come before long.

I never know which will be my last book, or when my time on this earth will be over. Therefore I want to make a double dedication of this book to Robyn and Isaac. I have dedicated books to all my children; it is Isaac's turn, but I want to acknowledge with this book, whose subject revolves so much around partnership, the incredible partnership between Robyn and our children. She has homeschooled them for years as she makes her way toward a brilliant career as an educator. Her partnership with each one of them is a marvel to watch, and in particular I want to acknowledge here her partnership with Isaac. I am deeply grateful for her talent and life dedication to these amazing children of ours. Robyn is an incredible woman and I love her.

Introduction

Hard-bitten political realists[1] question the political utility of conciliatory gestures, or moments of forgiveness, apology, and moral transformation. Such moments cannot have significant impact on the complex chain of events that lead toward or away from international wars, they will say. I would agree that it is never the case that one moment in isolation determines the world's fate in terms of war or peace.

Realists must admit, however, that one can also say this accurately about the endless moments of high-level negotiation. Yet realists never would consequently cancel such moments of negotiations with their endless and seemingly pointless twists and turns. They would add up all those "insignificant" moments of negotiation and build them into a crescendo of consequence.

I have many friends around the world who do the same thing, only they build a crescendo of change based on moments of reconciliation.[2] One such moment happened to me when I was as far away from my origins as I could possibly imagine. I am Jewish and from very conservative origins, and I am American with Eastern European grandparents. My background, in other words, is nowhere near the Arab Middle East. And yet, I found myself face to face one day in 2006 with three thousand poor Muslim worshippers in the "enemy" country of Syria in an ancient city known as Aleppo, as an honored guest of the Grand Mufti of Syria. But that is not all. Half the worshippers were refugees from Iraq, where my country had bombed their country, and their homes, and their lives, to pieces. They were among over four million Iraqi refugees as of 2006. As if that were not enough, the man I was introduced to and to whom I apologized was a survivor of American homegrown torture, having lived in a coffin, literally, for a month, in a certain place called Abu Ghraib.

I was shaken to the core, terrified, unsure of myself, and yet it was one of the most profound, spiritual moments of my life when I held his arm. Little did I know that it would also make front-page news in Syria, but it did. That moment and many others led me down a path of subsequent events in Damascus, Washington, and Jerusalem that created some significant ripples in the enemy system in operation between the United States, Israel, and Syria. Our initial work, confronted by strong resistance and skepticism from all sides, eventually gave birth to more and more fellow travelers both inside and outside several governments.

The Syria work is ongoing and has resulted in an unfolding series of events and relationships that have made war between Syria and the United States harder, despite one of the most extreme ideological periods of American foreign policy that ended on January 20, 2009, and despite some intentions at the highest levels of Washington to provoke such a war. This same period has also led to official peace conversations between Israel and Syria that are more realistic than at any time in almost a decade.

It is not so much that my partners and I changed the minds of the leadership in Syria, Israel, or the United States. But we set in motion a constellation of relationships, cultural gestures, and communications that made it clear to everyone but the most extreme on all sides that there was realistic room for a new set of nonviolent alternatives to war—including alternatives to the ongoing proxy wars in Lebanon and Palestine.

What I was doing in the mosque, and what I have been doing for twenty-five years, is best known as "citizen diplomacy." This is a specialized form of "conflict resolution" and "peacebuilding" that I believe is critical to the transformation of the world today, and essential to the planet's eventual transformation into a global community.[3] We have utilized a network of relationships across enemy lines to build the earliest foundations of cooperation and communication where there is little or no constructive contact between enemies. Based on my own ongoing practice and experience and that of my colleagues that has been documented elsewhere,[4] I will argue that the increments of positive change that are embodied in such moments of citizen diplomacy constitute critical building blocks of creating global community; a kind of social contract, even across enemy lines, that will be the basis eventually of a more cooperative world order.

This book takes previous investigations further and explores what it takes to create friendship across the barriers of enemies, when war, religion, civilization, and great powers are set up and designed to prevent that very friendship. It is in essence an investigation of how to create the foundations of a social contract across the most difficult barriers that divide human civilizations. We can demonstrate that this is done in individual circumstances, such as in Syria, but my hope in this book is also to stimulate further exploration as to how to move this shattering of the boundaries between enemies to ever-increasing levels of influence and impact on a global scale.

To investigate this very complex phenomenon we must combine narrative and analysis, story and reflection, practice and theory building. I will do this by introducing a set of theoretical principles and then investigating in-depth one very long experiment in social change based on work that I have been doing with partners in Syria from 2004 until the present time.

BACKGROUND ON SYRIA

Let me then first offer some background on Syria. The last French troops left Syria in 1946, several years after the formal end of the French Mandate in 1941.[5] In contemporary academic literature, Syria figures as a country that has come over time to provide some stability in the Middle East. Stability in terms of Syria's regional role has also indicated a certain internal political and ideological stagnation that has, to say the least, stymied political participation and hampered democracy. Ideological stability has certainly been a highlight of the Syrian political organization. Syria is staunchly Ba'athist and therefore secular, even if it is also home to one of the earliest Islamic dynasties, the Umayyads.

The establishment of stability really takes shape with Hafez Al-Asad's coup d'état in 1970 that ended a series of bloody challenges of power.[6] It was nearly a decade earlier, in 1958, that an ideologically inspired political twinning took place with Egypt, which was called the United Arab Republic. It failed, in part due to Nasser's attempts at "clipping Syrian Ba'athist power" in the new political arrangement.[7]

There is a certain ideological pragmatism in Syrian politics that is crucial to understand in terms of the challenges currently of war and peace. This pragmatism seems to explain the cooperative relations of a secular state, ruled by a staunchly secular party, with (a) militant Palestinian Islamic factions such as Hamas and Islamic Jihad (the leaders of which it hosts in Damascus), (b) Hezbollah, the Shi'ite anti-Israeli resistance movement in Lebanon, and (c) Iran.

The Ba'ath ("renaissance," in Arabic) party, founded in 1947 by a Christian (Michel Aflaq) and a Sunni (Salah al-Din Bitar), brought together what may have been an early indication of some of the contradictions in the Syrian body politic. It was inspired by Euro-nationalism, as well as fascism and Leninism, but at the same time it was contextualized within the budding Arab Nationalist movement, as well as the Umayyad and Abbasid dynasties from centuries ago. Aflaq and Bitar created what would be the ideological background for contemporary Syrian history for decades to come.[8]

Syria's contemporary relations to its neighbors, other than the neighboring Iraqi Ba'ath state and party, started to take shape in the 1960s as part and parcel of the Arab–Israeli conflict. Wars with Israel included the loss of the Golan in 1967 and the relative success of 1973 (which did not reinstate the Golan, however) as well as the continued proxy war with Israel, mainly through Lebanon in recent years. In 1976, one year after the eruption of the Lebanese civil war and presumably upon the invitation of Lebanese Christian factions (and the tacit agreement of the regional and international community), Syria entered Lebanon and effectively took control of the country.

The proxy wars on Lebanese soil between Israel and the Palestinians, the Arab states, and Iran (but also between Sunni, Shi'a, and Christian, as well as between Syrian and Saudi interests), have led to the suffocation of what could have been considered the single most democratic, even if terribly divided, country in the Arab Middle East.[9] The Syrian presence, or occupation, as the Lebanese began calling it, came to an abrupt end in May 2005 following the assassination of the former Lebanese Prime Minister Rafik Hariri. It is also during these years that the relationship between Syria and Israel has seen some progress toward a peace agreement, especially following the 1991 Madrid conference and the sometimes secret, sometimes open peace talks, even all the way to 2008 when indirect peace talks were mediated by Turkey.

Another factor of Syria's relationship to its neighbors relates to the American occupation of Iraq, which directly impacts the larger question of Syria's relationship to Iran and to the West. The Iraqi occupation certainly placed Syria on a greater collision course with the United States, although we will see later that it was Syria that studiously avoided conflict with the United States during the Bush years, not the other way around. From Syria being named by the Bush administration as a member of the infamous "Axis of Evil" alongside Iran and North Korea,[10] to what seemed to be a newly found rapprochement between Sunni (and Alawi) Syria and Shi'ite Iran, Syria found itself at odds with the direction of other Arab states. It saw itself as a last bastion of pan-Arab nationalism that was standing up to regional bullying by the United States.[11]

Having joined the coalition against Iraq during the first Gulf War and having participated in the Madrid conference as payoff for their war effort, Syria thought it could improve its stagnated relations with a belligerent United States since 9/11 and the accession of Bush to the presidency. It was at the start of the Iraq war that Syria believed its absorption of refugees from Iraq and the sharing of intelligence with the United States would lift its name from the "Axis of Evil" and relieve it from the political isolation it has felt by the West.[12] This did not happen and was a bitter disappointment to those in Syria who wanted a warmer relationship between Syria and the West, and who had put their reputations on the line to push for it. By contrast, Syria's relations have been warming with other Western countries such as Germany, but in the United States it continues to be subject to the ebb and flow of U.S. domestic political conditions that gave rise to a strong neoconservative bias against Syria.[13] It was in this context that my work between Syria, the United States, and Israel took place.

Much scholarship and writing about Syria has focused directly on Hafez al-Asad, as well as his son Bashar, who succeeded him as president in 2000 following the father's death. Much of the literature on Hafez al-Asad focused on his position as a long-lasting strongman of Syria, having been in power for nearly thirty years,[14] as well as his role in making his country central to the geopolitical changes in Middle East politics.[15] Another set of writings focuses on the transition of power from father to son, as the age limit for the presidency was amended to accommodate Bashar at thirty-four years of age. Scholars also look at the first years following Bashar's taking over as president. Some have had hopes for and expectations of reform by a young president against the old guard, but also observed a continuity of business as usual of a security state accompanied by cautious, very slow change.[16] Much of contemporary developments in Syria are captured by individual analysis of authors writing in internet-based journalism, among other media, which has been helpful in sidestepping tight controls of media in the country.[17]

STRUCTURE OF THE BOOK AND ITS RELATIONSHIP TO SYRIA

This book's central case study is the work of citizen diplomacy and peacebuilding in Syria, but I frame the case study with a set of chapters before and after the Syrian case study that provides the intellectual contexts and foundations for citizen diplomacy as a practice and a form of intervention that can be extended to many parts of the world. Chapter 1 begins the book with an overview of the state of religion, conflict, and peace. I define several fields of study, including "religion and conflict," "religion and conflict resolution," and "religious peacebuilding." In chapter 2, I explore the evolving phenomenon of religious militancy on a global scale, and I argue for short-term engagement with religious conservatives, even extremists, the world over. But I combine this with a long-term strategy of building a global social contract based upon a safe and open public space that will be inclusive of both secular and religious visionaries. In chapter 3, I explore new approaches to peacemaking, and in particular citizen diplomacy. To understand the phenomenon of religion and citizen diplomacy as a specialized form of religion and conflict resolution, I explore the virtues of social network theory. As a way of addressing the ongoing challenge of evaluation of this kind of social change work, I also introduce a new theory of "positive increments of change" as a very different way to view evaluation of both practitioners and their supporters.

None of this theory matters if there is not a working methodology for putting these values and visions into practice. There is no greater challenge to building global community than harsh political environments in which war and conflict are either at or near the surface, and where there are global forces arrayed *against* coexistence and peace. One example of such an environment is the borderlines of the Israeli–Syrian–American relationship.

That is why chapters 4 and 5, which make up the central section of the book, present an in-depth case study of experimentation in Syria with the theories set forth in the first part of the book. In my experience it is practice that creates theory, and my practice in Syria, combined with what I had learned previously and what I have learned from partners, colleagues, and students, led to the building of the theories that I present in this book.

The case study in chapters 4 and 5 gives rise to a crucial set of questions around the ethics of intervention, and what an optimal intervention in conflict is. In chapters 6 and 7 the ethics of intervention are analyzed from the point of view of both secular and religious ethical traditions, as well as from Eastern and Western perspectives. This is necessary if the interventions of citizen diplomats are to constitute an authentic search for global community, not just the mere imposition of one region's or civilization's values upon others. Progress in creating global community can only come with practice, theory building, and a respect for the wisdom and traditions of the world's cultures. Conclusions are discussed in chapter 8.

NOTES

1. See Hans Morgenthau's six principles, for example, at mtholyoke.edu/acad/intrel/morg6.htm.

2. More on this will come in chapter 2 of this book, but the list would consist of a group of actors who represent widely different forms of intervention and peace-building. They include, as examples, John Paul Lederach, William Ury, Yehezkel Landau, Eliyahu Mclean and Ghassan al-Khatib of Israel/Palestine, David Smock, Mohammed Abunimer, Hind Kabawat of Syria, Daniel Lubetzky of Mexico, Neamatollah Nojumi of Afghanistan, Prince Hassan of Jordan, Prince Ghazi of Jordan, Grand Mufti Ahmed Hassoun of Syria, and Friar Ivo Markovic of Bosnia. Morgenthau, referred to above, who is known for his principles of rational investigation into the true laws of nature that govern society and politics, should have realized that it is irrational to ignore the nonrational elements of collective motivation. Interests are surely the central governing motivators of national behavior, but the desire for revenge or for apology are every bit as real in the motivations of individuals and also nations.

3. I will define these terms in the next chapter.

4. See, for example, R. Scott Appleby, *The Ambivalence of the Sacred: Religion, Violence, and Reconciliation* (Lanham, MD: Rowman & Littlefield Publishers, 2000); Douglas Johnston and Cynthia Sampson, eds., *Religion, the Missing Dimension of Statecraft* (New York: Oxford University Press, 1995); Douglas Johnston, ed., *Faith-Based Diplomacy, Trumping Realpolitik* (New York: Oxford University Press, 2003); Marc Gopin, *Between Eden and Armageddon: The Future of World Religions, Violence, and Peacemaking* (New York: Oxford University Press, 2000); Marc Gopin, *Holy War, Holy Peace* (New York: Oxford University Press: 2002).

5. For a clear and updated timeline of contemporary Syrian history, see news. bbc.co.uk/2/hi/middle_east/country_profiles/827580.stm.

6. See David S. Sorenson, *An Introduction to the Modern Middle East: History, Religion, Political Economy, Politics* (Boulder, CO: Westview, 2008), 276–80.

7. Sorenson, *An Introduction to the Modern Middle East*, 279.

8. See Sorenson, *An Introduction to the Modern Middle East*, 278–79, as well as Yahya Sadowski, "The Evolution of Political Identity in Syria," in *Identity and Politics in the Middle East*, ed. Shibley Telhami and Michael Barnett (Ithaca: Cornell University Press, 2002); Youssef Chaitani, *Post-Colonial Syria and Lebanon: The Decline of Arab Nationalism and the Rise of the State* (New York: Palgrave McMillan, 2007); Raymond A. Hinnebusch, *Party and Peasant in Syria: Rural Politics and Social Change Under the Ba'ath* (Cairo: American University Press, 1979); Raymond A. Hinnebusch, *Authoritarian Power and State Formation in Ba'thist Syria: Army, Party, and Peasant* (Boulder: Westview Press, 1990); and Raymond A. Hinnebusch, *Syria: Revolution From Above* (New York: Routledge, 2001).

9. See Chaitani, *Post-Colonial Syria and Lebanon*, as well as other literature on the Lebanese civil war and Syria's involvement, including Robert Fisk's epic *Pity the Nation: The Abduction of Lebanon* (New York: Maxwell Macmillan International, 1990). For a more partisan view on the Syrian presence in Lebanon, see Marius Deeb, *Syria's Terrorist War on Lebanon and the Peace Process* (New York: Palgrave Macmillan, 2003); and Dilip Hiro, *Lebanon, Fire and Ambers: A History of the Lebanese Civil War* (New York: St. Martin's Press, 1993).

10. Bruce Cummings, Ervand Abrahamian, and Moshe Ma'oz, *Inventing the Axis of Evil: The Truth About North Korea, Iran, and Syria* (New York: New Press, 2004).

11. Robert G. Rabil, *Embattled Neighbors: Syria, Israel and Lebanon* (Boulder, CO: Lynne Rienner Publishers, 2003); Jubin M. Goodarzi, *Syria and Iran, Diplomatic Alliance and Power Politics in the Middle East* (New York: Tauris Academic Studies, 2006).

12. Ribert G. Rabil, *Syria, the United States, and the War on Terror in the Middle East* (Westport, CT: Praeger Security International, 2006).

13. Noam Chomsky, Gilbert Ashcar, and Stephan Shalom, *Perilous Power: The Middle East and U.S. Foreign Policy* (Boulder, CO: Paradigm Publishers, 2007); Mona Yacoubian and Scott Lasensky, *Dealing with Damascus: Seeking Greater Return on U.S.–Syria Relations* (New York: Council of Foreign Relations No 33, 2008).

14. See Eyal Ziser, *Asad's Legacy: Syria in Transition* (New York: New York University Press, 2001); on political conditions vis-à-vis globalization pressures, see Eyal Ziser and Paul Rivlin, *Syria: Domestic Political Stress and Globalization* (Tel Aviv: Moshe Dayan Center for Middle East and African Studies, 1999).

15. See, for example, Patrick Seale, *Asad of Syria: The Struggle for the Middle East* (Berkeley: University of California Press, 1989).

16. See David Lesch, *The New Lion of Damascus: Bashar Al-Asad and Modern Syria* (New Haven: Yale University Press, 2005); and Flynt L. Everett, *Inheriting Syria: Bashar's Trial by Fire* (Washington, DC: Brookings Institution Press, 2005); and Eyal Ziser, *Commanding Syria: Bashar Al-Asad and the First Years of Power* (London: Tauris, 2007).

17. See, for example, Josh Landis's *Syria Comment* at joshualandis.com and Sami Moubayed's *Mid East Views* at mideastviews.com.

Section I

FOUNDATIONS OF A GLOBAL COMMUNITY THROUGH CITIZEN DIPLOMACY

1

The State of Religion, Conflict, and Peace: Strategic Foundations for Building Community in a Militant Time

In this chapter I will explore the state of the field of religion and conflict resolution, present some working definitions, and suggest some new approaches involving citizen diplomacy and social networking. This and the following chapter on networks will then set the stage for an in-depth case study of my work with partners in Syria from 2005 through 2009.

It will then emerge from the four-year case study that without ethical reflection, the work of conflict resolution and building peace cannot be effective, especially in environments of war and oppression. Ethically reflective work also makes it more possible for interventions to steadily weave a more global community. This is accomplished through citizen diplomats, social networks, nongovernmental organizations (NGOs), and governments, and it requires constant adjustment based on experience, reflection, and—what Hind Kabawat always emphasizes—the centrality of flexibility.[1] Extrapolating from the Syria case study I will therefore address in the final chapters of the book the importance of ethics and reflection for the future of citizen diplomacy and an emerging global social contract.

OUTLINING THE STATE OF THE FIELD

I begin this chapter with several assumptions:

The religions of the world are inherently dynamic in their expression, both in the present and in the past. No matter how much there appear to be boundaries of authority and legitimacy, the fact is that religions have always been subject to a radical level of influence by historical context and the extraordinary variety of opinions and behaviors among the faithful.

In addition there exists a profound level of influence that religions and cultures have on each other. This interreligious influence is constantly changing throughout history, based in part on:

a. imperial conquests
b. trade routes
c. cultural revolutions in one place that affect other places
d. the adversarial and competitive relationship of religious communities that stimulates common but competing themes, stories, and philosophical ideas

This is as true for Abrahamic faiths as it is for Indian and Asian religions, all of which have interpenetrated at various points, but especially today in the era of unprecedented globalization.[2]

This represents an opportunity for peace in that if religious moderates and peacemakers are given a free voice, they can compete with each other across religions by demonstrating that their religion is most suited to global communal values, such as, for example, health care or environmental care. This kind of "competition in goodness"—to cite a common Muslim phrase from the Quran[3]—stimulated Western Christianity and Judaism in the nineteenth century to spearhead interpretations of their traditions that were more democratic, more humane, and more universal.[4] The same can be done today across the globe if three conditions pertain: (1) there begins to emerge an attractive concept of global community, (2) religious moderates become increasingly free to advocate for a commitment to global community, and (3) these moderates are welcomed into a global conversation by secular thinkers and political leaders.

The meeting point of religion and conflict resolution[5] or peacebuilding is just as often through key heroes or exemplars of religion and conflict resolution as it is through major organizations such as United Religions Initiative, Parliament of World Religions, or countless other interfaith and multifaith organizations.[6] The strength of organizations is in their capacity to gather many representatives from different faiths in mostly peaceful circumstances, with some gathering citizens and others gathering high clerics. In situations of destructive conflict and extreme separation of enemies, however, positive change is more often pioneered by key individuals of courage, what social network theory refers to as "connectors"[7] who are good at linking an infinite number of people, and "boundary spanners,"[8] or people who have the courage to move beyond their immediate closed network and reach out to others. The classic peacemakers combine qualities of both these types.[9] They pass over boundaries where many representative bodies of organized religions do not have the flexibility to venture.

There are a multitude of global exemplars, people who engage in or support religion and conflict resolution, each with their own style and contribution.[10] These extraordinary people comprise among them radically different approaches to religion and peacebuilding, from very conservative orientations to very liberal. Some have been government officials and even military leaders. Others are spiritual teachers of a new way of coexistence and nonviolence for humanity, and others are conflict resolution practitioners with a base in one religious tradition. Here is a small sample of the variety of people who I have worked with over the past twenty years: very progressive spiritual activists for peace who do not affiliate with any conservative tradition; conservative peacemakers operating within violent environments trying to influence autocratic regimes at the highest levels; influentials with the wealthy and famous stimulating them to invest in religion and conflict resolution; clerics taking unprecedented risks in violent war zones; actors in multilateral agencies trying to convince countries and major donors to buy into a global agenda of interfaith cooperation; members of leading elite religious families who search for new ways that regimes can guide religion away from violence or the use of religion by the state for violence; youth activists working with those who are most at risk for violent recruitment; and fundamentalists who believe strictly in nonviolence and peacebuilding even as they proselytize for conversion.

Some of these exemplars are completely committed to a roughly separate relationship of religion and state, whereas others earnestly believe in the advantages of religious states and societies as leading to the most peace and justice. In this way the latter group shares the short-term goals of this author but not the long-term ones in terms of a global social contract where religion has no coercive power.

As we explore later the ethical and strategic dilemmas arising from our main case study I will take up the issue of cooperation across ideological lines for religion and conflict resolution. In religion and conflict resolution we have often been confronted with long-term visions of the various parties that are at odds with each other, not only in competing religious messianic visions, but also in competing visions of religion's power over human lives in the modern world.

But all the exemplars that I have worked with are united by their investments in networks of deep relationships. Their work is suggestive therefore of a new method of effective conflict resolution that moves far beyond the impact of isolated workshops and conferences. As mentioned earlier, their networks create and maintain relationships between enemy groups where none would exist otherwise. This implies new ways to examine success and failure in the management and resolution of human conflict, as well as a deeper understanding of the course and direction of conflict and reconciliation processes. It is possible that examining the number of people who hear about, talk about, or are in some way networked to those involved in peacebuilding may be a better foundation of evaluation and quantification of the effects of conflict resolution efforts than examining those who participate directly in formal dialogue or negotiations.

An examination of the quantity of people affected by networks of relationships may yield interesting results about what is actually transpiring between enemy groups in their perception of each other.[11] We may be able to evaluate the time it takes between exposure of a critical mass of a group to new ways of relating to an enemy and a group's willingness, cognitively and emotionally, to entertain a vision of coexistence. We need to understand better what kind of relationships lead to profound changes in political attitudes, and how many people it takes to move a large group in a new direction. This research has yet to be done.

The research will depend in part upon evaluating the importance of tipping points in the relationship between adversarial groups.[12] As an example, we need a complete reevaluation of what led finally to the tipping point in South Africa or Northern Ireland, away from the perpetual state of conflict and toward a decline in active oppression or violence.[13] We know for certain that as time went on more and more thousands of people had been exposed, directly or indirectly, to relationships with enemy others, attempts at reconciliation, dialogue, and gestures of respect. We know that more and more people at both highly influential levels and popular levels were directly or indirectly linked in some way to enemy others in ways that were positive or constructive. What we do not know yet is whether there is some constant, a predictor of when exactly there are a sufficient number of connections quantitatively that can lead to a qualitative transformation in enemy relationships at the group level, and therefore a fundamental change in the political and military situation.

There are so many variables at work in violent conflict situations, especially international ones, such as the active role of outside funders and spoilers, the personalities of individual leaders, their flaws and positive qualities, the state of the economic condition of the various classes of each group, and the power asymmetries of conflicting groups that can change over time. For this reason no one has dared suggest a precise form of prediction on these matters. But it is clear that future work on this issue should examine, at least as an important variable, the tipping points of various conflicts in terms of how many people had been exposed positively to the enemy other before that tipping point occurred.

We need, more importantly, to understand the quality of that exposure.[14] We know that some dialogue leads to a transformation of relationship and attitudes and some does not.[15] But we also know that dialogue has been of limited value in changing large groups of people. It is capital intensive, affects only a few people, tends to be elitist, and is often unsatisfactory to the less powerful party.

What may be more consequential to the future of a world of six billion people is how to network in a positive way very large amounts of people over time. How many people need some sort of positive surprise regarding new possibilities, before political leaders begin to emerge who espouse a peace process, for example? Can religious or cultural gestures and unusual relationships have sufficient impact on large numbers who hear about this, or see it in various media, so that a new political space is made for negotiations and compromise? These and many other questions about networks of relationships and the critical mass necessary for peace remain unanswered.

What has become clear to me, based on observed experience in the last twenty years, is that religious exemplars have a wide effect on critical social networks that are involved in conflict, far beyond their numbers. The way they engage others is filled with symbolic significance that resonates emotionally with many people. This needs to be studied more, and we will examine important instances of this in the coming chapters. It is in the nature of an exemplar's identity that his or her public acts appeal to a very broad spectrum of religious people who would otherwise be unmoved by elite peace processes.

Religious peacemakers are often seen as symbols in and of themselves of a new way of being in the world, of being in between worlds as bridge builders. They are symbols of identity-based politics (a frequent culprit in today's conflicts) and yet they are simultaneously symbols of coexistence. This new way of being is directly competitive with the exemplars of religious violence, chauvinism, and exclusivity. It is often the latter that most people hear about in that they create the boundaries of a clear if benighted and irredentist identity. Their violence also attracts great media attention, and they are also very clever in providing social services.

But when the religious peacemakers are given the chance, when the public can see their work, they put the lie to a violent definition of religion, and they make it more difficult for ethno-nationalists to claim exclusive control over identity. Religious peacemakers create an alternative and challenging paradigm of identity. As we will see in the next chapter, these peacemakers give comfort and hope for a peaceful future to religious traditionalists who have no other role models for peaceful interaction with the world. For reasons of trauma, poverty, or both, most religious people may have no trust in their enemies *nor* in their secular political and national leaders.

It is for this reason that the religious peace exemplars have an impact far beyond their numbers, especially when what they do becomes known through the media or word of mouth in global religious networks. In other words, religious groups talk to each other constantly in their intensive communal places of worship and celebration, and that means that just one peace exemplar who has crossed enemy boundaries—and remained faithful to the group—often has an electric impact.

What one must conclude after observing the worlds created by these exemplars is paradoxical. On the one hand, pursuing conflict resolution with
members of organized religions has some serious drawbacks. The biggest
one is that religious communities have a particularly difficult time with
honest dialogue due to traditional, unquestioned dogma and myths about
the world. These myths are often predicated upon themes of chosenness.
Perceptions of chosenness and victimhood are a perennial problem in all
group conflict,[16] but they are especially acute between religions because so
many religions build identity precisely on narratives of victimhood, saintli-
ness of the elect, and chosenness. Positive, honest dialogue that produces
practical results is therefore somewhat rare. There are exceptions, such as
the work between the Jewish community and the Catholic Church in the
post-Holocaust era. Even here I would look for the role of exceptional individuals who developed the personal and spiritual determination to cross
over boundaries. I doubt, for example, that the Catholic–Jewish processes
of reconciliation would have proceeded so well under Pope Pius XII rather
than John XXIII or John Paul II. The latter two seemed driven to pursue a
transformed relationship to other faiths, especially to Judaism.[17] Individuals have a far greater impact on breakthroughs in group relationships than
is generally recognized.

To cite another example of networks and contagious ideas, the idea of
rituals to honor girls in the Jewish "public space," the synagogue, such as
with the Bat Mitsvah, is unprecedented in Jewish history. It began with a
radical Jewish thinker, Mordechai Kaplan, founder of Reconstructionist
Judaism, at the beginning of the twentieth century. But it has filtered into
the heart of right-wing Orthodoxy! Thus, the penetration of feminism into
Judaism sometimes achieves successes slowly, imperceptibly, indirectly,
through the migration of ideas and institutions over time through informal
networks. This is a more benign approach to change that has implications
for addressing militancy in matters of violence and conflict.[18]

Religious peace exemplars, especially when they work in pairs or groups,[19]
appear to have the power to weave together relationships between enemies
and their network of communities. The drive of their ethical principles propels them across borders that seem impossible to scale otherwise. A person
truly driven by absolute compassion, for example, does not care about an
adversary's political program, the extremity of his hatreds, but rather pur-
sues doggedly a simple compulsion to act with compassion. This stubborn
commitment to principles of love, compassion, honor, or humility, tends
to have a powerful impact on enemies. It often creates a corresponding
set of gestures from enemies who one would think should be incapable
of this, given their ideological rigidities. In effect, the power of ethical and
interpersonal relations seems to trump the power of radical ideology in
many instances.

This puts the lie to the myth that conflicts of ideology are impossible to resolve. It may very well be that we have prejudged this issue. We have focused so much on rationalistic concepts of negotiation and compromise that we have forgotten how much compromise may be based actually on the emotional will to reach out to an alienated other. How a person changes, once he is emotionally motivated to do so, is a phenomenon full of surprises. I have sat with men convinced that Jesus was the only path to salvation and others who believed that literally there was no history before five thousand years ago. And yet our relationship on key issues of conflict and peace proceeded apace based on our moral commitment to each other; the ideology meant nothing. If I stopped at every moment and asked if we were in the same intellectual universe the relationship with them would have never even taken place. But I ignored that and concentrated on the emotional bond and the bond of remorse for the wasted human lives in war; these turned out to be the only bonds that mattered in our building of trust, loyalty, and a common vision of the future.

What seems impossible ideologically becomes possible in the context of passionately devoted relationships across enemy lines that are generated by these exemplars. Their strength is not ideological compromise but rather overriding ethical emotions and behaviors. This is something that no amount of negotiations can do.

Exemplars often create, out of religious zeal, a passionate commitment to the value of all human beings and therefore a nonnegotiable worth of enemies. Their courageous actions set the stage eventually for larger and more formal negotiations between enemies.

A network-centered understanding of peacemaking that better explains the work of religious peacemakers may entail a very different approach to reaching militant communities. It would naturally accept the need of mainstream communities and governments to keep their distance from radicals. But at the same time the religious peacemaker approach would work on the penetration of new ideas and relationships through select individuals who are talented connectors of communities, people who are ingenious at the conciliatory moment of human relationship.

The only others who reach radical communities from mainstream culture, when it comes to matters of violence and war, are—paradoxically—representatives of security agencies. They often appeal to the worst militant instincts and empower their most violent representatives. But this relationship is destructive and fuels more violence. Military and intelligence agencies are always interested in buying their way into control of or use of radicals to do "their dirty work."[20] Radicals are attractive to military agencies because both of them focus on perfecting the use of force. Thus, secular, enlightened moderates are cut off from radicals, but the military and intelligence wings of governments sometimes deal with them and bring out their worst instincts for power, not their best ideals.

The only ones who appeal to the best ideals of religious reactionaries while not rewarding them with too much power are religious peacemakers who respect the former's religiosity but will not accept their militancy or violence. This is the only kind of bridge that can lead to a nonviolent future with such groups. But only rare, talented, and patient people are capable of this work with the most militant.

The field of diplomacy has focused exclusively on official negotiations. The field of conflict resolution has focused on unofficial prenegotiations. But few have focused on the very first bridges between enemies, and how those early bridges were created. Often they are created by individuals with no institutional affiliations who are prepared to go where no one else has gone. The bridges they create are eventually traversed by others who are more representative of parties to the conflict. These early pioneers are often driven by spiritual or religious zeal, and their impact deserves its own analysis.

What we are witnessing in the field is also a remarkable evolution of traditional Christians[21] and Muslims[22] who are becoming bolder in their own unique styles of conflict resolution, thus the work of many of those mentioned above. This means that many more very devout, conservative people will be entering the arena of international diplomacy.[23] This presents an opportunity for the short-term peacemaking that we have outlined above, and a challenge to the long-term creation of a global social contract and a public space that we can all share.[24] But the benefits of the entry of conservatives into diplomacy far outweigh the challenges, even in terms of the long-term needs of a liberal social contract. The world needs unconditionally both religious and secular visions of nonviolent coexistence. This is an essential prerequisite to negotiating the foundations of a global community.

Traditional religious peacemaking is also developing side by side with radically progressive approaches to spirituality and syncretism (deliberate mixing of religious traditions). One can see a mixture of both syncretistic and traditional strands of peacemaking in places like the Fez Sacred Music Festival in Morocco,[25] as well as at the *Sulha* reconciliation meetings in Israel,[26] or in the interesting merging of global musical traditions that are a new form of spirituality and peacemaking; these are all interesting innovations that go well beyond any formal processes of conflict resolution.[27]

There exists a unique position in religious experience and ethics of deeds, gestures, symbols, and rituals that accompany and sometimes supersede words, conversation, and dialogue. This is essential for understanding the special world of religion and conflict resolution, and also this world's potential to point the way to new forms of conflict resolution on a global scale.

Conflict resolution as a secular field is going through a profound metamorphosis as its lessons and contributions have been absorbed most especially by the field of international development and poverty relief.[28] It is this latter field that has best understood the need for a combination of conflict analysis and resolution as a part of pursuing the "deeds," the best practices, of development and economic empowerment.

Economic development and overseas aid are fundamental characteristics of the current relationship between rich and poor nations, peaceful and embattled nations.[29] That relationship can go very badly unless a deeper understanding of conflict is present at every stage of relationship building across international boundaries. This marriage of development and conflict resolution practices is a welcome innovation that is a direct result of terrible lessons learned through the Rwanda aid and genocide experience, among many other examples.

Religious practitioners of conflict resolution have always had a hard time separating the use of the word from the use of the deed, or, conventionally speaking, peace and the work of social justice. A significant number of the people mentioned above (not all) tend to operate with a keen awareness that deeds, both interpersonal gestures and the deeds social justice, are central to peace, and that, from both a religious point of view and an ethical point of view, talk cannot be separated from action.

Authentic relationship entails a range of religious/ethical principles of human engagement that are indispensable for true reconciliation. Thus there is an emphasis in the work of most peace exemplars mentioned above on moving relationships very quickly into gestures and concrete deeds that constitute evidence of new relationship.

In a word, the best exemplars of our work insist upon a religious recreation of social contract. Social contract can never be only about words and dialogue but rather about the necessary conditions of coexistence that include sharing, respect, honor, and compassion for those who are less fortunate. Religious social contract is a contract of word and deed. This emphasis on deeds, gestures, and symbols leaves the more typical work of dialogue and negotiation in the proverbial dust. It is impatient with talk only, and it drives toward engagements of a far more meaningful impact.

Often, it must be admitted that the religious social contract of words and deeds is circumscribed to a select group, and the outsiders to the contract can have no rights. This is where the positive elements of religious social contract must learn from modern conceptions of social contract that include all citizens, regardless of their behavior or beliefs.[30]

This foray into bold new actions, deeds, and gestures is highly experimental, however, and it usually must be attuned to the unique circumstances of every conflict situation. This is the kind of intervention that makes large organizations, foundations, and governments hesitate. It makes them uncomfortable to invest in dramatic human engagement that cannot be characterized by the predictable structures of workshops and staged conversations. But all authentic experimentation is radical—right up until the day that it is no longer radical, until its results become more and more clear. How can we make our interventions globally more effective if we do not experiment? And where is the modern commitment to science if there is no experimentation? Perhaps we are in a state of flux regarding new forms of conflict resolution that are being born in the field, without support, and often by impoverished religious exemplars.

TOWARD A DEFINITION OF THE FIELD
OF RELIGION AND CONFLICT RESOLUTION

To get a better understanding of the field, and to see its usefulness for building a strategy of "making the earth whole" or evolving a global social contract, we need to have working definitions of our subject.

One of the greatest challenges to resolving human conflict is not only defining success but also extrapolating consistent definitions of religion, conflict, and conflict resolution. I will attempt this and then revisit the issue of social networks.

It is difficult to define what religion is, let alone "religion and conflict," "religion and peacebuilding," or "religion and conflict resolution." The definitions below must, therefore, be understood as attempts to character-ize dynamic and ever-changing phenomena.

Definition of "Religion and Conflict"

Based on my past twenty years of experience in the field, I am going to tentatively define "religion and conflict" as any conflict in which religious beliefs and practices play either a minor or major role in the defensive or aggressive motivations of *at least some* of the parties to the given conflict. This means that there is no claim of religion as being a primary factor in the cause of most conflicts. Rather the focus is on religion as a partial motivator or catalyzer of conflict for at least *some* actors. It is also sometimes the major motivation for a minority of actors who, despite being a small group, may be playing a critical role in catalyzing or escalating a larger group conflict.

Most approaches to international relations, with roots in state-based analysis, tend to oversimplify the conflict environment. In other words they tend to make conflict about essentially one thing, such as power, land, or money. But the chaos of conflict is such that there are always multiple actors complicating the environment. And there are multiple motivations operating inside even one actor, let alone the constellation of people that usually comprise a conflict environment.

Research into conflict analysis and resolution must necessarily create a more humble environment in which to study the variety of actors and motivations. It may very well be, for example, that the primary conflict between Israeli Jews and Palestinians is over a single piece of land that they both want for deeply ethnic and material reasons. But it has been a serious mistake to underestimate the power of religious settler ideology to carry the banner of radical Zionism far beyond a rational cost/benefit analysis of the situation that may have guided earlier secular Zionists like Herzl. Early Zionists were more pragmatic, taking what they could get at any point in time, and some of them were also tempered by some commitment to universal socialist or democratic ideals. But those ideals are stripped away when a messianic fervor sets in and defies all rational analysis of a situation. Those values are utterly crushed when a fascist need to expel whole populations from their ancient homes becomes a burning desire, as it does for a minority of religious Jews today inside and outside of Israel.

It is also a mistake to underestimate just how far Salafist ideology and radical Islam has undermined rational cost/benefit analysis of Palestinian needs and aspirations through the introduction of suicide bombing. The action/reaction spiral of suicide bombing took the stalemate to a hardened place of barbarity that depressed even the most ardent supporters of the Palestine Liberation Organization (PLO) with whom I have worked.

In other words, religion is an intense catalyzer of human emotions, and it builds constructs of reality that will fly in the face of any rational calculation of survival. There is an aspect to religion—and any other absolute ideological system—that is suicidal, prepared to sacrifice everything for an ideal or belief, out of conviction that the righteous will triumph, either in this lifetime or the next. When other combatants may be exhausted and reevaluating the benefits of the use of force, the ideological, mythic, and "ethical" constructs of a religion may catalyze the conflict further in the hands of some believers. It will also tend to create a mirror of itself on the other side of the conflict which polarizes the vying populations, descending further and further into barbarism.

Religious zealots need not be anywhere near the majority to catalyze violence. It is simply a function of the radical behavior that they set in motion, and the psychological processes of fear and rage that result from this in every person caught in the midst of the violence. This is why religion can affect conflict all out of proportion to the actual number of religious extremists. Be they secular or religious Palestinians, the zealous occupation of more and more land on the West Bank in the name of Judaism will unite Arabs in revulsion and corresponding aggressive actions.

Let's take another example from the United States. Be they secular or religious, Americans who witnessed religious suicide bombing on 9/11 united together in astonishing submissiveness to misguided and misleading wars in the Middle East inaugurated by the White House. Americans need not have all read the Christian extremist Tim LaHaye or believed in

Armageddon to give into an extreme foreign policy. They simply needed to be caught up in the shock of religiously motivated mass murder *directed at them* to begin to react rather suicidally themselves to their global standing and situation.

Why would I call the American reaction suicidal? Today the American is hated *exponentially* more on a global scale than on the day of September 11, 2001. This is due in no small measure to the "defensive" response of the "global war on terror," which has been everything but defensive. This must be seen in some ways as risky or suicidal behavior on the part of a very religious, mostly Christian society of the United States, with the Jewish religious community mostly supportive.

Religious zeal was a central catalyzer of this action/reaction spiral of violence, and one cannot ignore the sheepish way in which the majority of the American population went along with rather apocalyptic and irrational decisions to "take on" and assault the heart of the Arab world. There was nothing sheepish about the response of American religious radicals. What is surprising is how quickly the broad middle of American pragmatic think-ing went along for the ride; this happened, shockingly, both at the popular level and at the policy level.

Almost everyone allowed themselves to become caught up in ideo-logical warfare rather than rational defense. Rational defense has both violent (measured use of force against terrorists such as in Afghanistan, or a global coalition of policing against terror) and nonviolent forms (diplomacy, alliance-building, negotiations with enemies) that have char-acterized American pragmatism in the past; but both were suppressed in favor of apocalyptic revenge in Iraq. In fact, the vital resources to carry on the antiterror campaign in Afghanistan were siphoned off completely to fight the war in Iraq. It still defies the imagination that an apocalyptic war of revenge against Iraq could supplant the rational campaign against Al Qaeda in Afghanistan.

One cannot say, however, that most of America became plagued by Pat Robertson's religious apocalyptic mindset; the ill effects of violent religious ideology are more subtle in their effects. One *can* say that President Bush's war plans in Iraq, and the passive way in which they were accepted, suggest a broad and perhaps unconscious succumbing to apocalyptic approaches to a complex world.

Apocalyptic politics is characterized by isolation, universal distrust, militancy, and deliberate defiance of real world consequences of behavior. Consequences do not matter if one already knows what the end will look like based on faith. We cannot ignore the way in which extreme religious behavior catalyzed this action/reaction spiral of self-defeating behavior on both sides of the 9/11 tragedy. This is an example of the complex interpen-etration of religion and conflict.

Definition of "Religion and Peacebuilding"

Moving on with definitions, I understand "religion and peacebuilding" as any effort by people to engage the values, texts, traditions, and communities of faith to build peace between enemies. This effort can be considered religion and peacebuilding whether or not its primary proponents are religious themselves. It is the constructive engagement with religion that is the key. Such peacebuilding centers on building relationships and networks that can become a better basis of trust and negotiation between groups in conflict.[31]

Generally speaking, the most innovative religious peacebuilders, like Canon White, Menahem Frohman, Sheikh Bukhari, and Eliyahu Mclean, assume what has become standard in social network analysis.[32] They will deliberately, and with great spiritual discipline, cut across endless boundaries of all the networks that divide societies and civilizations. They will appeal to the widest potential group of friends and partners, as they globalize their constituencies. Therefore they each, as a node (central axis point)[33] in the conflict network, assume that the loose ties generated by their initiatives, that their friendships, prayers, ceremonies, or collaborations, will generate a far broader impact than their numbers might indicate. Long before the publication of the *The Tipping Point*, they have been aggressively innovating in the contagion of new ideas. Their venue is new relationships that cut across every conceivable line of division. Evidence of new and unusual relationships spreads by word of mouth, but unlike isolated idealists, they actually create substantial networks globally. Sometimes this is a conscious plan, and other times it is actually unconscious or instinctive to who they are.

THE POWER OF RELIGIOUS NETWORKS

Let us do a study in contrasts between a religious peacebuilder and how he or she operates, as opposed to more typical negotiation and prenegotiation approaches to peacemaking. As an example, an academically based secular peacemaker who privately recommends a set of negotiation tactics to two enemies may be quite gifted and creative. But he may also be quite limited in the extent of his ties to the world, mostly inhabiting the world of left-wing academia and progressive policy makers. He may have ties to the State Department but not to the Pentagon, or perhaps just to some ambassadors.

This is unlike religious connections in any given congregation, which tend to cut across all walks of life. The same congregation, and certainly the same denomination, could have lawyers, doctors, draft dodgers, mechanics, cab drivers, policy makers, military staff, and antimilitary public protesters. Any sermon that is spread among them immediately affects dozens of separated networks. But if you add to that a religious peacebuilder who *with great intention and skill* cuts across all boundaries in her own religious group even as she reaches out to other religions of enemy groups, then we will witness a phenomenon that cuts across hundreds of networks.

The dialogue workshop social network is another example. The dialogue workshop between privileged members of enemy groups has become a classic form of conflict resolution in recent decades. But it is often limited to those who analyze and negotiate the details of conflicts at a very sophisticated level. It impacts the few who are involved politically, or who can even comprehend the complexity of a proposed agreement.

By contrast, let us think of the impact of:

a. a religious peace ceremony
b. a group of religious enemies who plant trees together in defiance of their deliberate destruction
c. a small set of religious peacebuilders that build a network of relationships between enemies over a period of years, and who then build houses together for the poor or the displaced. Then the same group says prayers in the process that have resonance in both enemy communities and the broader cultures.

In all these cases the religious peace networkers are broadcasting an image or a message that is broadly comprehensible to millions of adversaries *at every intellectual and economic level.* The message, therefore, has a fundamentally different trajectory than elite relationships. It has the potential in principal to spread like a virus among an extremely wide set of loose, indirect ties numbering in the hundreds of millions. The numbers of the actual networkers, or nodes, may be quite small, but their "expansive ties"—or "weak ties" in the classic social network sense—are of the broadest potential.

The prayers, for example, would be known immediately to millions of people familiar with those prayers; the significance of the trees would be recognizable to anyone on the planet who appreciates the living symbol of hope and life that is a tree; housing for the poor would be understood by virtually everyone as a conciliatory gesture. If the kind of tree they are planting symbolized a special gesture to an enemy, like an olive tree for a Palestinian that is planted by a Jew, then this too would carry weight with anyone who heard about it, educated or not, rich or poor.

To be sure, recognition of a symbol does not equal acceptance or agreement to it by millions of people; it does not replace agreements, negotiation, or reconciliation. But the shared understanding of deeds, symbols, and prayers would create conversation, consternation, controversy, and the struggle of competing paradigms of relationship to enemy others—as opposed to a closed meeting of a few people in an elite workshop. Instead, bombs would be in competition with trees and housing for the images in the mind of the average person. This is a victory in itself, but it is more. It spells the potential to shift paradigms and to eventually create tipping points toward a new vision of the enemy and of one's future.

If this were amplified and advertised by a willing network of government agencies, powerful third-party states, NGOs, and the media, the effects would increase geometrically. But so far there is little courage to do so on the part of the establishment players in global relations.

Let us take another example of social network. Any time a priest, rabbi, or imam makes a public statement either in action or deed, there are millions of people who could *in principal* understand and take special notice of that. This is simply because there are billions of people on the planet who, based on faith or even culturally rooted habits, pay special attention to what clerics do and say.

This is why the Arab press notes especially what every chief rabbi in Israel says about them,[34] but secular, intellectual Israelis who are rooted in Western culture and who disparage their chief rabbis scratch their heads in consternation. "Why are the Arabs in an uproar over what Reb Ovadiah said this time? We laugh! They should be more concerned about their pragmatic situation." Liberal Israelis want their progressive academic conferences to be noted throughout the Arab world, not the words of a former chief rabbi, but the world they are in does not work that way. Most of the world is religious, and therefore what religious leaders say and do has great resonance, whether the minority of secular people like it or not.

It goes without saying that just how broad the impact is of religious symbols and gestures might depend upon the level of respect—or disrespect—that religious exemplars or clerics generate in a given population. The intellectual elites, for example, are continually shocked by the massive following of preachers and clerics because they are completely removed from those networks. Nevertheless these massive traditional networks exist, and they can be used for good or for ill.

Furthermore, when there is a public religious deed broadcast to a large network, and it is inherently peaceful, focused on a path toward reconciliation, justice, and tolerance, this generates a broad range of ties among those who are inspired and who become activist supporters.

The next crucial point is that the strength of these expansive ties depends less on authority and more on the dedication and talent of networkers. Positions of authority are less important than how the peace networkers position themselves among and between others.[35] Much of their challenge therefore is not so much religious rejection as much as how much the secular world of media actively ignores their work because they are not shedding blood. Religious peacemaking is simply not newsworthy, as opposed to religious violence, and this gives an unnatural voice and advantage to extremists. There are no simple answers to this imbalance of media exposure to the masses.

There are lessons to be learned from the extremists, however, when it comes to media. One is the power of symbol and gesture in today's world of religious enthusiasm. The religious world is not anywhere near as centrally controlled as it once was. In today's world where, on balance, the absolute authority of religious leaders has been weakened by the state as well as by globalized information, choices, and globalized networking, it is the symbols and gestures that resonate. It is symbols that challenge most people, symbols that feel to them as authoritative and grounded in their culture. The impact is even more enhanced if the peace networkers can induce religious clerics to embrace such peace gestures.

For example, in the winter of 2008 Rabbi Frohman was trying to generate movement in Israel and the United States to embrace a religious ceasefire between Hamas and the Israeli government during a vicious cycle of reprisals.[36] He had all the details worked out, and had a serious text, based on consultations with innumerable networks, from military to political to populist, on all sides. From those trying to release Israeli soldiers, to intelligence experts, to politicians left and right, to the PLO, he was endlessly networking.

But Rabbi Frohman was still hoping that senior chief rabbis would publicly embrace the move because it would only enhance the effort. Again, he got a fraction of the press that Bush administration "peace process" representatives received, despite the fact that the Bush administration had played such a destructive role for so many years. Frohman's networks were excellent, but he still needed larger venues to create a paradigm shift. Ironically, if the press had taken it as seriously as Hamas representatives were taking it, the senior rabbis may have felt safer politically to take a chance on a shift toward indirect negotiations with Hamas on a ceasefire.

It is not so much the authority of clerics that matters to millions of people today. Rather it is entrance into the world of religious networks that can happen if symbols and gestures of a conciliatory move toward alienated others become widely publicized. It is the symbols and gestures of inclusion of religious sensibilities that matter to religious enthusiasts, from Hamas supporters, to Orthodox Jews, to evangelicals. If they see themselves in the picture, if they see their God in the picture, then the risky process of peacemaking becomes more palatable.

The most clever networkers for peace, therefore, are not necessarily those in positions of religious authority, but it is rather those people who are passionately committed to expanding their networks and reaching out through gestures. That is why a religious peace activist, even if he or she is not a cleric, may have a very large network indeed, especially if her work receives a boost of global attention from media.[37]

Millions of traditionalists across the world today are not simple robotic adherents to this or that religious authority. They may venerate authorities but they are more often than not making their own moral calculations about complex issues in the world. That is why religious symbols of reconciliation that resonate with their culture and their worldview will enter into their calculus of right and wrong.

Symbols of reconciliation may not weigh in the average person's mind as much as a militant religious authority who *also* happens to be providing his children with meals and schools, however. And this is why the most important conciliatory gestures are gestures of justice, going much farther than words, for they are especially geared to the satisfaction of basic human needs. What is most effective, therefore, are gestures that are geared toward the poor, who have the least amount of their basic human needs being met. Simultaneously, the fact that there may be a religious view that is conciliatory, if it becomes known through the media or some trusted network, will give the average religious person, poor or wealthy, a religious choice that he does not currently have.

The average religious person in many conflict regions sees religious extremists around them, and the extremists are very clear about their political positions. They are also very willing to provide help. Then this average person sees the State which could care less about his family's survival and does not speak his religious language. This does not present him with a fair choice.[38]

If the same person sees a real choice between competing religious worldviews, and the peaceful exemplars express interest in him and speak his language, then something else can happen. Then his moral religious reasoning is in a better position to make independent decisions about adversaries, about the use of force, about interpretations of what his religious mythic heroes, or his God, would or would not want him to do about coexistence with others who are different.

In cab rides across the world I have been astonished at the range of traditionalists I meet from quite patriarchal and rigid religions. They are continually making their own judgments and interpretations of right and wrong. They never quote me obscure religious law about exclusive or racist positions. They always cite their own interpretations and impressions of what is right, drawing on a variety of influences, from their own news analysis to their memories of favorite religious stories or verses.

There is then more freedom of religious conscience in the world today than we think. But those secular and modern global citizens who want a nonviolent democratic world are not connecting with most religious adherents who may share a surprising number of values. And they are certainly not connecting with these people's basic needs.

Definition of "Religion and Conflict Resolution"

"Peacebuilding" is generally considered to be the broader work of building relationships over time in such a way as to create a peaceful society. "Conflict resolution," however, is specifically focused on intervening in an ongoing conflict in an effort to: (1) stop the destructive elements of the conflict,[39] (2) manage the conflict in a way that leads it in a more constructive direction, and (3) help point the parties toward a vision and path of reconciliation of their own making.

I will therefore define "religion and conflict resolution" as (1) any effort designed to integrate classical forms of conflict resolution with a religious overlay that will appeal to religious combatants; (2) any effort designed to elicit from religious traditions indigenous forms of conflict resolution that may creatively interact with secular forms of conflict resolution. An example might be combining conflict resolution practices together with classical forms of Arab and Islamic reconciliation, *sulha*, as a means to develop culturally authentic conflict resolution in the Arab and Islamic worlds.[40]

The inherent problem of such an approach is the fact that a religiously indigenous form of conflict resolution may be appealing to only the party for whom it has meaning.[41] However, as stated above, there is a remarkable level of creativity among religious interfaith peacemakers who regularly network with many religious parties to a conflict. There is a creative adjustment of traditional rituals and deeds to interfaith circumstances. This is constantly evolving in the field, and I have been surprised at the flexibility of traditionalists in this regard. It seems that what is essential for success among traditionalists today is their commitment to peace. If they become committed to peace then they tend to come up with creative but traditional ways to create "interfaith moments," gestures, or experiences that carry meaning across religions *but* that will also avoid violations of traditional rules of conduct.

As a rather extreme example, I was told recently of an encounter between Franklin Graham and a very brutal leader in the hinterland of Sudan. There was also an American senator in attendance. The senator, when it was his turn to speak at a planned gathering of the parties, appealed to United Nations resolutions and urged the leader to cooperate. The senator was angrily rebuffed in public by this local leader. Then Graham's turn came to speak and apparently he professed his commitment to Jesus Christ *and that only this could solve the problems of the region*. Astonishingly, this received a quiet, intrigued response from this Muslim leader.[42]

It never ceases to amaze me how many religious people in the world, no matter how extreme, seem to respond positively to *other* religious traditionalists *when they come in peace*. One would think that these competing proselytizers would be the ones to push the most for war. But it turns out that religious traditionalists and even extremists have a common language that they long to connect to.

This example should not be construed as an endorsement of proselytism as a form of conflict resolution! Far from it. The overwhelming facts continue to suggest that proselytism in many regions is a major cause of tensions, resentment, and jealousy. At the same time, if even Graham's rather crass appeal was appealing to an extremist, then how much more so could be a constructive and subtle approach that combined spirituality and conflict resolution.

The mutual influence of religions that occurs in such circumstances appears to evolve unusual religious interpretations, and this seems to create the possibility of integrated forms of religious peacemaking across faith communities.[43] Although mixing religions may be common in the lived, traditional experience of some religions, such as in Indian villages, it certainly represents a relatively small percentage of religious traditionalists, especially in the Abrahamic religions. Indeed, many religious people in rural regions that had forms of coexistence as a long-standing component of village experience come to the cities by the millions today, culturally displaced, and come under the sway of much more chauvinistic expressions of their faith.

Experience in recent years, however, suggests that even the most traditional adherents, when positively motivated by trusted networks to reach across enemy lines, appear to be interested in some forms of interreligious experience. These are modest but significant expressions of the fusion of religious horizons.[44] Recent interchanges of imams and rabbis, as well as the recent outreach of leading Islamic traditionalists to Christian leaders, suggest that interfaith efforts are moving more and more into very traditional worlds [45] There have also been internal processes of change, an emerging consensus on what is and what is not a legitimate ruling regarding war in Islam, that have clear implications for interfaith relations.[46]

These are welcome developments. The untold story is how much these bold gestures are based on quiet networks across the divides within and between religions that have been developing slowly for years. There are quiet figures at work here, such as Prince Ghazi of Jordan, a strong traditionalist but a serious man of peace, who have played a central role in some of the gestures just mentioned.

Everything begins with quiet networks, and then the important documents and gestures of coexistence begin to emerge when the time is right. Let us turn then in the next chapter to an in-depth study of the power of networks to create transformational change through increments of positive human engagement and peacemaking.

NOTES

1. Hind Kabawat's work will be featured prominently in chapters 4 and 5 on Syria.

2. Marc Gopin, *Between Eden and Armageddon: The Future of World Religions, Violence, and Peacemaking* (New York: Oxford University Press, 2000).

3. Quran 5:48.

4. See Henry O. Thompson, *World Religions in War and Peace* (Jefferson, NC: McFarland, 1988), especially his descriptions of each religion's contemporary approaches to peacemaking; Marc Gopin, *The Religious Ethics of Samuel David Luzzatto* (PhD dissertation, Brandeis University, 1993).

5. Oliver Ramsbotham, Tom Woodhouse, and Hugh Miall in *Contemporary Conflict Resolution*, 2nd ed. (Cambridge, UK, and Malden, MA: Polity Press, 2006) note that the term "conflict resolution" has been defined by conflict studies literature in a number of ways. For the most part it can be seen as a term that is more comprehensive than "conflict settlement," "containment," or "management." It implies that "the deep-rooted sources of conflict are addressed and transformed. . . . Behavior is no longer violent, attitudes are no longer hostile, and the structure or conflict has been changed" (p. 29). Ramsbotham et al. also note the ambiguity of this term in that it often refers simultaneously to both the *process* and the *end-state* of conflict. When I use the term in this book I refer to the process. For the term *peacebuilding*, Ramsbotham et al. define it as an effort that underpins the work of peacemaking (moving toward settlement of armed conflict) and peacekeeping (the interposition of armed or civilian forces between belligerents) by addressing structural issues and the long-term relationship between the conflictants (Ramsbotham, Woodhouse, and Miall, *Contemporary Conflict Resolution*, 30). Gopin, *Between Eden and Armageddon*, also notes that the term *peacebuilding* is seen in connection with the "conflict transformation" school of thought, and emphasizes long-term relationship building with a broad spectrum of people in enemy societies as the key to peace (pp. 234–35). That is what I mean when I refer to this term in this book. In terms of the deeper meaning of *peacebuilding*, John Paul Lederach proposes an integrated framework for peacebuilding that is comprised of two axes. The vertical axis, *structure*, is taken from Maire Dugan's nested paradigm, beginning at the zero point with issue, relationship, subsystem, and system. The vertical axis, *process*, begins at the zero point with crisis intervention, preparation and training, design of social change, and desired future. Lederach then argues that the two axes intersect at five points, each conforming to a school of thought: root causes (high structure, low process), crisis management (low structure, low process), prevention (low structure, high process), vision (high structure, high process), and ultimately transformation, which is a middle-range point between all four other points. The latter integrates all four schools of thought and ultimately signifies an integrated framework for peacebuilding. See John Paul Lederach, *Building Peace: Sustainable Reconciliation in Divided*

Societies (Washington, DC: USIP, sixth printing, 2004), 79–85. My interest does not easily fit into any of these paradigms. I am interested in the most elemental, primitive stages of change in enemy systems where individuals reach out and create relationships, sometimes just one at a time. This comes well before processes of peacebuilding are underway. The relationship building that I describe in this book also sometimes comes *after* everything else has failed. I am exploring the role of the individual who steps in when nothing has even been tried yet, or when all else is failing, *either before, during, or after* more formal structures of conflict resolution or peacebuilding have been operationalized. My interest is how individuals and citizen diplomats can get the more formal structures of conflict resolution, peacebuilding, or diplomacy either started or back on track.

6. For an adequate list of some of these organizations, see rfpusa.org/links/other.cfm (accessed October 2, 2007).

7. I mean this term in the sense that Malcolm Gladwell gives to it. See gladwell.com/tippingpoint/tp_excerpt2.html.

8. This has become a common phrase to refer to a certain kind of individual who reaches beyond the boundaries of his organization or group. See Paul Williams, "The Competent Boundary Spanner," *Public Administration* 80, no. 1 (2002): 103–24.

9. A good place to begin studying these peacemakers is David Little, ed., *Peacemakers in Action: Profiles of Religion in Conflict Resolution* (Cambridge: Cambridge University Press, 2007). This volume, published by the Tanenbaum Center for Interreligious Understanding, dovetails their projects of highlighting the work of pioneering religious peacemakers. They announce a yearly, well publicized set of awards for heroic action in religious peacemaking. As chair of their Program Advisory Council on Conflict Resolution, it has been my privilege to work with wonderful colleagues in moving the work of our field away from a fixation on programs, conferences, and workshops and toward support for the heroic peacemakers, their path-breaking relationships, and their extraordinary bridges and gestures. See tanenbaum.org/conflict_resolution.html (accessed November 27, 2007).

10. A very small list includes the Dalai Lama, John Paul Lederach, Rajmohan Gandhi of India, Yehezkel Landau, Eliyahu Mclean of Israel, David Smock, Mohammed Abunimer, Ihab Balaha of Northern Israel, Samuel Doe of Liberia, Hind Kabawat of Syria, Bryan Hamlin, Daniel Lubetzky of Mexico, Neamatollah Nojumi of Afghanistan, Rabbi David Rosen, Sharon Rosen and Rabbi Menahem Frohman of Israel, Nasser Youssef of Palestine, Talal Sidr of Palestine, Prince Hassan of Jordan, Prince Ghazi of Jordan, Grand Mufti Ahmed Hassoun of Syria, Thich Nhat Han, Sheikh Shehadeh of Syria, Bill Ury, Shamil Idriss, Lisa Schirch, Joseph Montville, Gabi Meyer of Israel, Sushoba Barve of India, Canon Andrew White of Great Britain, Reverend Brian Cox, Ron Kraybill, Doug Johnston, John and Susan Marks, Sheikh Bukhari of Palestine, Rabbi Michael Melchior of Israel, Friar Ivo Markovic of Bosnia, Imam Yahya Hendi, Eboo Patel, and Patrice Brodeur of Canada. In this small sample I have deliberately listed people with very diverse approaches to peacemaking and conflict resolution.

11. A good start here would be Marc Granovetter, "The Strength of Weak Ties," *The American Journal of Sociology* 78, no. 6 (1973): 1360–80. Also for foundational books on Network Theory, see Manuel Castels, *The Rise of the Network Society*, 2nd

ed. (Oxford: Blackwell, 1996); Mario Diani and Doug McAdam, eds., *Social Movements and Network: Relational Approaches to Collective Action* (Oxford: Oxford University Press, 2003); Charles Tilly, *Identities, Boundaries, and Social Ties* (Boulder, CO: Paradigm Publishers, 2005). A tight cluster of individuals will tend to have strong bridges between them, but the diffusion and flow of ideas remains in a circular, group-centrist ethos and pattern. On the other hand, while loose networks of individuals might have weaker ties among them, these ties provide lesser constraints on information diffusion and sharing outside of the main group. This is what makes them so useful for shifting the opinions of large populations. Furthermore, the kind of individuals who connect the most networks can have very wide impact, as we will see later. It is also important here to link social network literature to some broader conceptions of social capital. For a complete discussion on this, see Robert Putnam's influential work *Bowling Alone: The Collapse and Revival of American Community* (New York: Simon & Schuster, 2000) as well as David Halpern, *Social Capital* (Cambridge, UK: Polity Press, 2005).

12. Malcolm Gladwell, *Tipping Point: How Little Things Can Make a Big Difference* (Boston: Little, Brown, 2000); David Demers and K. Viswanath, eds., *Mass Media, Social Control, and Social Change: A Macrosocial Perspective* (Ames: Iowa State University Press, 1999).

13. The concept of "tipping point" is related to but not identical to the term "ripeness" in conflict resolution, which implies a ripeness for intervention by others in a conflict. Tipping points or paradigm shifts seem to be phenomena that occur on their own due to a constellation of complex causality. But there is enough similarity here to invite further comparison. On "ripeness," see William Zartman, "Ripeness: The Hurting Stalemate and Beyond," in *Conflict Resolution after the Cold War*, ed. P. C. Stern and D. Druckman (Washington, DC: National Academy Press, 2000), 225–50. Another related idea is the more positively inclined notion of "readiness," as proposed by Dean G. Pruitt and Sung Hee Kim in *Social Conflict: Escalation, Stalemate, and Settlement* (New York: McGraw-Hill, 2004), 172–73, note 3. Instead of Zartman's mutually hurting stalemate and the parties then, when the time is ripe, seeing a way out of the conflict, Pruitt and Kim use "perceived stalemate" and "optimism" as reactions that make the parties ready to de-escalate.

14. Conflict resolution based on the belief that exposing populations to each other leads to reduction in conflict is technically referred to as the "Contact Hypothesis." This hypothesis has its limitations. Those who utilize this approach may strive to reduce prejudice by equal status contacts between majority and minority groups in the pursuit of common goals, but this rarely happens. The effects are greatly enhanced if this contact leads to the perception of common interests and common humanity between members of the two groups, but again this is difficult to achieve, at least in the broad experience I have had in dialogue and contact experiments. See David Halpern, *Social Capital* (Cambridge: Polity Press, 2005), 261. Halpern adds that in situations of conflict, contact equality can rarely be secured as a condition for mutual reduction of prejudice. Furthermore, it is my experience and that of many others that contact between groups that are either unequal, or are perceived to be unequal or unfairly treated, will lead to reentry into situations where groups will feel that the contact that they had was an illusion, out of step with reality, even a trick. Therefore they may become even more embittered. This is as true for the ma-

terially more empowered group as it is for the disempowered. The disempowered group returns to systematic prejudice and abuse. The empowered group may very well return to random violence at the hands of members of the enemy group, and thus also feel that the isolated island of contact was an illusion. By contrast, the positive networks that I have witnessed move well beyond contact to rather profound and equal moral relationships in which collaboration, sacrifice, and risk are central. This kind of relationship has a much more profound impact on those who witness it. They are also able to get past the endless divide of enemies in dialogue situations in which one group has an especially strong grievance. The more powerful side, the winners, if you will, "just want peace" and do not understand the anger, rage, and barbarity of the other side. But the more aggrieved side sees this "peace" conversation as offensive, as a cover-up to theft, humiliation, deception, denial of history, and large-scale injustice. This is as true in interpersonal relationships as it is in group relationships. By contrast, the more profound relationships that spiritual peacemakers create get past all of this with a level of intimacy, respect, common purpose, and solidarity so that love of peace and pain over grievance become a source of bonding, not a divide.

15. Mohammed Abu Nimer, one of the most preeminent scholar/practitioners of intergroup dialogue, argues that certain basic principles must be met for effective interfaith dialogue (as well as other kinds) to occur. They include: symmetric arrangements in the process and design of the encounter between the parties, selection of appropriate participants, examination of both similarities and differences, inclusion of a collaborative task, having a flexible process of interaction, healing and acknowledgement of collective and individual injuries, and having "uni-religious" (in-group) preparations and forums. See Mohammed Abunimer, "The Miracles of Transformation through Interfaith Dialogue," in *Interfaith Dialogue and Peacebuilding*, ed. David R. Smock (Washington, DC: USIP, second printing 2007), 21–26.

16. See, for example, Vamik Volkan, *Bloodlines: From Ethnic Pride to Ethnic Terrorism* (New York: Farrar, Straus, and Giroux, 1997), and *Killing in the Name of Identity: A Study of Bloody Conflicts* (Charlottesville, VA: Pitchstone, 2006), for analysis of phenomena such as "chosen trauma" and multigenerational transfer of traumatic experiences and its various manifestations.

17. The relationship between Jews and Christians, mainly the Catholic Church, has seen positive and encouraging developments in the twentieth century, but that has not always been the case due to the history of the Jewish experience from theological demonization, discrimination, and misrepresentation. It is a pervasive feeling among Jews that Catholic action or inaction in the early twentieth century either fueled or failed to stop anti-Semitism in Europe, which in turn became a contributor to the Holocaust. For an adequate bibliography of Jewish–Catholic relations in history regarding anti-Judaism and anti-Semitism, as well as on the positive developments in ecclesial statements and commentaries, see the Institute for Christian & Jewish Studies' annotated bibliography at icjs.org/info/bibliog.html. Jewish–Protestant relations have also had their ebb and flow. The relationship between Jews and Presbyterians in the United States is one such example where recent discussions have included such contentious items as Presbyterian groups evangelizing activities among Jews and implicit or explicit support for groups such as Jews for Jesus. Political issues have become a central reason for tension among Jews and

Presbyterians following the Presbyterian Church's (USA) successive General Assembly calls for divestment from companies that are seen as aiding Israel's occupation of the West Bank and its construction of settlements. Nonetheless, agreements between the Jewish community in the United States and the National Council of Churches (including PCUSA) have been reached. See, for example, ncccusa.org/news/050525christianjewishdialogue.html on Jewish–Christian dialogue "showing signs of maturity." See also pcusa.org/pcnews/2006/06644.htm on Presbyterians and Jews reaching an accord on a "new season of dialogue and understanding." All of this interfaith progress is ambivalent in a certain way. The confrontation of the Church and the Jew had already reached a horrible level of failure by the time that 90 percent of European Jewry were exterminated in World War II. We are at a stage of history now when all state power has been removed from the Church. Reconciliation is less exemplary when the parties are no longer in power. Truly successful conflict resolution removes active conflicts between parties who are in a position to do each other damage. After the fact and after the parties no longer have the power to destroy, it is more of a "mop-up" operation consisting of expressions of remorse and promises of a better future. I do not mean to belittle the benefits of interfaith dialogue, but I do mean to emphasize that organized religions, as opposed to individual religious exemplars, have a rather terrible record of self-regulation, self-limitation, and self-imposed sanctions. On the other hand, religious individuals, both clerical and nonclerical, present some amazing examples of courage under fire, sacrifice, and prophetic vision that has and continues to be a model for millions of spiritually oriented citizens; it is their paradigm that is more the subject of this book. It is also noteworthy that Christian–Muslim relations as well as broader interfaith cooperation efforts have flourished in the past two decades. Examples of this would include the establishment of the Pontifical Council for Interreligious Dialogue (PCID), founded in 1964 by Pope Paul VI as the Secretariat for non-Christian people and renamed in 1988 as PCID. In 2006, PCID seemed to be headed for demotion and consolidation into other Vatican councils, but it was reinstated in 2007 with the appointment of a new director. At the global level, initiatives such as the United Religions Initiative continue to grow and flourish.

18. It is worth noting here the value of Taoist wisdom, as embodied in the *Tao Te Ching* and *The Art of War*, that lends credence to indirect forms of acquiring power that seem invisible and weak but are actually supremely strong. The contagion of ideas through loose networks is an example of this. Indirect power and the contagion of networks and ideas undercut the most important cause of destructive conflict, the action/reaction spiral of aggressive actions and counteractions. There is a self-evident tendency of aggressive actions and counteractions to radicalize all positions. Loose, informal approaches to shifting ideas and institutions, however, undercut the action/reaction spiral of conflict in exactly the way that the *Tao Te Ching* intended. It does not attempt control and domination through programs and predetermined methodologies. It merely insinuates new ideas and new relationships, and allows this to percolate inside the minds and hearts of many people on an informal basis. Lao Tze, the traditional author of the *Tao Te Ching*, often associates this with a feminine principle. See this excerpt, for example:

Giving birth and nourishing,
having without possessing,
acting with no expectations,
leading and not trying to control:
this is the supreme virtue.

Tao Te Ching, trans. Stephen Mitchell (Harper: New York, 1988), 12. For Lao Tze this is a moral position, a virtue, and we will see the value of ethical principle for citizen diplomacy and intervention in the last chapters. But simultaneously this approach is also strategic with powerful possibilities for successful, nonviolent outcomes in the struggles of social change.

19. See, for example, the trip of the former president of the Egyptian Protestant Churches, Samuel Habib, together with the Grand-Imam of Al-Azhar University, Sheikh Mohammed Sayyed Tantawi, to the United States in the 1995 where both also received honorary doctorates from Westminster College, PA. See wrmea.com/backissues/0395/9503049.htm. Also note such interfaith projects as the Presbyterian Church's (USA) Interfaith Listening Program, and the work of pairs of peacemakers in the Israeli/Palestinian conflict, documented at jerusalempeacemakers. org. See especially the work of Menahem Frohman and Eliyah Mclean, and their work with Sheikh Bukhari, Talal Sidr, Nasser Youssef, among many others. See also below, chapters 3 and 4.

20. See, for example, Jessica Stern, *Terror in the Mind of God* (New York: Harper-Collins, 2004), 77–79, 116, 118, 205, 211, 221, 226–29, 234, 252–54.

21. See, for example, the work of Chris Seiple, an evangelical, former Marine, and president of the Institute for Global Engagement on "Engaging Conservative Islam" at globalengage.org/media/article.aspx?id=6276. See also Douglas Johnston and Cynthia Sampson, eds., *Religion: The Missing Dimension of Statecraft* (New York: Oxford University Press, 1994, and Douglas Johnston, ed., *Faith-Based Diplomacy: Trumping Realpolitik* (New York: Oxford University Press, 2003).

22. For example, Imam Feisal Abdul Rauf is the Founder and Chairman of The Cordoba Initiative, a multifaith organization formed to improve the relationship between the Islamic World and United States. He is also the imam of Masjid Al-Farah, a mosque in New York City. Rauf is the author of *Islam: A Search for Meaning* (Costa Mesa, CA: Mazda, 1996), *Islam: A Sacred Law* (Watsonville, CA: Threshold, 1999), and most recently, *What's Right With Islam: A New Vision for Muslims and the West* (New York: HarperOne, 2004). He was born in Kuwait in 1948 into an Egyptian family steeped in religious scholarship, and then was educated in England and Malaysia; he also has a degree in physics from Columbia University. Rauf is working tirelessly behind the scenes at high levels, especially with the government of Malaysia. He lives in New York with his wife Daisy Khan, who is also a powerful reformer. See asmasociety.org/about/b_dkhan.html. Eboo Patel is an important young innovator who will be making more and more of an impact on this field. See ifyc.org and his *Acts of Faith: The Story of an American Muslim, the Struggle for the Soul of a Generation* (Boston: Beacon Press, 2007). See also the work of an important and courageous Palestinian Muslim philosopher, Moustapha Abu Sway, who has shown great courage. His vision of the relationship of state and religion is decidedly different from mine or other Muslim reformers mentioned above; nevertheless

his efforts at peacemaking in Israel and Palestine and his efforts intellectually to develop a relationship of equality and dignity between citizens is all the more admirable given the environment in which he finds himself. For a dated biography, see cis-ca.org/bios/mustaf~1.htm. Mufti Ahmed Hassoun, the Grand Mufti of Syria, is another important and little-known innovator in the West, and we will address his role in much greater detail in chapter 3. For now, see drhassoun.com.

23. See this astonishing statement from the National Association of Evangelicals:

> Recognizing both the immediacy of the danger and the cultural mandate of Genesis 1:28, the National Association of Evangelicals vigorously affirms that ecology is not merely founded upon an instinct for human survival, but expresses man's responsibility under God to act as a faithful steward of the natural world. The commandment to fill and subdue the earth (Genesis 9:1) implied a trust which we believe is violated by any wastage or spoilage of the environment detrimental to the welfare of mankind in the present age.
>
> We pledge our cooperation to any responsible effort to solve critical environmental problems, and our willingness to support all proven solutions developed by competent authorities. We call upon our constituency to do the same, even at the cost of personal discomfort or inconvenience.

nae.net/index.cfm?FUSEACTION=editor.page&pageID=199&IDCategory=9 (accessed November 27, 2007).

Note the evolution of interpretation of Genesis. They have taken the classic text that has been used to justify human domination of the earth at whatever cost, and have evolved it instead into a notion of responsible *stewardship*. This notion of "stewardship" rather than domination has been migrating steadily from progressive monotheistic sources to even the most conservative organizations. This process takes time but the effects of new interpretation and response to new challenges is unmistakable, even in the most conservative camps.

24. I will address later the theoretical implications of this. I will look at an approach to conflict analysis and resolution that evaluates the effect of networks, as opposed to evaluation of individual programs, workshops, or negotiation processes. Evaluating the success of peacebuilding lies in tracking ever-extending networks that create a tipping point of peace, rather than static phenomena like conferences, workshops, or other staged events, which do not really demonstrate change. This parallels the move of science toward uncovering the deeper nature of natural phenomena as manifestations of dynamic organization, such as energy flows, rather than static phenomena, such as molecules or stars. See the discussion ahead in chapter 3. Our systems of critical analysis and evaluation must come to reflect this reality.

25. See spritoffes.com. While not the official site, it mentions building bridges through sacred music. For the official site, go to fesfestival.com/en/Frame1.htm.

26. See the Sulha Peace Project at sulha.com.

27. See for example Goffredo Plastino, ed., *Mediterranean Mosaic: Popular Music and Global Sounds* (New York and London: Routledge, 2003); and the website of international musician Idan Raichel, idanraichelproject.com/en/index.php.

28. See Connie O'Brien, "Integrated Community Development/Conflict Resolution Strategies as 'Peace Building Potential' in South Africa and Northern Ireland," *Community Development Journal* 42, no. 1: 114–30. It is worth noting that the term

"development" is becoming more associated with the term "conflict prevention." This may be due to a number of factors including the rise in priority of the "prevention" paradigm among foreign ministries such as in Scandinavia, and also the slow but visible shift in the United Nations' perspective on roots of conflict. The latter is epitomized by UN Security Council Resolution 1325 on "Women, Peace, and Security" (October 31, 2000), coupled with Kofi Annan's 2001 Report to the UN General Assembly and Security Council, entitled "Prevention of Armed Conflict." Furthermore, it is no accident that the most important office in the U.S. State Department concerning conflict, the Office of Conflict Management and Mitigation, is housed within the Agency for International Development. Speaking there in November of 2007, I was impressed by the serious thought that is going into the ways in which conflict prevention and resolution need to be combined with development and reconstruction.

29. Peter Uvin, "The Development/Peacebuilding Nexus: A Typology and History of Changing Paradigms," *Journal of Peacebuilding & Development* 1, no. 1 (2002): 5–24.

30. There is a paradox, however. The secular social contract excels at inclusion *as long as* a person is a citizen of a country. Once beyond national borders, however, such as where a national army is slaughtering some hapless group, where is the legal authority of the secular social contract to protect the defenseless? The appeal must then be to international global social contracts which are still very weak. By contrast, religious representatives can easily move their moral appeal across state boundaries and defend passionately the victims of one's war against some group who are not citizens. Thus, while religion has much to learn from the inclusivity of the secular social contract at the domestic level, at the global level, it is religious visionaries like Amos, Grotius, Kant, Gandhi, King, and the Dalai Lama who have pioneered an inclusive conception of universal care and respect.

31. For a more complete overview of religion and peacebuilding, see R. Scott Appleby, *The Ambivalence of the Sacred: Religion, Violence and Reconciliation* (Lanham, MD: Rowman & Littlefield, 2000); Douglas Johnston and Cynthia Sampson, eds., *Religion: The Missing Dimension of Statecraft* (New York: Oxford University Press, 1995); Douglas Johnston, ed., *Faith-Based Diplomacy, Trumping Realpolitik* (New York: Oxford University Press, 2003); Marc Gopin, *Between Eden and Armageddon: The Future of World Religions, Violence, and Peacemaking* (New York: Oxford University Press, 2000); Marc Gopin, *Holy War, Holy Peace* (New York: Oxford University Press, 2002).

32. See Marc Granovetter, "The Strength of Weak Ties: A Network Theory Revisited," *Sociological Theory* 1 (1983): 201–33; Valdis Krebs and June Holley, "Building Smart Communities through Network Weaving (2002–2006)," at orgnet.com/BuildingNetworks.pdf; Barry Wellman, "Network Analysis: Some Basic Principles," *Sociological Theory* 1 (1983): 155–200.

33. A node is the person who has links to either a tightly woven cluster, or who can have broad links to many other nodes and clusters depending on the behavior, values, and capacities of the node; see Krebs and Holley, "Building Smart Communities," 2.

34. BBC News covered the story of Rabbi Ovadiah Yosef, who apparently called for the annihilation of Arab enemies of Israel. See news.bbc.co.uk/2/hi/world/

monitoring/media_reports/1272343.stm. His defenders claimed that he was only referring to terrorists, but the damage was widespread. It is ironic in that this is the same rabbi who supported the Oslo Peace Process and was in favor of exchanging land for peace if it would save Jewish lives, a liberal position for an Orthodox rabbi in Israel. He is also well known for many outrageous statements about non-Orthodox Jews. See rac.org/Articles/index.cfm?id=2507. So non-Orthodox Israeli Jews are used to his antics and laugh at them. But the Arab reaction is not laughter because the enemy system, the cycle of hatred, is immediately stimulated by such remarks. In the Arab world, what a religious leader says is of great significance. This downward spiral of religious attitudes that moved toward hatred since the Millennium has been apparent in Judaism as well as in Islam. The endless Palestinian/Israeli conflict has been a major fuel of this fire of hateful rhetoric.

35. For more on positioning theory, morality, and action, see Rom Harre and Luk van Langenhove, eds., *Positioning Theory: Moral Context and Intentional Action* (Oxford and Malden, MA: Blackwell, 1999). The most important point is that power is sometimes less important than how someone positions themselves in human relationships. This is why an obsession with high clerics that one sees in interfaith dialogue is often so misplaced. It is not the person at the top who may matter as much as the person who has positioned him or herself the most to be an agent of change. This is why it has been clear in my work that inducing a shift in army or police behavior, for example, has much more to do with who is most widely influential with the security services, not what the head of a country, or even the head of the army, says that he wants.

36. What made the ceasefire "religious" was a deeply Islamic frame to the arguments, combined with Jewish religious frames, and especially extensive citations from the Koran and the Torah. The text, originally drafted in Hebrew and Arabic, was beautiful, and at the same time clear in its argument that it was by God's blessing that both Jews and Muslims have come to live in the Holy Land. God, the Greatest, will provide solutions to the problems between the Israeli and Palestinian people. This divine solution calls on people of faith from both sides to take the initiative in advocating and working on such a solution. See Marc Gopin, "Israelis Are Talking to Hamas," Middle East Online, May 16, 2008, at metimes.com/Opinion/2008/05/16/israelis_are_talking_to_hamas/3606 (accessed May 16, 2008).

37. See, for example, the range of networks affected by the work of Eliyahu Mclean, at jerusalempeacemakers.org/eliyahu/writings-recent-0412.html, and see there also the networks affected by the other Jerusalem peacemakers (accessed April 13, 2008).

38. It should be noted that extremist groups that have no social service arm, such as Islamic Jihad, are doing far worse in terms of recruitment than Hamas and Hezbollah, for example. But they all provide generous life insurance policies to suicide bombers, a powerful motivator to a family man who can provide far more to his family by dying than by living.

39. Conflict itself is often quite constructive in human relations, leading people toward shared goals, greater efficiency, greater justice, and greater trust. It is the destructive aspects of conflict, such as the verbal and physical abuse of the parties, that is the most damaging and which creates a cycle of retaliation. Intervention is required to break that cycle or spiral of retaliation.

40. See Elias Jabbour, *Sulha: Palestinian Traditional Peacemaking Process* (Montreat, NC: House of Hope, 1996); Mohammed Abu Nimer, *Non-violence and Peacebuilding in Islam: Theory and Practice* (Gainsville: University Press of Florida, 2003); Abdulaziz A. Sachedina, "Is There a Tradition of Pacifism and Nonviolence in Islam?" Paper presented at USIP workshop on Religious Perspectives on Pacifism and Nonviolence in Washington, DC, July 28, 1993; Sharon D. Lang, *Politics, Honor, and Peacemaking in Israeli–Palestinian Society* (New York: Routledge, 2005); Ralph Crow, Phillip Grant, and Saad E. Ibrahim, eds., *Arab Nonviolent Political Struggle in the Middle East* (Boulder, CO: L. Rienner Publishers, 1990). Also see Paul Salem, ed., *Conflict Resolution in the Arab World: Selected Essays* (New York: American University of Beirut, 1997) for a critique of Western conflict resolution and the importance of contextualizing conflict resolution in the Arab world through its indigenous practices. For peace and reconciliation in Palestine/Israel, see Elias Chacour, *Blood Brothers* (Grand Rapids, MI: Chosen Books, 1984), and Elias Chacour with Mary Jansen, *We Belong to the Land: A Story of a Palestinian Israeli Who Lives for Peace and Reconciliation* (Notre Dame, IN: University of Notre Dame Press, 2001). See also Ayse Kadayifci, "Living Walls: Among Muslims Peace Building Takes on Its Own Forms," *Harvard Divinity School Bulletin* 35, no. 4 (Autumn 2007): 22–29.

41. That is why Christian-to-Christian forms of peacemaking that Lederach has utilized in Nicaragua are best suited to Latin America more than anywhere else in the world. Conflicts in Latin America always involve parties that are all Christian. See Bruce Nichols's account of John Paul Lederach's religious conciliation between the Sandinistas and the East Coast Indians on Nicaragua, the importance of the Christian spiritual dimension in this effort, and the occasions where members of the negotiating teams in fact prayed together. Bruce Nichols, "Religious Conciliation between the Sandinistas and the East Coast Indians in Nicaragua," in *Religion: The Missing Dimension of Statecraft*, ed. Douglas Johnston and Cynthia Sampson, 73–74.

42. This story is based on the report of an anonymous eyewitness, but see Stephanie McCrummen, "U.S. Evangalist, a Critic of Islam, Reaches Out to Sudan's President," *Washington Post*, February 14, 2007, and washingtonpost.com/wp-dyn/content/article/2007/02/13/AR2007021301255.html (accessed May 16, 2008).

43. What we are witnessing among these people is a creative fusion of their spiritual and moral horizons. I mean this in the Gadamerian sense. See Mary Ann Stenger, "Gadamer's Hermeneutics as a Model for Cross-Cultural Understanding and Truth in Religion," in *Religious Pluralism and Truth: Essays on Cross-Cultural Philosophy of Religion*, ed. Thomas Dean (Albany: State University Press of New York, 1995), 151–68.

44. These include the actions of the World Congress on Imams and Rabbis for Peace. Reports and statements are found at imamsrabbis.org. Also see the reverberation of this positive development in the conservative newspaper *The Jerusalem Post* at jpost.com/servlet/Satellite?cid=1139395659456&pagename=JPost%2FJPArticle%2FShowFull (accessed April 13, 2008).

45. See islamicamagazine.com/Online-Analysis/Open-Letter-to-His-Holiness-Pope-Benedict-XVI.html (accessed April 13, 2008).

46. The Royal Aal Al-Bayt Institute for Islamic Thought in Jordan organized an international Islamic Conference in July 2005 that brought together religious leaders of the Sunni, Shi'ite, Zaydi, Ibadi, and Thahiri schools of jurisprudence. They

called collectively for a clear observance of *fatwa* issued by the Sheikh of Al-Azhar (the highest Sunni Muslim authority). This *fatwa* prohibits Muslims from declaring other Muslims apostates or committing violence against them, particularly those subscribing to more heterodox creeds such as the A'sharis, Sufis, or Salafis. See the full text of the statement at aalalbayt.org/en/conferencesandsymposia.html. Another development in October 2007 was the publication of *A Common Word*, a document signed by 138 Muslim scholars and sent primarily to the Vatican as a response to Catholic–Muslim tension arising from Pope Benedict's Regensburg, Germany, address. The Papal address on September 12, 2006, had angered Muslims around the world for insinuating that Islam was an irrational religion and hence susceptible to violence. *A Common Word* argues that reconciliation between Muslims and Christians would bring about world peace. The basis of this reconciliation is "love of God and love of neighbor," as documented in their respective sacred texts, the Quran and the Bible. See the full text at acommonword.com/ (accessed April 10, 2008). Prince Ghazi of Jordan, whom I had worked with closely to bring together King Abdullah and one hundred American rabbis in 2005, has been the principal force behind these efforts.

2

Religious Power and the
Future of Global Society

AN AGE OF SLOW PROGRESS

In this chapter I will outline the challenges of religious extremism to the future of human civilization. I will then present the need for short-term and long-term strategies to weave together a global social contract that includes as many religious traditionalists as possible. An inclusive social contract requires an ongoing process of conflict prevention and resolution with religious members of every civilization.

We live in an age of religious extremism that is indeed worrisome. Many of us had hoped that by this time in history, with the extremes of twentieth-century fascism and communism behind us and the Cold War a fading nightmare, we would be well on our way to democratic societies steadily emerging across the planet. We hoped for the development of a global consensus on basic democratic freedoms, and we sought a commitment to pluralism, in terms of ethnic, religious, and racial coexistence.

Many observers of the last two hundred years of modern history thought that traditional cultures, which often house intolerant prejudices, would slowly become fellow travelers to a progressive evolution of democracy and tolerance. That may still turn out to be true despite all the contrary indications, because progress in history has often been hard to perceive with the naked eye. Social progress is agonizingly slow in the history of human civilizations, and it is rarely linear in direction. One longs to see evidence of irreversible progress, but this often eludes the short-lived human being.

There are pushes and pulls of history that make it hard to trace a progressive direction of social consciousness. Yet there do seem to be massive shifts afoot in a positive direction. Slavery is now an embarrassment in most cultures and religions, despite the fact that some form of slavery was perfectly acceptable in most traditional religions until recently. In fact the laws governing slavery are still "on the books" for many religions, even though most clerics will vigorously deny their applicability today.

In every high-level interfaith dialogue I have ever participated in, and there have been many, even the most conservative representatives trip over themselves to profess the dignity and honor of women. In practice, many laws stay on the books that indicate something less than this claim, but there is hardly anyone left in a respectable position who *advocates* the inequality of women. This is a massive shift from just a half century ago.

There are extensive global rules today outlawing "crimes against humanity" that used to be acceptable practices of warfare according to many religious traditions, as well as acceptable in the most established democracies. Noncitizens used to be considered effectively nonpersons, but increasingly there is at least official recognition that noncitizens are something more than nonpersons, governed by numerous international agreements on human rights. One can see this seeping into the domestic American debate on illegal aliens, referred to now by many advocates as "unregistered citizens."

These are very slow moves toward the globalization of social contract and citizenship. The means of enforcement of these laws and trends is currently missing, however. But the fact that most nations on earth agree to new rules of war, law enforcement, and imprisonment and have to hide their violations, is a significant development. Preaching is not practice, but preaching sets the stage for future change in practice.

Murder rates in the major developed cities of the world are going way down, when seen from a very long view of history.[1] *This means that the foundations of the basic social contract between all human beings in a globalized community, together with the principle of the rule of law, are strengthening very slowly over time.*

The steady decrease in the acceptability of murder means that the most basic ethical assumptions of a liberal world are become stronger and more widespread. "Honor killings," such as killing a daughter who "violated" her virginity or who dared go on a date, are an embarrassment that is being covered up more and more by local cultures, even though these killings are still widespread.[2] But laws remain on the books in many countries that do not consider the murder of women in families under these circumstances to be murder.[3]

Duels to satisfy honor, once common in the West and practiced by its most distinguished citizens, including American presidents, would simply be considered second- or first-degree murder now. The real shift over time is not even in the murders themselves but in the public attitude toward murders for so-called honor. There are still many "honor killings," but they are not publicly as embraced by religions or communal representatives in most places.

A decrease in the acceptability of murder also means a much more widespread commitment to the value of every human life regardless of race, religion, or personal choices. This did not used to be the case when human beings lived as religious or ethnic groups in countries and regions that were largely monochrome: one dominant race, one ethnic group, or one dominant religion, with tiny unthreatening minorities interspersed here and there. One could consider oneself civilized, duly horrified at the killing of a member of one's own group or religion, but unmoved by the killing of others who you may not even consider quite human, or who legally may not even be considered quite human, like Africans or slaves.

But something dramatic has happened. Our major cities across the earth consist of unprecedented mixtures of minorities, all of whom are equally bound by the laws of the city and country. Effectively, minorities, viewed as a collection of groups, are becoming the majority.[4] This means that police and judges the world over are getting more and more used to colorblind and tribe-blind law.

This represents a major increase in a very basic and abstract idea that has never been so widely applied before in history to all of humanity. The commitment to a social contract, to the unacceptability of any human being's murder, for example, is a broad commitment to all of humanity as it appears in every major city. It is not just a commitment to one's religious, ethnic, or racial group. Black, white, or brown, gay or straight, Muslim or Wicca; if you kill someone you have committed murder in all the major capitals of the world today.

This is the early foundation of a global, enlightened community. This foundation seems to be steadily growing deeper legally and spreading in popularity. It is true that extremism is still a major attraction, and there are major setbacks of war and ethnic strife in specific locations that we will take note of throughout the book. In the midst of conflict, war, and political oppression, all the old instincts of fear and hatred come out.

This is precisely why citizen diplomacy, conflict prevention, and resolution are the embodiment of a war for enlightened civilization. These gestures and skills embody our attempts to cross all tribal lines, secure the global social contract, and prevent its dissolution.

Progress in the idea of the tolerant social contract, when seen over long periods of time, is unmistakable. We must recognize and internalize the fact of this progress, and not let it be overshadowed by our fears and disappointments with everything else that is wrong with human civilization.

We are disappointed, for example, with the behavior of large swaths of the Abrahamic religious communities today: those of Judaism, Christianity, and Islam. But often, in our disappointment and in our eagerness to make

utopia, there is a tendency to overfocus on the negative, on what is dangerous, without having an accurate sense of what else is real, what has *become
real because in our minds we willed it to be real.*

What *has* become real? We as a human community have willed it to
be real that human rights are a universal ideal, and we have enacted laws
globally to institutionalize them. The majority of religious leaders have embraced this as well. We have, on the other hand, failed so far to set in place
an adequate means of enforcement, because that appears to be a long-term
challenge to the absolute sovereignty of states. But the tendency to only
see the negative right now in history, the barbaric counter-trends, is a part
of the problem. Our minds focus on what is missing. Like the local news,
obsessed only with murder, rape, and assault, it is a distortion of the trends
of reality. This distortion must be resisted as we conceive of a realistic set
of alternatives in the future of humanity. Pessimism is just as unrealistic as
Panglossian[5] flights of fantasy. We need realistic pictures to conceive of effective plans for the global community.

UNRESOLVED ISSUES

Despite overall signs of progress, the twentieth century left many deep
problems unattended and unresolved. It is as if through the many world
war years of the twentieth century we had saved up for solution a whole
series of threats to sustainable life on this planet. These include, especially,
environmental degradation, but also chronic inequality of opportunity,
women's inequality, inequality of races, overpopulation, ineffective health
care and maintenance, and an inadequate economic strategy that can realistically maximize prosperity for the global south as well as the north.

Most of us have also come to understand that radical capitalism without
any restraints led to too much inequity. We seemed unable by the beginning of the twenty-first century to devise the kind of free enterprise that
would maximize freedom and prosperity for all in a globalized economy.

We managed to escape the Cold War without the feared catastrophe
of nuclear holocaust, which in many ways is an amazing achievement
considering how armed both sides were for the complete destruction of
humanity. But we now live in an age of resilient religious militancy that
threatens a chaotic slide into global confrontations that could yield untold human suffering. We do not face a doomsday threat of fifty thousand
nuclear warheads unleashed at once, but we face a threat of falling into
civilizational confrontations with weaponry that could destroy the lives
of millions. This will not stop the long-term march of progress, but millions may suffer needlessly, and we must devise new ways to confront
this challenge.

The Pervasive Scourge of Extremism

Religious militancy has some very nonviolent expressions and some very violent ones, as Appleby has emphasized.[6] The nonviolent expressions in terms of a life of devotion, prayer, and sacrifice have become increasingly prevalent, with many people searching for meaning in postmodern environments, such as big cities, that are bereft of deep culture and a sense of belonging. But this is benign.

What *is* a threat to everyone is the decidedly material and martial expression of religious militancy which is interested in taking over the public space, taking over and controlling land, and taking over bodies, especially female bodies.

Religious militancy most often expresses itself as a vehicle of promoting some national or ethnic interest, and it is amazingly capable of riding the horse of national or ethnic injury, ethnic pride, and ethnic rage. It is astonishing how resilient the destructive use of religion is in political history, and how easy it is to shift whole cultures and religions toward militant state and ethno-national agendas.

The most obvious example of the resurgence of religious militancy as a tool of social control is in the Islamic countries, and among Muslim minority communities globally, that are experiencing an unprecedented crisis of leadership, identity, and relative deprivation.[7] Much of this is deadly but artificially created by the distortions of oil wealth, and the subsequent infusion of Gulf-funded radicalism that assaults these communities in various pockets of the world with massive funds. Ironically, our excessive worship of carbon-based energy—which is killing the planet—is also assaulting the religious fabric of billions of lives; the radicalism of the few overtakes the relatively benign traditionalism of the many. The addiction to oil empowers a few radicals to ruin millions of small communities around the world by offering funds to the poor that must be accompanied by radical clerics. The damage done will not be quickly eradicated.

What does not meet the naked eye is that this crisis is taking place in a more subtle form in all the major religions and civilizations. From the cooptation of Christianity in the United States for a militant imperial agenda at the beginning of this century to the merging of Rwandan Catholicism, Serbian Orthodoxy, or Croatian Catholicism with an agenda of ethnic cleansing, to the pernicious effects of Hindutva on India's minorities, to the merging of Judaism and an ultranationalist agenda in Israel and the United States, we are seeing countless examples of how religion has become in recent years a handmaiden of exclusivist political ideologies and militant agendas.

It would seem that religion is also filling a void in national identities. Old nationalist and patriotic ideas that lost their fresh appeal now tend to use supplementation from religious ideology to motivate large numbers of people to extreme patriotism and violent behavior; it is as if religion often gives a booster shot to vapid nationalist rhetoric.

This is what happened with secular Zionism, for example, which lost its sheen and appeal to younger generations who either got tired of war or discovered the humanity of the Palestinian "other." The zeal of the first generation needed a booster shot from religious radicalism, and got it from religious Zionism, hence the continuing roadblocks to authentic coexistence in that tragic country.

Something Wrong with Modern Life?

But this infusion of religious radicalism has happened all over, and it suggests something missing or empty in modern life. The modern idea of the nation promised so much to people a couple of hundred years ago. Coupled with industrialization and modernization, nationalism promised prosperity and empowerment to all who were citizens, as well as personal fulfillment through pride in and defense of one's country.

But it turns out that this was a bit much to promise. Human fulfillment is more elusive than material prosperity, and more importantly, modernization led to massive dislocations of family and community that made meaningful fulfillment hard to find.

Liberal expressions of cosmopolitanism led to greater fulfillment of the individual but also to dislocations of the individual from family and community. Capitalism demanded great mobility to be educated and to succeed, further adding to disappointments in terms of community and a sense of belonging. This has been especially the case in experiments in modernization that were brutal, forced, and rapid, such as in Iran under the Shah, and in oil-rich countries.

At the same time that nationalism suffered some real setbacks as a vehicle of fulfillment, it seems that religion gave new life to nationalism as a vehicle for motivating millions of people to militant beliefs and behavior. But it is also the case that religious militancy is outpacing any one nationalism as a form of extreme devotion, thanks to the Internet and unprecedented levels of mass communication. Religious militancy also offers much more in terms of creating a sense of community, belonging, and fulfillment to rich and poor alike, connected to each other across the globe.

The strange thing about the modern world is that all of this is happening even as the trends of liberalism continue to increase their appeal to millions of others. On the one hand there is a resilient appeal of classical liberalism that is appealing to people across the globe, and it expresses itself in how many societies are experimenting with democracy, civil rights, and the steady extension of the social contract to more and more minorities. The reversals of the last decade cannot undo the trend of centuries toward an insatiable appeal of human rights and freedoms. But reactionary militancy is also vigorous and appealing.

There exists a vast contest across the globe right now between the idea of an open, democratic, egalitarian, pluralistic society, and the idea of a society that is controlled by a militant ideological agenda rooted in ethno-national, patriarchal, or religious exclusion.[8] The latter often uses traditional religious texts, but just as often distorts them for militant purposes.

The Fragility of Emerging Modern Democracy

There are those who are attracted to fundamentalism but also want to benefit from the globalization of democracy. There are millions of religious people who are in fact attracted to democracy.[9] But sometimes they mistakenly entrust their hopes for democracy to antidemocratic militant movements that promise to liberate them from unjust political and military regimes.

It is often the case in history that the first stages of experiments in democracy turn out to be vulnerable to antidemocratic ideologues and organizations. They make expansive promises to the masses, only to fail them when these organizations come to power. The moral bankruptcy of what I would call "demagogic democracy" certainly was best exemplified by Hitler. But it has been an ongoing lesson in recent times since the Iranian revolution robbed democratic moderates of their hopes and dreams. Elections that do not lead to civil rights for all will often become "demagogic democracy." I am sure that many Iranians hoped and believed that Khomeini would have had everyone's interests at heart when he took over, but he intended no such thing. He wanted a theocracy, pure and simple.

Many religious populations across the world seem doomed to learn about the dangers of democratization the hard way. It is difficult to imagine how so many religious people fall prey to a clever combination of a clear formula that consists of four elements: politicized religion, generous social services, militant behavior, and the promise of a perfect future.[10] But a few days inside a repressive regime helps make more sense of the choices for naïve hope that people make. After working in many difficult countries I can now appreciate a little bit more the stifling sense of desperation that police states impose on the human psyche.

It is also true that religious passion has always been easily manipulated. When you live your life day to day in poverty and misery with no hope of economic opportunity, it is easy to have a religious authority make you believe that there is a way out—so much the better if this person comes with generous help in the way of food, medicine, or child care. Even better still if all they want from you is to do something as benign and progressive as a vote for them in democratic elections. How could that not be a better alternative to a selfish capitalist culture, allegedly democratic, that is crushing them underfoot?

What has come to haunt us in the twenty-first century are the so-called "emerging democracies." These societies will often be dominated by a corrupt elite who may prevent any development of economic freedom for the vast majority. And yet a hungry globalized economy in search of raw materials and cheap labor will support the elite of this society by doing business with them, even as they crush millions into grinding poverty. (Indeed, the absurd gap between the highest and lowest paid has become extreme in the United States itself. So what stops emerging economies from doing the same in the face of such irresponsible role models in the major democracies?) We have learned that this is a perfect atmosphere for the development of religious militancy.

The truth is that transitions to greater empowerment through democracy in the West have always been a rough ride for those who were weak and vulnerable. Western industrialization brutalized millions of people before adjustments were made. Significant forms of empowerment through unions and the steady maturation of popular democratic power and legislative protections eventually improved the situation of average workers to a more tolerable level. People were also given educational ways out of the cycle of poverty, but all of these adjustments took time and struggle, and some of these positive adjustments are reversing themselves now in the wake of absurd discrepancies between rich and poor.

The Temptation of Extremism

The great danger today in the developing world is the degree to which radical religion is mobilized right now to take advantage of widespread misery. Followers are recruited to allegedly democratic political movements *without* the protection of a well-established democracy that upholds a permanent regime of civil rights. More importantly, radical religion is providing the social services that emerging economies fail to provide. It takes advantage of a simplistic equation of elections and democracy. In this it is aided by superficial Western enforcement of elections to the detriment of a deeper establishment of democracy.

We cannot afford as a global community to unwittingly aid this process of destruction. This is not to say that there are not many legitimate religious movements that authentically care about people and are also committed to democratic governance. But the distinctions between what is religiously moderate and what is radical are lost on most young people. They easily get trapped by radical groups, and this endangers the future of human freedoms around the world.

This explains the success of the Iranian revolution with idealistic students, as well as Hezbollah and Hamas. In fact, I have met Christian supporters of Hezbollah's Nasrallah! They like his strength, his honesty, his personal commitments, and his lack of corruption. This indicates that the problem is often not so much religious extremist impulses as much as a lack of attractive alternatives.

BUILDING GLOBAL CIVILIZATION IS ESSENTIAL AND ATTAINABLE

Building the foundations of a social contract for a global community is vital at this moment in history precisely for this reason. We cannot afford so much hopelessness among millions of people that religious extremists are the only ones they trust. We can no longer afford to intensify our economic interdependence as a globe without building a corresponding moral and social interdependence.

We need a global social contract that presses autocratic regimes to move in the direction of greater freedoms and greater opportunity for empowerment. But the contract we forge must also challenge religious movements to equally share the countries they inhabit with nonbelievers and a variety of religious communities.

If we start to create this contract we will begin to see an alliance of stronger democracies and more progressive religions in the developing world who could more effectively stand up to the selfish core of the north–south relationship. Tyranny and extremism in the developing world offer good excuses to take advantage of the south. But stronger states with better governance in the south, along with the vital input of moderate cultural and religious traditions, would be able to embarrass the selfish northern states into a better balance of economic power.

The lack of human rights and democracy in the developing world are the excuse of richer countries to take advantage of poorer ones. Remove that excuse and some profound changes will occur. The emergence of a global social contract will constitute a call for the taking of responsibility by all players on the global stage, rich and poor, religious and secular.

Our very survival is dependent upon this kind of global negotiation toward a new social contract. Now more than ever the human community is utterly interdependent, and the earth, in turn, depends upon a greater unity of our goals for its health and survival.

The utter interconnectedness that we are beginning to experience will lead possibly to self-destruction, a war of all against all. Or it just may lead to a new sense of human community that we have never achieved before. The choice to buy into a war of all against all or into a new cooperative community is something that every human being will have to face, as far as his actions and attitudes are concerned. Will she be contributing to one or to the other? This is a stark choice and the ultimate responsibility for the future.

What I would define as the most basic element of a global civilization would be a series of common ethical and political commitments that would be embraced by most every nation. We have the foundations of such commitments in the form of many international agreements, but very few tools of implementing these commitments.

The most obvious impediments to identifying with the commitments of a global civilization are exclusive tribal and national commitments. Not any less important are the prior commitments of powerful nations to the preservation and enhancement of their own wealth at the expense of others.

This book will deal with one of the other impediments standing in the way of an emerging self-conscious global civilization, and that is the historical role of religion as a divider of humanity, oft-times a quite violent divider of humanity.

THE PROMISE OF HUMAN WISDOM AND RESILIENCE

All of these obstacles, taken together with the unprecedented technology of destruction in the last hundred years, raise a central concern, which is whether humanity and its earthly habitat will survive. There are indicators suggesting both survival and destruction. Human civilization has always been awash in contradictions of resilience and destruction. Some of our tendencies have always militated toward a level of self-destruction unseen in the animal world. We commit genocide, often with little gained in the long run, but animals do not. On the other hand, human resilience, the astonishingly creative response we sometimes muster to challenges and near catastrophes, introduces an unknown quantity into predictions of our future.

We simply do not know when we as people will sink or swim, how badly we will fail and what resources we have for recovery. Who could have predicted that out of the barbarous blood fest of the American Civil War would come a vision of Lincoln's that has inspired generations of progressive Americans to fight for social justice? Who could imagine that Ronald Reagan, the relentless anti-communist warrior, dissatisfied with a stalemate with the Soviet Union, would be the one to have the political capacity and interpersonal skill to reach out to the "enemy," Gorbachev, and to thus prevent the greatest world war in human history? With ashes behind us, and ashes in our nightmares, we humans often create the most surprising tides of resilience.

That is what we are called upon to do now. We see before us a world that is in many places fragmented and violent, where mutual suspicions abound across civilizations. We waste astonishing amounts of resources on outmoded forms of militarization, waging aggressive wars of "defense" unilaterally. Our primitive defense policies bleed precious economic resources when robust collective forms of international security based on integrated policing and prevention would be far more efficient, not to mention moral. All this as the planet's life-sustaining capacity, its oxygen, is overwhelmed by carbon dioxide, which is a symbol of our own neglect.

But right beneath the surface of an earthly crisis, which is crystallized and symbolized by global warming, there abounds creative global human interactions by the millions every day. We talk to each other, love each other, and live with each other, across the globe and across civilizations more than at any time in history.

This adds up to at least the possibility of a paradigm shift in human civilization: the potential of a global civil society. There are countless international nongovernmental organizations (INGOs) spanning the earth, uniting people of every race and religion, who work on worthy causes of dizzying variety. Average life expectancy is way up as a result, and infant mortality is way down. This is our resilience at work, and it suggests great possibilities for the future.

There is a paradigm shift that seems to be at work in all this international cooperation, but as in all paradigm shifts we cannot easily evaluate it in midstream. All these dizzying changes make it harder to make a clear-headed assessment of our own potential. We require therefore a vision of our future that can be rationally aspired to.

Here is the essential paradox we must confront to move forward. There appears to be great sophistication at work today in the brainpower of millions of human beings *as individuals*. Millions of people engage in technical advances. Most of us, educated and simple alike, intuitively know the essential truth of the freedoms of democracy. We also sense the truth and value of scientific inquiry, and we therefore often display the requisite skeptical humility before what we do not know. Many people across the globe see the need to balance wealth with responsibility for others, and also the need to pursue technology but recognize its limits. We have come to see the benefits of mature society-building by way of democracy and the rule of law. Yet *as collective groups* we are still behaving like barbarians.

THE PERIL OF COLLECTIVE BARBARITY

Most of our political and religious leaders seem curiously behind in joining this emerging human wisdom. Our wisdom as individuals seems to be far ahead of our behavior as groups because we seem to direct leaders to act in our name with a far more primitive set of impulses.

We pay lip service to wise visions as individuals, but our actions as groups suggest a primitive approach to the world, as if the world is a wild frontier of "winner take all," with no rules, no limits, no responsibility, and no negotiation. Both organized religions and governments run wild with the fantasies of conquest. The vast majority of countries train their diplomats to pursue not much beyond the so-called "national interests" of big business, for example. And the major missionary religions treat proselytizing as big business as well—the business of conquest.

It is this unscrupulous behavior of nations and cultural collectives like religion that allow autocratic regimes to flourish with wealth and weapons and power. There is a collusion of primitive collective behavior that sets the atmosphere for cruel regimes to persist. The world is not unjust because a few dictators tyrannize the planet in the developing world. This is a failure of our collective will, of our behavior not as individuals but as collectives, especially as nations, as a community of nations, but also as communities of the religiously faithful.

As far as my native United States is concerned, the Bill of Rights sits before the conscience of every American, proudly, but the Wild West has been more the stuff of global fantasies and foreign policy miscalculations in recent decades. This is a dangerous mix when one realizes that American citizens are the most powerful people on earth, overseeing a military that simultaneously operates in over 160 countries.

All of this suggests that on a very large scale we are still growing up as a species, and that we need to push harder at a fundamentally new way of thinking about our planetary organization. Reaching a global scale of community will involve some unprecedented psychological challenges and choices, *especially around the integration or coexistence of our greatly varied identities.* Our sense of responsibility will need to integrate our identities as individuals, as national citizens, as religious beings, and as citizens of the planet.

Here we will deal with one of those choices involving the interaction of religion, culture, and power. The task is to live together with others who share much with each other, but differ in other substantial ways around religious belief and practice. The challenge is essentially one of forging the rules of equal coexistence between people when so many of those same people are members of religious traditions that promote an exclusive superiority of revelation, mission, and even human worth.

THE UNPRECEDENTED CHALLENGE OF EQUAL COEXISTENCE

There have been many forms of *unequal* coexistence in the past, between civilizations and between religions, but rarely equal coexistence. There have been times when one religious group dominated but tolerated the other religions, but that is different than the challenge we face today. We face a world of major cities, from Beirut and Jerusalem to New York and London, in which multiple groups must either sink in a swamp of hatred or swim in coexistence.

In addition there is the question of self-limitation. Can religions that are used to limitless expansion and self-promotion become self-limiting?[11] Can they become used to a world that can no longer afford aggressive efforts of one religious group to dominate others?

One way to begin to answer these questions is to ask a simple historical question. Are these challenges of coexistence, of the need for religions to be self-limiting, an unprecedented challenge? Not really, but the precedents are buried in obscure places and times of human history.

Old Wisdom beneath the Sands

Answering this question fully would require a separate study, but I want to respond by sharing the story of a place I have come to know in Syria called Dura-Europos. I dream of Dura-Europos often even though it is long gone now. It was an ancient town in Eastern Syria not far from the Iraqi border. It flourished over two thousand years ago, from the last centuries before the Common Era, the time of Jesus, to a couple of centuries after the Common Era.

When Dura-Europos was unearthed in the 1920s it was discovered that there was a synagogue that had been buried in dirt for almost two thousand years, with the result that all the paintings of the walls survived intact. The synagogue abutted the protective wall of the city, and when the city was attacked they buried the synagogue in dirt to protect the outer walls. The discovery of these intact synagogue paintings was unprecedented, for almost all other synagogues had never had paintings, as far as we know, due to Jewish rabbinic laws discouraging religious painting. But this region had a specialty in religious art that influenced all the religious sites.

The Damascus Museum now houses the remnants of those synagogue walls, and they are in a closed room behind dark curtains. It was the winter of 2005 as I stood motionless before those walls for what seemed like an eternity, unable to move. My eyes began to water in the presence of a painting, as they had done before only once in front of Van Gogh's *Starry Night*. It was like being alive two thousand years ago with vivid portraits of faces and vivid synagogue scenes. There are exquisitely painted memories of then recent calamities, such as the destruction of the central Jewish Temple of Jerusalem in 70 AD, and also past glories like the reign of Solomon.

Not long after staring at the synagogue portraits, I found myself attending services at a synagogue in Old Damascus on Saturday morning. I noticed

two men with some of the exact same distinctive facial characteristics that
I had seen on those ancient walls, and I thought to myself that there is so
much that is miraculous about the continuity of human life. We go into
countries that are strange to us, and all we think of is politics or the quality of the hotel. We get excited about a few ancient bones from long dead
humans that we may see at the museum, but we fail to see the living monu-
ments to history walking past us on the street at every moment.

The most extraordinary thing about Dura-Europos is that there were no
less than sixteen different temples in the city.[12] There were temples to three
different versions of Zeus worship, to Artemis, and many other forms of
worship, including a Christian church.

What astonished me the most, however, was the *layout* of this Middle
Eastern city. It appears that the city was *planned* in such a way to have every
one of these religious forms of worship represented, all along a geometric
pattern in the *center* of the city. Over two thousand years ago this city was
planned for equal coexistence of religions.

Try to imagine the sight. One cannot see this kind of planning for religious pluralism in any major Western city, now or then. The center of
cities is always dominated by one church or another, with others being
built later, competitively. For this reason Dura-Europos has captured my
imagination in terms of the age-old question of religious pluralism, of human coexistence, of majority and minority relations, and the primeval fonts
of human wisdom.

I have been brought up as a monotheist, but I must say that recent
manifestations of monotheistic intolerance and self-righteousness in all
three Abrahamic faiths have made me sick with anger, especially in the last
two decades of my life. From Bosnia to Rwanda to Saudi Arabia to Israel
to the White House I have sensed the fatally corrosive effects of the abuse
of power on Abrahamic faiths. It has left me with a decisive loss of faith
in the wisdom of absolute power residing in any human construct, especially religious constructs. After millennia of human emulation of Divine
omnipotence it seems that religious human beings are at their worst and at
their least wise when they are the most powerful.

Wisdom emerges from powerlessness not power. That is why I like being
a minority, and I like experiencing difference. Monotheism has its tendencies toward intolerance but it is especially the case when it is in the hands of
the majority. Minorities, however, tend to develop more benign interpretations of their religion. In my case, being a religious minority means that I
always know a great deal about others, more than they know about me, and
so I can never be lulled into the self-delusions that majorities often fall into.
The safety of the majority is always a false safety. Majorities are unprepared
for destruction that may be coming because they do not know or care to
know the strangers in their midst.[13]

The New Wisdom of Human Rights

Another challenge of traditional monotheistic thinking has always been that it is strong on extensive responsibilities that human beings have toward one another, and weak on rights. By contrast, liberal society has been weak on personal responsibility, perhaps by design. On the other hand, the evolution of liberal thinking on human rights in the last few hundred years has been a breath of fresh air *for the major Western religions*. Human rights simply do not allow for the many categories of hatred or persecution of minorities that seep into most organized religions. The power of the human rights perspective in the development of modern liberal states has forced many a theologian, therefore, to revision his religious constructs, to reinterpret old categories of exclusion. Even more radically, human rights have turned into something sacred in the modern period at the hands of liberal religious theologians. A commitment to human rights became a way to affirm the sacredness of every human being. This is a remarkable development at the hands of courageous believers of conscience.

Science and free inquiry, however, have not been consistently beneficial to human rights. The technical mechanization of mass murder and torture has been the bane of modernity's contribution to human rights abuses. Human rights abuses have been magnified by the machine gun, poison gas, napalm, and helicopter gunships. But the boon of modernity has surely been an unprecedented confluence of secular and religious thinking on human rights.

This may lead in the long run to an irreversible human commitment to the concept and practice of human rights. One could not say this, for example, on the eve of World War II, with the Church's official preference, for example, for fascist over communist parties in most countries that subsequently participated in an unprecedented slaughter of innocents across Europe. By the time we reach the 1990s, however, Croatian and Serbian nationalist forces' employment of Christianity to justify ethnic cleansing was seen by most other Catholics and Christians as a spiritual travesty.

This is where hope lies. Hope lies in the evolution of global commitments to every human being. Hope also lies in a consensus, religious and secular, that some deeds are evil, but not human beings as such. Human beings are not inherently evil, and in fact they are rather similar across cultures in both their positive capacities and their failings. This too has become the basis of common understanding by many millions of people, both religious and secular.

Some of our institutions, religious and secular, still behave, however, as if this truth is not accepted. States and religious collectives can behave as if primitive wars of domination are still the only way to exist, where evil is not about a crime but a way to define whole groups of others.

Despite our legitimate fears of contemporary religious extremism, many classical representatives of conservative organized religion the world over have embraced human rights, *at least in principle*. No self-respecting cleric of the major religions would publicly spurn the *concept* of human rights today. The detailed extension of human rights to everyone in every aspect of their lives, however, such as for women and homosexuals, will be fought over for decades to come.

The extension of human rights to everyone has been a steady battle for hundreds of years that appears to be on a relatively linear path to completion. Human rights were long ago accepted, but only to be savaged by "exceptions" that were made for native Africans, native Americans, and so on. This has been a long struggle of ideals versus selfish realities.

Organized religion will always be the space of the last holdout for full extension of rights, because human rights represent to guardians of the faith a surrender of control over private and public morality.[14] The irony is this: spiritual religious principles were a foundation of thinking for many of those, as early as Grotius, who championed human rights. But conservative religion's representatives will generally be the last to surrender control over the individual's conscience. Human rights depend for their continued existence, however, on the free exercise of individual conscience. In my opinion, a long view of history suggests that the die has been cast for human rights as a universally dominant moral construct, and it is organized religion that will be on the defensive in this regard.

Human rights are honored often in the breach the world over, but this is still a significant shift in human history, and in religious history. First theory, or our cognitive constructs, change, and then, slowly, very slowly, our institutions of survival and competition will adjust to the cognitive moral constructs that we set in stone. Just as big business, despite great protests, always adjusts to environmental laws, so too will organized religions adjust eventually to the freedom of the public space.

In a certain sense, we are witnessing a tug of war between three forms of leadership in the matrix of the biblical universe: the prophets, the priests, and the kings. These three nodes of biblical leadership also form nodes or points of departure for the Western psychology of leadership. (1) The prophets, social critics, poets, and bohemians conceive of a radical new world of justice and equality, and they are very good at provoking the imagination of the average person to join their democratic vision. But this is also threatening. (2) The priests resist the vision because it threatens the power of their religious rituals and strictures over the lives of citizens. (3) The monarchs resist the social justice because it interferes with their desire to accumulate as much power and wealth for themselves as possible.

Who in this matrix truly stands for the voice of God, or for Truth, or for Conscience? This has been completely contested in history. Today, I would argue, in the age of democracy, the locus of truth becomes a decision inside the heart of every citizen as to where he or she places their ultimate allegiance. Is it with prophets, priests, or monarchs, with social critics, with clerics, or with "the national interest" as embodied by powerful lobby interests? More and more the vox populi, I believe, will be with human rights and democracy because it is so irresistibly beneficial to every human being. There is far more of an intuitive grasp by large swaths of humanity of John Rawls's "original position" approach to political justice than is generally acknowledged.[15]

The Central Space of "The Strange Other" in the New Contract

Human rights, housed in documents such as the Bill of Rights, are the sine qua non of the survival of minorities, not constitutions or free elections. The prophetic voices of the United States, such as Martin Luther King, whom I admired as I grew up, were the prophets of a minority. The Jewish religion I grew up with was a religion of a minority—an oftentimes persecuted minority that was trying to recover from the worst genocide in its history. But Israeli Judaism (and its pervasive impact on contemporary Judaism) is so different than the Judaism that I experienced as a child.

Israeli Judaism is the religion of the majority, and it is suffering the same tragic effects that other religions of the majority experience. Whenever and wherever Christianity, Islam, or Judaism dominate and lay claim to whole states or regions, they tend to corrupt the thinking of the majority, and they easily forget that love for the stranger—or what I like to call "the strange other"—those who are fundamentally different, was actually a litmus test of decency for the Bible. It was *a divine litmus test for the very right to possess land*, at least in the dozens of texts about the stranger, the fellow resident who is not of your religious group.[16] Love of the strange other is certainly the litmus test of any civilization today that dares call itself a democracy and that hopes to organize itself around inalienable human rights.

Invariably the minorities in our midst carry a bizarre and strange narrative of history that is at odds with the majority's narrative. Minorities carry the history of inconvenient truths. But these truths, if embraced honestly and debated by the majority, have great potential for healing. The minority can become the bedrock of the entire community's evolving conscience—but only if they are not silenced. That is why majorities and minorities must occupy the public space *equally*, for it is in their dialogue and debate of competing narratives as equals that a society can grow spiritually and evolve away from its flaws and failings.

Returning to Dura-Europos, I think to myself how almost two thousand years ago in the Middle East, in a region now embroiled in the most dangerous conflicts in the world, a large group of Syrians knew how to design a city that was *by definition*—not by happenstance—culturally and spiritually pluralist, a place where strangers could almost assuredly find a form of worship right for them, and that they would undoubtedly mix in public in a context of radical pluralism and equality.

Then I think of our contemporary world, and the world wrought by our civilizations, and I say that the Middle East of today, in all its monotheistic manifestations, cannot hold a candle to Dura-Europos. Iran cannot hold a candle to the Persia of Cyrus, and the Gulf cannot hold a candle to Al-Andalus. And if biblical holiness entails the vision of God inside every human being, then the Holy Land is not a very holy place these days. The Abrahamic religions, taken as a whole, are hardly promoting the kind of tolerance that polytheistic Hellenistic civilization promoted over two thousand years ago (at least through some of its voices and institutions).

Monotheistically infused nationalism, that new religion of the last couple of hundred years, is among the most destructive of all. Friar Ivo Markovic, a Croatian Franciscan hero of peacemaking, refers to this kind of monotheistic ethno-nationalism as a retreat to magic and paganism, though this may be too insulting to pagans.[17] Surely this must produce some soul-searching from all of our monotheistic institutions today. But it does not, at least not yet.

Wisdom comes from everywhere, and it is sometimes buried beneath layers of two-thousand-year-old sand in Syria, but it is no less real. The sands of the Middle East cover up oil, carbon energy that should probably remain buried because it is killing the region and our planet. But those same sands also cover up experiments in human living, some negative and some positive, that can still teach us moderns a thing or two. That is why I keep coming back to this haunted place called the Middle East, why I respect it for what it has to teach me, even when it is mired in trouble that is engulfing all of our lives.

STEPS TOWARD THE SOCIAL CONTRACT

The question remains, however, even if we find historical precedents for authentic and equal coexistence, how do we take effective, realistic steps in this direction right now? The steps must be pragmatic, but they must also be preceded by a clear vision. So many international efforts have failed because they are reactive not visionary. We need (1) a vision and then (2) practical steps to get there. These two aspects must live in dramatic tension since what is required of both does not easily cohere.

In terms of vision, there has been a dream for centuries that humanity is heading toward global community based on a social contract. The notion of society-wide covenants between God and community is as old as the Bible itself. But the foundational works of Hugo Grotius, John Locke, Immanuel Kant, and Jean-Jacques Rousseau, among many others, pushed these ideas further, toward the dream of *global* covenant and community. Their ideas about covenant were often inspired by commitments to spiritual values, such as the sacred value of every human being, which at least implies absolute equality of worth and rights.

The twentieth century saw efforts to experiment with a global social contract with the creation of the League of Nations, the United Nations, and the International Criminal Court. These experiments remain incomplete because there is still not enough power in global institutions to enforce global commitments. They also lack a parallel set of institutions that represent a popular global voice; instead they cater to states that comprise the United Nations. And just as democracies recognized the need for two kinds of representatives, those representing states' interests and those representing individual citizen interests (Senate and House in the United States, House of Lords and House of Commons in Great Britain), so too do the peoples of the world need representation at the global communal level. Nevertheless the institutions of global community appear to be growing.

There are some religious parallels to this slowly evolving global community. Take, for example, the Parliament of World Religions in the last hundred years, or the more recent movement, United Religions Initiative.

These are all unprecedented, certainly for the rigid monotheistic faiths. They intimate an evolving acceptance, even in conservative monotheistic circles, of a global communal covenant. This is not just based on utopian, messianic dreams that appear universal but are often exclusive in terms of salvation. Rather we are seeing the evolution of regularly engaged relationships.

Here is another important point. A fortunate byproduct of global multistate institutions that are officially secular is that their growth has led many a religious conservative religious leader to seek out allies from *other* religious communities. There is now a healthy competition afoot between secular globalization across state lines and interreligious globalization, a kind of unionization of religious traditionalists. The latter see that they have a common adversary in secular states that do not take them seriously. Thus, religious pluralism may be on the increase if only because religious conservative leaders in secular states increasingly see themselves as misunderstood minorities!

This is actually a wonderful development from my perspective as a scholar/ practitioner of conflict resolution. It *requires* religious traditionalists to increasingly shelve fantasies of domination, and instead focus their efforts jointly with other religions on their right to freely practice religion *as minorities*. But this puts them squarely inside the universe of human rights discourse!

Interreligious leaders are arguing to be recognized and respected using the human rights language of weakness, or victimhood. By this I mean that (following Nietzsche's critique of ethics, but inverting it) the language of rights and social justice, from the Bible to our own day, is the language of the weak; it is the claim of the weak against the strong. It is an argument for fairness to all, especially those who are vulnerable and have human rights as their only recourse to empowerment.

The more that religious and interfaith leaders engage this kind of language and justification the more they are buying into a worldview where everyone, no matter how weak or small or weird, has inalienable rights, *including those who have been condemned by religious texts*. This necessitates interpretive development and the liberalization of religion. Ineluctably, this is creating secular/religious bridges of understanding, by contrast to exclusive salvation fantasies that can only divide. Those exclusive fantasies can and will continue. The key to a peaceful future, however, is that these exclusive fantasies play a secondary role to a pragmatic social contract of universal commitments that includes religious and secular alike.

The twentieth century has proven that the road to a democratic future, which includes both religious and secular covenants of global cooperation, is filled with potholes and reversals. Nevertheless it appears to be inexorable as the planet becomes smaller and humanity becomes larger. This is a difficult road that requires a vision of something that has not yet been created. We have been very good at pouring large amounts of resources into our international business relationships, but that is not the same as creating a more profound social vision of global community.

Building a vision of global community requires thought on our behavior as human beings. In other words, how will we act and treat each other in this globalized community? How we behave depends on how we agree to behave. We are searching then for a global community based on an interactive web of national and international social contracts.

We already have the basis for the behaviors required to uphold these contracts at the national level that can serve as a model for international relationships. In essence we are looking for a social contract that is based on democracy and freedom, which guarantees rights to every individual regardless of race, religion, color, or sexual orientation. This implies a radical right of all people to choose their own identity religiously and sexually. It also assumes freedom of inquiry that gives an unfettered right to thought, speech, research, and political organization.

Can Religion and the Liberal Social Contract Coexist?

The ideological founders of this model in the West, such as Adam Smith, never assumed that such freedoms and the attendant capitalism of a free market would satisfy all aspirations of the human spirit.[18] Furthermore, there was never an assumption that rights and radical freedom would satisfy moral obligations of one person to another. Indeed, especially due to widespread economic imbalances, as well as the emptiness of unfettered materialism, the search for deeper forms of spiritual fulfillment and social obligation is as alive as ever.

The problem is that this unfulfilled aspect of human aspiration has been the basis of millions of people turning to illiberal forms of religion as a radical answer to the disappointments of both capitalism and Marxist materialism.

Does such a search for spiritual fulfillment necessarily lead to an undermining of the radically free society? Yes and no. There are some blatant contradictions between science and spiritual systems that claim mythic or magical explanations for what science cannot accept. There are basic divides on the very nature of cause and effect.

There does then appear to be a contest of sorts between science and religion, but does it have to be a fight to the death for the public space? And has the contest been exacerbated by those who seek power over others through the use of religion?[19] The answer to these questions is, in a word, yes and no. Yes, religion has been used for power, but, no, this does not have to be a fight to the death for the public space. There are ample models of nonviolent religion that do not require coercion of others or their manipulation.

The real challenge for the future, however, is to develop a coalition globally that *wants* to create a social contract that includes religious and nonreligious people alike. The goal is the empowerment of those people—religious and nonreligious alike—whose commitment to equal coexistence along the lines of a social contract and civil rights is paramount, serious, and proven.

Less important is how each person or group nuances the balance of scientific and religious explanations of cause and effect in the privacy of their own thoughts and worldviews. Less important to us should be whether a person's moral judgments as he debates dilemmas such as abortion is religiously based or based on some other form of moral intuition. Less important should be the differences between people on what social, moral, and ritual obligations they take upon themselves as part of their spiritual fulfillment. Much more important is the question of whether or not she can live peacefully in a universe in which others, without coercion, come to their own conclusions about these matters. Can he live peacefully as he watches equal citizens debate difficult moral dilemmas of life and death, war and peace? That is the litmus test of the new social contract.

Short-Term Strategies of Religious Inclusion Combined with Long-Term Strategies of Empowerment of the Individual

In the coming chapters I will offer illustrations of inclusion of religious traditionalists in the formation of civil society discussions and debates. This is a *short-term* strategy of inclusion of conservative religious communities in the process of building a new global civil society, even in very politically re-pressed countries. I will demonstrate how this can lead to wider, interfaith consensus on nonviolent solutions to major political conflicts, as well as how we can utilize this consensus to build progressive civil societies even in conflict regions.

At the same time history has proven time and again that the only viable *long-term* way for religion to play a positive role in building civil society is for clerics and religious communities to have very little power over the indi-vidual. Otherwise, freedoms are always diminished or eliminated, the mind is stunted, science suffers, and minorities are always persecuted.

There is no way around the conclusions of major Enlightenment figures that religion is at its worst when it has absolute power. My own more posi-tive conclusion is that religion can be at its best when it plays the role of peaceful social critic and conscience of a civilization. In fact, it is indispens-able to have prophets to remind imperfect political, military, and economic leaders of their fundamental social obligations, or of the need to nurture the nonmaterial side of human needs and aspirations. But it is deadly to turn any society over to priests and clerics.

The past several hundred years of Western history, and now global his-tory, have demonstrated the vital importance to human progress and pro-ductivity of the basic freedoms and empowerment of all human beings. The freedom of the individual is the litmus test of progress, and it is clear that many religious traditions, as traditionally interpreted, stand in the way of this march toward freedom of the individual.

As I have intervened in regional conflicts where religion plays an impor-tant role, I have tried to balance short-term respect for traditional religion, on the one hand, and, on the other, a way to secure the steady march of in-dividual freedoms by avoiding undue support for repressive representatives of a religion. This is the balancing act that I will address in this book based on the trials and errors of field experience and experimentation.

My experience in the field has proven to me that most everyone is err-ing in this balancing act. Secular liberals in charge of multilateral interna-tional agencies and government institutions lack the skill and *tolerance* to include religious traditionalists in their efforts to promote development and positive social change. On the other hand, the apologists for organized religion are legion, especially in the United States, failing to see the danger to women and minorities of glossing over organized religion's numerous intolerances.

There is no clear-headed strategy to combine two objectives: (1) respect for religion and (2) caution at the same time. Put another way, it is the distinction between (1) a near-term strategy to respect and include reli-gious representatives in civil society building (especially in mostly religious countries), and (2) a long-term strategy to progressively liberate vulnerable individuals from the clutches of repressive social and cultural orders.[20]

These two objectives and strategies sometimes contradict each other, and that is precisely why reflection on ethics and wisdom feature prominently in later chapters of this book. We need study of wisdom literature, study of precedents, reflective practice,[21] self-examination, and a familiarity with ethical reflection over the centuries to wend our way through the labyrinth of imperfect progress. Reflection and self-examination are essential when there are competing goals and high stakes.

The best experiments in the field intuitively balance these two objectives and strategies, based on the lessons of experience. But the best experiments also require a finely tuned deliberation of what is most right to do in each situation, with a reflective background in ethics and wisdom.[22]

Whenever there are competing objectives and multiple goods one must consult the deliberations of ethics literature and wisdom literature. The history of wisdom literature and ethics comprise the collective human effort to learn from experience. But experience is inherently complicated and often suggests competing courses of action based on the circumstances.

Practical ethics most often should have a basis in knowledge of and balance of many schools of ethical reflection, as well as learning from experience, one's own and that of others. I will examine this more fully in the last chapters when I outline the experience of learning from ethical dilemmas that my partners and I face in the field. For example, there are issues concerning cooperating with autocratic regimes, in terms of self-censored speech, to have access to people to promote ideas of coexistence, conflict resolution, democracy, or interfaith tolerance, or to even be a mediator between enemy groups.

There is not a diplomat in the world who has engaged in peace negotiations, for example, who does not keep his mouth shut about the dirty laundry of the people he has to work with, despite what Immanuel Kant, as the champion of absolute moral laws, may have expected of them. There is hardly any way to achieve the laying down of arms without some dishonesty and cover-up in these deliberations. And yet, there are degrees of dishonesty, cover-up, silence, and collusion. How does one construct an ethic and style of intervention that does not subvert the very principles of a just civil society that you are trying to foster? I will address this in detail later, but for now I will say briefly that this kind of balancing act can only be done by trial and error.

This balance also requires vision, a view of where one is headed. And that vision (and this is a bow to John Stuart Mill, the champion of consequentialist balancing of positive and negative outcomes) requires an evaluation of each action in terms of its long-term costs and benefits.

Where I want to be headed as an ethical/political goal might be, for example, the greatest happiness for all, or the greatest peace, or the greatest amount of lives saved, or the prevention of the most suffering, or the generation of the most social justice—or some balance of all of these laudable outcomes. Balancing such goals requires imperfect calculation, guess work, and intuition, very messy things that necessitate submission to the very scientific but deeply frustrating experience of trial and error.

Finally—in a bow to Kant—it requires a commitment to "red lines," things that you will never do under any circumstances. If, however, you violate your own red lines, as many of us do in war, you must have the kind of reflection in place that will help you acknowledge your failure and help you move back to your red lines. This is hard because the outcomes you are working for lie before your eyes like a treasure, like an obsession. Often peace becomes so wrenchingly enticing, so seemingly within arm's reach that it is easy to flee across red lines in the pursuit of high-minded goals; I know I have. Yet, once you cross these lines you may be in league with the very political and military leaders whose own compromises you tend to despise, even as you smile at them. At the very least, the simple ethics of your childhood seem dead and buried. This is hard, and it requires recovery. It requires consultation with those who are wise and compassionate, both alive and in the past.

One important premise of this book—to honor religion but also contain its power over the public space[23]—is complicated in terms of ethical choices. It suggests that we can include religious people, even conservative people, in the building of global civilization, even as we curtail the power of religion to tyrannize the individual in the public space. How this can be done honestly and forthrightly is a difficult calculus. Deciding when one's efforts at inclusivity have spilled over into aiding those who would subvert the rights of others has been inherently complicated and imprecise in my own work in Israel and Palestine, for example. I never knew when working with very patriarchal, narrow systems of religion was bringing more peace or more tyranny. And I simply had to judge my own interventions on a case-by-case basis.

Achieving some success, therefore, requires the wisdom of experimentation and experience, a strong dose of humility, but also a fairly clear vision of the kind of society that we want to move toward. The latter is essential for creating the ingredients of a social contract, which, in turn, is essential for a nonviolent path to the future.

In a word, all of my experience of twenty-five years in the field of conflict resolution and religion suggests that the separation of religion and coercive power is essential to a peaceful future, but that traditional religious people must wherever possible be actively pursued and included in the process of building a peaceful social contract.

Religious Peacemakers across the World Are an Essential Link in Building a Global Civilization with All Parties

Because organized religions have so often become tools of dividing civilizations, and billions of people adhere to them, it is essential that religious representatives committed to peace play a role in weaving together a global civilization. Religious moderates and peacemakers are the ones who can counteract the corrosive effects of religious militancy because they have the capacity to entice religious people into the larger community of humanity.

The bedrock ingredients of a global community must ultimately include commitments to children's welfare, equality of opportunity, women's equality, empowerment through development, anticorruption, environmental protection, energy and water innovations, and so forth. But these broad objectives on a global scale require local meaning systems, local philosophies, and ideologies that embrace these goals. That is where spiritual and religious approaches to peacemaking,[24] diplomacy, and coexistence are the glue that will hold together all of these other efforts at social change.

The long-term goals of civil society must be aided by traditional meaning systems that give a deep and persuasive frame to these goals. Conservative religion does change over time, and institutions such as slavery, which were once widely embraced by religions, can also come to be disallowed by those same systems.

A politicized Christianity that sees environmentalism as a communist threat in one generation can see it in the next generation as a natural expression of manifesting the glory of God's Creation. A hated minority, such as Jews, can be the incarnation of evil in one generation, and in the next a necessary partner in the worship of God. Organized religion, including the Abrahamic faiths so deeply implicated in political violence of the last two thousand years, are capable of these shifts. But they must be cultivated in the context of a civil order in which religion has less and less power over the individual.

The only way that positive change has occurred for the freedom of minorities or individuals is when the interpretive imagination of the individual has been able to express itself in a public space free from religious coercion or intimidation. The only way that the religious imagination breaks forth in millions of people is when they can proceed *freely* to recast the emphasis of a religious ideology, even very conservative ones. This is the great potential of religious creativity.

Where this gets held back, sometimes for hundreds of years, is where religious authority tyrannizes the public space. Then it becomes a threat to life, career, or position, such as during the height of the Church's power in the Middle Ages, or in some places today in the Islamic world, or in parts of the Jewish world today regarding a progressive spiritual approach to the Land and State of Israel.

In this chapter I have outlined the critical importance of cautiously engaging religion if we are to build a peaceful global community of the future.
In the next chapter I will introduce the central importance of understanding
religious networks and their role in conflict and peacebuilding. This will
provide the basis for a new strategy of engagement with religion and social
change. The discussion of religion and social network in chapter 3 is a
natural outgrowth of understanding new and novel approaches to religion,
conflict resolution, and citizen diplomacy. Citizen diplomacy will emerge
as a key method of global intervention that is especially suited to social networks and traditional cultures. From there we will move on to the book's
central case study of citizen diplomacy in Syria. We will then examine the
essential role of ethical reflection and wisdom literature in perfecting the
art of citizen diplomacy and global engagement.

NOTES

1. Steven D. Levitt and Steven J. Dubner, *Freakonomics: A Rogue Economist Explores
the Hidden Side of Everything* (New York: Harper Collins, 2005), 4–5.
2. Terminology and framing are important in the designation of right and wrong
and the development of social consciousness. For example, it is unwise to refer to
murder of women and girls as "honor killings" which implicitly and linguistically
offers some justification. It should just be called "murder of girls by families." "Suicide bombs" should just be called murder, and American "waterboarding" (sounds
like a sport in the American media) should just be called "drowning" because the
lungs fill up until the person is murdered—or saved at the last minute; this is an
ultimate form of terror and torture. Cleaned-up language is always an accessory to
regimens and cultures of human rights violations. The first place to contest this is
through our own use of language.
3. Human Rights Watch, among other local and international human rights
organizations, has been documenting the practice of "honor killings" and the laws
that permit them in many countries. Examples include Jordanian law, articles 98
(partial or full exoneration for committing a crime while in a "fit of rage") and
340 (receiving a reduced sentence if a man committing a crime against his
wife or any female relative having caught her in the act of adultery). See hrw.
org/reports/2004/jordan0404/4.htm. In Pakistan, similar laws are on the books
and their amendment has found great resistance from some circles who regard
any change to them as against tradition. The practice of honor killings is called
Karo-Kari, literally translated as "black-male black-female," a metaphor for
adulterer-adulteress. See islamonline.net/servlet/Satellite?c=Article_C&cid=11
68265536796&pagename=Zone-English-News/NWELayout. The International
Campaign against Honor Killings documents these trends in different countries,
stophonourkillings.com.
4. For example, 280 out of 3,141 counties in the United States now have a majority of minorities. See usatoday.com/news/nation/2004-09-30-census_x.htm.

5. Pangloss is a character in Voltaire's satire *Candide, ou l'Optimisme* (1759) who epitomizes for Voltaire naïve forms of optimism that claim that everything that happens is for the good. This is an implicit attack on Leibniz, but it is also an ancient theological position. The Talmudic sage Akiba claimed that everything that happens is for the good. *Talmud Bavli Berakhot* 60b. Also there was a Talmudic sage by the name of Nahum who was referred to as Nahum Ish Gam Zu, because whatever evils befell him he would claim, *gam zu le'tovah*, "this too is for the good." See *Talmud Bavli Ta'anit* 21a. What Voltaire may have missed is that this kind of optimism and search for the good may be a very adaptive human behavior. Research suggests that blaming yourself for everything is quite destructive, whereas seeking explanations that avoid blame increases one's health and happiness. See Martin Seligman, *Learned Optimism* (New York: Free Press, 1998), 49–53. Of course, taken too far, such explanations can cause someone to evade personal responsibility. At issue here is also a fine line between realism and cynicism. Cynicism, however, is quite often just as unrealistic as naïve optimism. It seems very difficult to balance realism with optimism, but it is equally difficult to embrace realism without it spilling over into pessimism and cynicism. This will have relevance as we address later the cognitive constructs of both conflict and peacebuilding. Focusing only on conflict can make a person realistic but also quite cynical. There is a pervasive tendency of journalists to overreport violence and underreport peaceful relations, for example. Exposing violence and human degradation not only sells, it also seems to fit a certain cognitive construct of the world that is reinforced by the practice of reporting and journalism. This puts them at odds with peacebuilders, whose cognitive construct of reality is often decidedly more optimistic. It is easy for reality to be skewed just as much by such cynicism as it is for reality to be skewed by naïveté.

6. Scott Appleby, *The Ambivalence of the Sacred: Religion, Violence, and Reconciliation* (Lanham, MD: Rowman & Littlefield, 2000), 121–65.

7. Relative deprivation refers not to measurements of absolute poverty but to the chasm between the richest and the poorest. Nowhere in the world is this more grotesque than in the Middle East. It is relative deprivation that has the greatest effect on frustration and aggression. See Ted Robert Gurr, "Why Minorities Rebel: A Global Analysis of Communal Mobilization and Conflict since 1945," *International Political Science Review* 14, 2 (April 1993): 161–201.

8. See, for example, George Soros on the idea of the open society and its values and principles, in "Toward a Global Open Society," found at project-syndicate. org/commentary/sor4. See also Abdullahi Ahmed An-Na'im, *Toward an Islamic Reformation: Civil Liberties, Human Rights and International Law* (Syracuse: Syracuse University Press, 1990).

9. James Zogby, *What Arabs Think: Values, Beliefs, and Concerns* (Washington, DC: Zogby International, 2002). See also Saad Eddin Ibrahim, *Egypt, Islam, and Democracy: Critical Essays, With a New Postscript* (Cairo, Egypt, and New York: American University in Cairo Press, 2002); also Saad Eddin Ibrahim's extensive writings on Arab democracy, civil society, and militancy, mainly at eicds.org/english/publications/saadarticles/drsaadarticles.htm.

10. John Donohue and John Esposito, *Islam in Transition: Muslim Perspectives* (New York: Oxford University Press, 2007); James DeFronzo, *Revolutions and Revolutionary Movements* (Boulder, CO: Westview Press, 1996); Carrie Rosefsky Wickham,

Mobilizing Islam: Religion, Activism, and Political Change in Egypt (New York: Columbia University Press, 2002); Christian Smith, ed., *Disruptive Religion* (New York: Routledge, 1996).

11. See, for example, Victoria S. Harrison, *Religion and Modern Thought* (London: SCM Press, 2007); Ghassan Salame, *Democracy Without Democrats: The Renewal of Politics in the Muslim World* (London and New York: I.B. Tauris, 1994); Aziz Azmeh, *Islams and Modernities* (London and New York: Verso, 1993); Abdulaziz Sachedina, *Islamic Roots of Democratic Pluralism* (New York: Oxford University Press, 2001); Noah Feldman, *Divided by God: America's Church–State Problem—What We Should Do About It* (New York: Farrar, Straus & Giroux, 2005).

12. For an extensive piece on the art, history, and literature of the city, see Michael Ivanovitch Rostovtzeff, *Dura-Europos and Its Art*, (Oxford: Clarendon Press, 1938). Also for a first-hand account of its discovery, see Clark Hopkins, *The Discovery of Dura-Europos* (New Haven: Yale University Press, 1979). For some illustrations, see le.ac.uk/archaeology/stj/dura.htm.

13. This despite the fact that loving and caring for fellow residents whom you do not know is an ancient biblical precept that has profoundly influenced the legal and spiritual resources of all three Abrahamic faiths. See extensive citations regarding *ger* in the Hebrew Bible, including Exod. 22:20, 23:9; Lev. 16:29, 18:26; Deut. 10:19. On the implications of biblical thinking about minorities for religious approaches to human rights see Leroy S. Rouner, *Human Rights and the World's Religions* (South Bend, IN: The University of Notre Dame Press, 1988). Also see the five-volume work by Moddathir Abd al-Rahim, Harold Coward, Robert E. Florida, Peter J. Haas (authors), and William H. Brackney (series editor), *Human Rights and the World's Major Religions* (Westport, CT: Praeger, 2005). For a Christian perspective, see Jurgen Moltmann, *God for a Secular Society: The Public Relevance of Theology* (Minneapolis: Fortress Press: 1999).

14. There are some exceptions. Pious Christians played a pivotal role in the American abolitionist movement.

15. John Rawls, *A Theory of Justice* (Cambridge, MA: Belknap, 1971).

16. For an extensive discussion of the concept of the resident stranger and the biblical *stranger*, see Marc Gopin, *Between Eden and Armageddon: The Future of World Religions, Violence, and Peacemaking* (New York: Oxford University Press, 2000), 6, 7, 9, 97, 148, 179, 277n44; for the concept of "stranger" as a metaphor for peacemaking, see Marc Gopin, *Holy War, Holy Peace: How Religion Can Bring Peace to the Middle East* (Oxford: Oxford University Press, 2002), 22–28. Citation of the "stranger" or *ger* sources in the Bible is the extraction of one set of progressive sources that are easily counteracted by the selected sources commanding ethnic cleansing in the name of God, for example. Nevertheless, what interests me is how monotheisms of the majority, or the empowered group, within a fairly short time of achieving power tend to hide from view the humanitarian sources and instead highlight sources justifying the worst crimes against humanity, be it slavery, ethnic cleansing, or simpler forms of racism in the courts and in citizen entitlements. This happens across the world, in nonmonotheisms as well, such as in the Sri Lankan Sinhalese Buddhist case.

17. David Little, ed., *Peacemakers in Action: Profiles of Religion in Conflict Resolution* (Cambridge: Cambridge University Press, 2007), ch. 4.

18. See Adam Smith, *The Theory of Moral Sentiments* (1759), and the importance of moral sentiments in his classical work *The Wealth of Nations* (1766). Capitalism in practice has never come close to living up to his moral and social vision.

19. Scientists and social critics have weighed in on this matter in a number of interesting ways. See Francis Collins, *The Language of God: A Scientist Presents Evidence for Belief* (New York: Free Press, 2006); Richard Sloan, *Blind Faith: The Unholy Alliance of Religion and Medicine* (New York: St. Martin's Press, 2006); Richard Dawkins, *The God Delusion* (Boston: Houghton Mifflin, 2006); Sam Harris, *The End of Faith: Religion, Terror, and the Future of Reason* (New York: W.W. Norton, 2004).

20. I have found repeatedly in recent years that the European and American legacies are quite paradoxical. It seems that America is a far more hospitable place for religious and ethnic minorities than is Europe, indeed it was founded (at least as a white European outpost) for the sake of escapees of religious persecution. But European experience diplomatically with foreign cultures has deep roots that make their diplomats far more skilled at the balancing act that I am aiming at, an ironic advantage of their long experience with imperialism. European diplomats whom I have worked with tend to be both more secular, less fundamentalist about faith, but simultaneously more respectful of the importance of understanding culture and religion. I have specific experience with the Swiss, the Canadians, the Swedes, and the Norwegians, among others. But it seems to me that a nonviolent approach to managing difference with a less arrogant tone seems to be more common in European approaches to diplomacy in difficult regions of the world. This may be due to many factors: centuries of lessons learned the hard way, Europe's greater facility with soft power due to their lack of hard power, American isolationism and overreliance on hard power and "sticks"; the corrupting power of being a superpower. Isolationism and global naiveté have always dogged American use of power. On the use of American soft power, see Joseph Nye, *Soft Power: The Means to Success in Global Diplomacy* (New York: Public Affairs, 2004). It would be interesting to do further comparative study on American and European choices of diplomats, and especially their training.

21. See, for example, David A. Schon, *The Reflective Practitioner: How Professionals Think in Action* (New York: Basic Books, 1983); Sandra I. Cheldelin and Wallace Warfield with January Makamba, "Reflections on Reflective Practice," in *Research Frontiers in Conflict Analysis and Resolution* (Fairfax: Institute for Conflict Analysis and Resolution, George Mason University, 2004), 64–78; James Laue and Gerald Cormick, "The Ethics of Intervention in Community Disputes," in *The Ethics of Social Intervention: Goals, Values and Consequences,* ed. Gordon Bermant, Herbert C. Kelman, and Donald P. Warwick (Washington, DC and London: Hemisphere Publishing Corporation, 1978), 205–32; Wallace Warfield, "Is This the Right Thing to Do? A Practical Framework for Ethical Decisions," in *A Handbook of International Peacebuilding: Into the Eye of the Storm,* ed. John Paul Lederach and Janice Moomaw Jenner (San Francisco: Jossey-Bass Publishers, 2002), 213–23.

22. This is captured most often by what is referred to as "situational ethics." See, for example, Joseph Fletcher, *Situation Ethics: The New Morality* (Philadelphia: Westminster Press, 1966).

23. I often refer to "the public space" in my lectures, and students and members of other cultures have pointed out to me that the meaning of this term is not universally apparent. What I mean by "the public space" is the physical shared space of

community in which the tolerance and freedoms of the social contract are tested. It is the place in which true equality among diverse citizens is apparent or not apparent. It does not include private clubs or religious institutions, but it does include just about everything else. It is the space in which human rights is tested. (I am not attempting a legal definition but a moral and political one). A church, for example, is not a public space. I enter into it voluntarily (if the public space from which I enter is truly free!) and, once in, I need to abide by the particular rules and traditions governing that church. In that church I may not be considered equally good in the eyes of God if I am gay. I can either lobby to change that and stay in the church, I can stay and accept my status, or I can walk out the door to "the public space." That ability to walk out the door into a public space that is governed by a social contract based on a Bill of Rights is the essential difference historically between freedom and tyranny. The legal subtleties of private institutions that receive federal funding being bound by the Bill of Rights and antidiscrimination laws are important developments of civil society in the United States, but not as essential as the basic right to *exit* institutions. It is the first stage of exiting to a free public space that provides us with our most essential freedoms. A second stage of antidiscrimination consists of the ability to pressure institutions, such as private colleges, to be nondiscriminatory. Most of the world's citizens, however, still labor under public spaces and governments (including democratically elected governments) that do not adhere to equal human rights for all citizens in the public space. In other words, they have no exit, which is tyranny. That tyranny, that inability to exit to a free public space, is what haunts me the most in my work in the Middle East. The lack of space to exit discriminatory or occupying forces, the inability to exit from patriarchy, to exit from the clutches of police and informants, the inability to exit from the informants and networks of tyrannical religions, subcultures, and tribes. It is pervasive and ever-present beneath every conversation.

24. I distinguish between religious and spiritual approaches to peacemaking because this reflects the empirical reality of our work. Some activists are consciously associated with one religion, in either its liberal or conservative manifestations; I would call them "religious." Others are consciously anticlerical, or "postdenominational," or syncretistic in their religious outlook and practice; they often refer to themselves as spiritual, preferring not to identify too closely with traditional religion's power constructs. This is especially the case because women are so frequently excluded from leadership in traditional religions, and many men today who value women's equality tend also to veer away from organized religious structures as a result. At the same time, there are many feminist movements afoot within organized religions. There is a paucity or near absence of women studying religion, war, and peace, for example, as well as in the practice of interfaith peacemaking. This requires some surveys and polls, but it may be due to the natural discomfort that most women analysts and practitioners of conflict resolution feel within the bounds of organized religions, their dominance by male clerics, and the preponderance of interfaith peacemaking programs that focus on male clerics.

3

Networks That Build a Peaceful Future: A New Approach to Incremental Change[1]

I want to delve a little more deeply into the importance of social networks. But I will do it by taking a small detour into the world of international development, by which I mean the global antipoverty interventions that focus on village-based programs. International development is a classical form of intervention that is relatively easy to quantify. This includes diverse interventions, such as support for small businesses and cottage industries through low-interest loans, revolving loan funds, child survival interventions, or educational/literacy initiatives.

Such interventions are easily subject to quantification and evaluation because you can count child survival, school attendance, and other social-change indicators. But as anyone in development will tell you, without a peaceful environment all of the quantifiable gains can be destroyed in an instant by violence and war. Thus, everyone knows how important conflict prevention and resolution is to the weaving together of peaceful civilizations into a new form of global interaction.

That does not mean that intervention for conflict resolution is easily quantifiable, however. It is extremely difficult to quantify what constitutes progress when it comes to conflict resolution and peacebuilding, and therefore the field of conflict resolution has had a very hard time with the question of evaluation.[2] When can something be safely considered to be successful?

The answer may lie in a complete reassessment of how the field of conflict resolution looks at its own interventions. It is possible that we as scholars, advocates, and practitioners have asked too much of peacemaking, that we are too utopian in our demands. In our zeal to find the deep roots of conflict and solve them we have been unimpressed with facile governmental attempts to paper over real needs and real problems. And so we have demanded a commitment to radical peace, "peace on earth and good will toward man."

We asked too much of "conflict resolution." Worse, *we promised too much* and thus set ourselves up for failure. We insisted that real conflict resolution address the root causes of conflict. That is certainly the right goal, but we also set ourselves up for failure with funders and realist critics by making this the first goal, and not the final goal.

By contrast, when it comes to international development we do not consider child survival programs a failure unless all children cease to die of unnatural causes in a country! Nor do we look five years after an inoculation when the child is killed violently from child abuse, or indirectly through contamination of a nearby waste dump, and then say the inoculation was a failure!

We look at survival issues incrementally. We judge interventions based on *how well that intervention did for that child at that moment in time, but also, more deeply, whether this effort was playing a constructive role in a larger effort at social transformation.*

The same judgment must be made in the area of conflict resolution. We must look at each intervention in its own place in time, but also quantify the networks of human beings who we are exposing by our interventions to a new way of viewing their world and their enemies. Essentially we must judge our conflict resolution work one increment at a time, and *then* move resolutely with each increment toward lasting change that indeed addresses the deep roots of conflict through paradigm shifts in attitudes, behaviors, and worldviews.

I have noticed a broad-based pattern in my field of work that if we do not achieve an end of conflict and settlement of all issues to the satisfaction of progressive actors and progressive observers, then we see the resolution as merely a settlement, or worse, a ruse to trick the less powerful side into capitulation. But this is because we are confusing long-term ends and short-term tasks.

This obsession with utopianism is not just a problem among progressives; it is actually quite pervasive in Western culture, and perhaps in many others. And Abrahamic religions may have some responsibility for this by promising utopia at the end of days.

This has an insidious impact on peacemakers that sets them up for failure and disappointment. For example, I am constantly bombarded at a personal level by cynical neighbors, cousins, and colleagues, both from the right and the left, who know what I do, with a question as they pass me on the street or in hallways, grinning and winking, "Have you made peace yet?"

Why do they ask me this? They treat doctors with reverence, never taunting them by asking, "Did you save everyone's life yet? Did you cure all the diseases of your patients today? Did you give us all the capacity to live to

120 years?" No, they are respectful and grateful that the doctor saved one life this week, or even this year. Why the difference in attitude? Why no questions to government workers or policy makers working for social welfare or education, "Hey, what did you do today? Come up with a cure for poverty?"

Perhaps it is because most people are skeptical about progress in making a more peaceful planet. Perhaps it is guilt, because everyone knows that they are complicit in enemy systems on a global scale, and they have given up on doing anything about it; perhaps they are therefore threatened by those who keep trying. This remains a mystery to me.

Perhaps it is also the fault of religious utopian fantasies. But those of us working in the field of conflict resolution must take some responsibility because we set ourselves up for disappointment. If we had made our public goals more modest, such as emphasizing relationships, and establishing a measurable goal of incrementally weaving relationships among individual enemies, then we would be able to point to success at every turn. Perhaps this could make what we do far more attractive and inspiring; resembling the way that a doctor inspires. She never completely defeats the deadly effects of viruses and bacteria, but certainly she makes at least some people survive them and flourish every day, and it is this that induces respect, emulation, and trust.

A DEFINITION OF CONFLICT RESOLUTION REVISITED: TOWARD THE NEW INCREMENTALISM

We need a new approach to conflict resolution that I would like to call "incrementalism" or "incremental conflict resolution (ICR)." The new approach establishes first-order goals and practices and higher-order goals and practices. The most important point is that it evaluates each increment of intervention on its own terms.

First-order goals are more closely related to present challenges, while higher-order goals address long-term transformation of societies and civilizations. Most importantly, first-order goals and practices are evaluated on their own terms *without any regard* as to how events unfold in the long-term in a particular conflict setting, a setting which may be uncontrollably complicated.

At the same time, higher-order goals are stated from the beginning of any first-order practices, and are constantly revisited to evaluate to what degree first-order goals and practices are serving higher-order goals.

Higher-order goals include all the most profound and utopian goals of conflict resolution, including justice, the satisfaction of basic human needs, and the creation of a peaceful society that is egalitarian.

An example of a first-order goal might be building housing together between two religious communities, when one of the communities is more privileged than the other. A higher-order goal would be building a broad-based coalition of citizens to commit to an economic relationship in the society in which all ethnic and religious groups are treated fairly.

More than one first-order goal may need to be introduced in a conflict setting to move toward the higher-order goals. Let us say, for example, that you bring together two religious groups to build housing together. You build, but it turns out that as a result of their new relationships and common values they unite in prejudice against homosexual or atheist citizens of the region! Unintended consequences result that make your higher-order goal more distant. So you have to introduce other first-order goals such as stimulating an interfaith conversation on tolerance. Thus you can see successes for some of your first-order goals while acknowledging others to be more stubborn.

On the other hand, you may evaluate and discover that your first-order and higher-order goals are perfectly aligned. But many factors *beyond your control*, such as riots in a nearby community, or an earthquake, or an oil boom enriching someone corrupt, undid all of your work.

Here is the crucial point. The increments you have accomplished are a success anyway, pure and simple. It is the stubborn complexity of advancing the quality of human community that remains a challenge, or the perennial problem of too few resources in the hands of the true change makers. This is analogous to a new form of cancer emerging in a body that you had already successfully treated for another form of cancer. You had worked hard to successfully excise the first form of cancer. It does not mean your first treatment was bad, but that carcinogens continue to exist in the human environment that are beyond the control of both the doctor and the patient. In a word, ICR requires a determination to evaluate the positive increments of change (PICs) on their own terms.

From Positive Increments of Change to Paradigm Shifts

ICR does not neglect the issue of long-term change or fundamental paradigm shifts. It merely releases the individual PIC from responsibility for surrounding uncontrollable circumstances. At the same time ICR posits that there is an arithmetic to PICs. Positive change transforms human social life with the steady accumulation of PICs, given the right circumstances.

This means three things: (1) We must now look at how change is detectable at its most elemental level of increment. We must look for small indicators that something transformational has occurred between two or more enemies who have met, helped each other, or worked together, something much more significant relationally than mere contact. (2) We must look at when those changes reach some saturation point that triggers utterly new relationships, transformed from hostility to tolerance to friendship and even to love. In other words, how and when the PICs add up to true reconciliation between enemies. (3) Finally, ICR must look at when those true reconciliations add up to fundamentally new structures of equality in the larger relationship between enemies.

A critical element of ICR, for example, would be creating and tracing networks of incremental relationships of true friendship between enemies. Addressing the deep roots of conflict, it is said, requires a fundamental restructuring of society.[3] This is true, but it begs the question that is most asked by ICR. *How* do such structures actually change in the real world? And how does structural change *begin* at its most elemental level? What are its mechanics, especially at the interpersonal level?

Certainly the change of society as a whole, away from destructive violence or war, involves political activity and organizing, protests, and shifts in legislation and political leadership. But this observation also begs the question. *How* do groups of people even get to this level of consciousness and motivation? My experience with these very elemental levels of change in oppressive circumstances (and what I have learned from thousands of students who came from conflict regions) is that this shift begins only based on the transformation that occurs in friendships between members of disparate or adversarial groups or classes. Only the exchange of experience between unusual friends from groups separated by ethnicity or class leads to a new conception of how their world should be *structurally* different.

True friendships—and sometimes only true friendships—lead to an authentic level of empathy, solidarity, and loyalty. This in turn over time leads to the organized effort to address the deepest roots of conflict, dehumanization, and inequality.

This means that we cannot escape ICR and the PIC as the fundamental unit of evaluation. It is the building block of all change, no matter how profound or structural that change may be in the long run. Discovering the most foundational PICs of peace is the Rosetta Stone of peace, because it is the transformational increment of change that can be seized upon as the basis for steady, measurable change, even when structural paradigm shifts prove elusive for decades or even generations. The engine of medical and health revolutions in terms of the efficacy of a cure is all to be found at the microscopic level. Get that wrong and the health revolution will flop. It is the same with conflict resolution.

There are other kinds of PICs to engage besides the building block of friendship between members of adversary groups. For example, if we can assume that each positive gesture made between groups, when conceived and accomplished by the best innovators of peacemaking, *and* when we have evidence that it is well received *by at least some* in both enemy groups, then we have in our hands a precious PIC, an invaluable increment of positive change. The key criterion of evaluation is that the effect of the increment is transformative, meaning that it profoundly changes the attitude and approach *of at least some people* toward peace and away from destructive forms of conflict. That is all it need do to qualify as a PIC.

At the end of the day, it does not matter *how many* people have been transformed but that this increment is *inherently* transformative. The transformative impact on some, and only the transformative impact on some, is what must be evaluated and then embraced.

Reproduction of the Positive Increment of Change and the Abuse of the Peacemaker

The next critical component of a new approach is this: replication and mass reproduction of positive change is an entirely separate challenge. The burden of evaluation of effectiveness *leaves* the single positive increment and its authors when transformative impact on some parties to the conflict has been established. The larger societal impact becomes actually a question of investment, mass production, and persuasion, namely the extension of this increment to millions of more people and thousands of more opportunities in and between the enemy groups. That means that the burden of change and evaluation *leaves* the conceiver and implementer of a particular increment of positive change, such as the innovative NGO or peacemaker.

The burden of evaluation and the moral responsibility for large movements of social change is placed rather on the very significant group of bystanders, governments, and private donors, and especially the wealthy owners of most of the world's assets. It is they who must be challenged to fund the replication of a positive increment of peacemaking or conflict resolution. They must fund the right instruments or organizations that will take a successful increment of positive change and fund the expertise necessary to reproduce it on a massive scale.

The reproducers should naturally consult extensively with the original conceivers of the increment. But it is equally vital that the funding strategies of reproduction, the bureaucracy of replication, and the mass production itself be seen inherently as based on a special and different expertise than that of the original innovators. It also involves a different set of moral and professional responsibilities.

It is exactly the same as what must happen and who must step in when a new cure is found for a disease. To think that the genius who discovered the cure also needs to be the funder, the corporate CEO, chief financial officer, and chief engineer of the company that mass produces it, the Food and Drug Administration that regulates it, the secretary of Health and Human Services and the surgeon general who oversee its legitimate reproduction, would be manifestly absurd.

Yet donors, foundations, and governments have done precisely this to our geniuses of peacemaking all over the world. Rather than taking responsibility and looking at their own need to raise the requisite funds or political assets for the replication of change on a massive scale, donors shift this burden onto the innovative peacemakers and scholar/practitioners. This is not only professionally absurd, but it is also morally bankrupt.

I am suggesting an utterly new level of responsibility or sharing of responsibility on the part of donors both small and large—in other words, the rest of us. I am also suggesting expanded sets of expertise that are involved in a vast chain of production. We must outline exactly how an elemental and transformative method of change in enemy relationships moves from PICs to mass production, from the moment between two people, to a society-wide change. Then we must differentiate the expertise necessary for each stage of replication and reproduction.

This is the true way to move from first-order goals to higher-order goals, from incremental change to structural change. It must be done by a detailed outline of what it takes to move from the transformative interpersonal relationship all the way to society-wide tipping points and paradigm shifts that we may refer to as structural change.

This is very different than the current mode of evaluation, which places the whole burden of utopian peace on every NGO and every individual peacemaker. Peacemakers must not only be geniuses of human relations, not only courageous to the point of risking all their relations and even their lives by living and working in between enemies. They must also be fundraisers, writers, politicians, and ruthless competitors for funds. Lately they must also show that they are collaborators with the very people they must ruthlessly compete with for funds (!) because now the donors want to see evidence of "collaboration."[4] Last but not least, geniuses of peacemaking who study the human heart, the face, the moment of human relationship, and discipline themselves to read people at every critical moment of an enemy encounter, must also be top-notch administrators of grants.

Most importantly their successful combination of all of these must lead to "peace in our time," or at the very least a Gandhian Salt March or a King March on Washington to show evidence of paradigm shifts on the ground. It is absurd how we have set them up for failure because we need to blame someone for the sorry state of human relations. More often than not, NGOs comprised of such peacemakers have done their job of conceiving and implementing some kind of valuable PIC, but they have been unsupported in the necessary replication on a massive scale. The failures that we have seen in recent years in global relations may very well be due not to some failure of peacemakers or their paradigms, but to their support being a fraction of the support given to violence in all its forms.

How can major donors pull out of peace work after 9/11, blaming the peace innovators, when it is they, the donors, the wealthiest people on the planet, who have not yet persuaded their own community of wealth to put in the appropriate funds for mass production on a global scale of these extraordinary PICs? It is they who have yet to persuade the global community of wealth that at least a decent fraction of money must go into peace as compared to what goes into war for peace to even have a fighting chance of capturing the hearts of the masses. How did they ever imagine that we could defeat the wealthy forces of militarization and extremism on this planet with a tiny fraction of the assets available for violence? Was 9/11, and the loss of momentum for positive global change after the Cold War, truly a failing of peacemakers, or rather of the bystander and donor community?

Too many people and organizations have been used as scapegoats for civilization's failures, with expectations of expertise and mastery far beyond what peacemakers possess—*or should possess.* The absolute genius that I have witnessed with my own eyes of a peacemaker eliciting a moment of sincere sorrow or apology between two adversaries is victory enough in the context of human history. Why do we expect more than that from someone who can elicit this increment of the most profound cultural, moral, and spiritual significance? Why do we sacrifice the peace innovator on the altar of our own failures in the wealthy world, imputing to him or her utter failure because he or she or they could not do the impossible—mass produce their ingenious moment to the point of political, economic, and military paradigm shifts?

How cruel we have been to the brave, innovative artists of peacemaking on this planet. Why did we not celebrate their achievement, and then launch in with massive resources, with the same capitalist drive for mass production that drives the sale of every other valuable discovery on the planet today? Perhaps because the challenge of the ingenious peacemaker to our way of life, to our political and tribal comfort zones, to our cynicism, is so—terrifying.

This is not to deny that the question for every positive increment of change, in terms of its contribution to higher-order goals, is its traction, how much it is contributing to major shifts in overall group relationships. But if the increment, in and of itself, has had a transformative and permanent effect on at least some people then it gets a positive evaluation. It suggests massive possibilities for reproduction that must be attempted, just as surely as science would require experimentation with any promising drug. If it has little traction *because no one came forward to reproduce it properly* then this is a burden of failure that must be placed on a much broader range of actors and third parties who are failing to support this successful increment.

Let us say that a doctor discovered an amazing cure to a major disease, but there were no corporations and no government funds and no personal patrons

available to mass produce the cure. Would the cure then be thought to be ineffective? Of course not, for that would be outrageously unscientific. It would
be irrational and unscientific to say that the cure is ineffective because no one
came forward to mass produce it.[5] But that is what has happened to the evaluation of numerous conflict resolution interventions, especially the experimental
kind that are part and parcel of religious peacemaking. We have confused critical evaluation of the cure with critical evaluation of its mass production.

The Core of the Peaceful Paradigm Shift Is Not Linear

Another question raised by the difference between (1) an increment of positive change, (2) its mass production, and (3) paradigm shifts in society, is that
the mechanism for how we go from one to the next is not straightforward.
Increments of positive change do accumulate, but not in a simple way. There
is instead a chemistry of change in organisms and organizations. And this is
often complicated by increments of violence in conflicts that are also present
and quite overwhelming. There is no contest with increments of violence unless they begin to be matched by countervailing increments of positive change
that are replicated enough to give the average person a true choice between a
path of violence and a path of peace. But *how* they accumulate to the point of
presenting a clear choice to the average person is harder to nail down.

Increments of positive change do add up over time, affecting more and
more people, but we know from chemistry that saturation points of change
are not linear. They are hidden, with fundamental change building to a crescendo that is hidden from view right up until the super-saturation point.

This resonates with my experience of many conflicts that is encapsulated
by the common wisdom perception, "it is darkest before the dawn." Quite
often, you almost cannot see peace coming. Something profound is going
on right before peace breaks out, but people are actually becoming *more*
agitated by violence, more fed up, and it does not feel like peace. Then
something amazing happens, and there emerges a consensus on ceasefire,
on dialogue, and on reconciliation. There is in these cases a nonlinear accumulation of positive changes that seem to suddenly converge and spring
forth to create a different reality.

Human relationships are not mechanistic; they are organic, and we are
starting to see nature today not as mechanistic but as a collection of organic
systems with a high degree of sensitivity to subtle change that is dynamic
and highly interactive. Freeman Dyson has noted a paradigm shift emerging in our understanding of nature that moves away from particles and
toward organization of systems that are complex and interactive.

This picture of living creatures, as patterns of organization rather than collec-
tions of molecules, applies not only to bees and bacteria, butterflies and rain

forests, but also to sand dunes and snowflakes, thunderstorms and hurricanes. The nonliving universe is as diverse and as dynamic as the living universe, and is also dominated by patterns of organization that are not yet understood. The reductionist physics and the reductionist molecular biology of the twentieth century will continue to be important in the twenty-first century, but they will not be dominant. The big problems, the evolution of the universe as a whole, the origin of life, the nature of human consciousness, and the evolution of the earth's climate, cannot be understood by reducing them to elementary particles and molecules. New ways of thinking and new ways of organizing large databases will be needed.[6]

Dyson also quotes Carl Woese, who states, "it is becoming increasingly clear that to understand living systems in any deep sense, we must come to see them not materialistically, as machines, but as (stable) complex, dynamic organization."[7]

This will have a profound effect over time on how we see human conflict and peacemaking. We are beginning to see the interactive power of the small elements with the largest trends. Small increments of change, when they become known through networks of relations or loose networks of knowledge such as the web or media, can have a dramatic effect on entire systems of human interaction. It is as if it is a living organism that is interactive. This means that small but astounding increments of transformation in relations can have an impact way beyond their actual size.

Here is an excellent proof that is familiar to any American who examines his own thought patterns. We freely acknowledge the power of 9/11 as a small increment of change that profoundly altered our consciousness and our systems. Small? How can anyone say it was small, I will be asked. But let's look at more closely 9/11. It had no real strategic or military impact on the immense power of the United States or on the continuing vitality of its population of three hundred million. Its impact on the United States' gross domestic product (GDP) was small, infinitesimal. It cannot compare even fractionally to the Cold War arms race, with thousands of nuclear warheads poised to destroy the United States and the earth, five times over. It cannot compare even fractionally to the hundreds of the thousands of premature deaths every year in America from smoking.

And yet 9/11 changed everything! Small increments that are widely disseminated into consciousness can have a dramatic impact that is not linear. We in the United States were profoundly and permanently changed by 9/11, but we also *willed it by our consciousness and focus to be a matter of profound change*. As Dyson noted, our consciousness mattered a great deal to the construct of reality. Our decision to consider it a turning point in history was a part of our own making it a turning point in history. There is an interactivity to how we change that suggests the power of individual components over larger systems and over human consciousness itself.

Perhaps more importantly, our decision to accept the terminology "global war on terror" instead of say, "global police engagement," changed the way we think and our construct of the world. What this means is that how seriously we take the symbols of positive human change in relations, of PICs is as important as how seriously we take the negative symbols of human interaction, such as a terrorist incident like 9/11.

From funders to diplomats and policy makers, many people are beginning to understand the impact of increments of positive change, especially when they are new and novel.[8] We need then to acknowledge the power of these positive increments, harness their power, and have them run a course toward tipping points of human change. This takes great vision, reverence for the visionaries of peacemaking, and revolutionary capacity building by the public or private sector for mass production.

The Special Networking Impact of "Unusual Pairs" as Symbols of a Different Future

One symbol and instrument of positive change that bears special mention is what I refer to as unusual pair conflict resolution (UPCR). This entails the surprising friendship and alliance of two people from adversary groups who team up to work together, speak, teach, and intervene in places of conflict and violence; this will be explored in our major case study in later chapters. Not only are two better than one in terms of interventions, but *their pairing becomes a living symbol of the vision they are proposing for the future.*

People become symbols of violence, but they also become symbols of peace in their lifetimes and beyond. But the increment of positive change that I am exposing here is a double symbol. It is given life in the inner workings of friendship, of interpersonal struggle. It is rooted in the boundaries of partnership and interactive identity formation and growth. It is played out in the dynamics of tolerance, forbearance, forgiveness, and reconciliation between two people, two enemies. And it thus becomes emblematic of much larger conflicts. It is also played out on the public stage, as it were, in the face of everyone with whom the pair works and with whom they struggle for positive change.

The building block of life over death in the world of human violence inheres in the powerful friendship of two enemies. Often it results in profound debate and negotiation, vicarious conflict, deep love, devotion, and, above all, loyalty to the point of self-sacrifice. Self-sacrificing friendship between enemies is the quintessential opposite of war.

The friendship of enemies as an instrument of peacemaking and peace advocacy astonishes witnesses who are transformed by its shocking reality. And that is why news of unusual friendships between enemies appears to spread rapidly among loose networks, especially if it is augmented by video and web reports. The unusual relationship completely inverts the mental construct of our world. It subverts our notion of an enemy system that we need to have in order to make sense of a chaotic world.

I know that my own inner world was turned upside down when I met Rabbi Frohman of Israel together with General Nasser Yousef of Palestine. These were not the left-leaning "new age" progressives from different religions whom I was used to dealing with in Israel as of 1998. These were military men, a founder of a militant Zionist movement, and the other an active Palestinian general, both veterans of many battles. And here they were beloved of each other in the true sense, not through superficial diplomacy, but with families in tow, and with risk and sacrifice for each other at every turn.

My world changed when I saw this as a possibility in life. To this day it breaks my heart to visualize them together in my mind's eye, because their living symbol is so opposite of the Jewish–Palestinian reality that we all must endure every day and every moment that we read in the news the litany of violence, hate, and the ever-present dead.

An enemy system where there is no intimacy of enemies seems compelling to our mental construct of the world. In fact it makes us feel safe inside a set of false certainties about "us" and "them" (or for bystanders who dismiss enemies as "those groups who just cannot get along with each other." How neat and unchallenging!) We may not be happy about such polarities and stereotypes, but at least they make sense of a frightening world.

That is why the Cold War made so much sense to analysts and common citizens alike, whereas in the twenty-first century we cannot easily comprehend the enemy systems at work. So we struggle to create simplistic antimonies, polarities of enemy identities, and we often do a bad job of it. "The West and the Rest," "those who love freedom and those who hate it," "Jihad vs. Mcworld"; these polarities are inaccurate, superficial—and we know it deep down. But the polarity is still intoxicating. It certainly intoxicated President Bush.

Along comes an unusual pair, and they upset our sense of what in this world is real and what is possible, especially because our constructed universe of enemies is so paper thin. The unusual pair is deeply threatening to some, but hopeful to others. In most people, it generates a profound emotional reaction. This is the kind of increment of positive change that may have a highly interactive effect on larger systems of human relations, beyond its arithmetic significance.

The unusual pairs abound in the work that I have witnessed for twenty years in the Middle East. From General Nasser Yousef and Rabbi Menahem Frohman, to Eliyahu Mclean and Sheikh Bukhari, Sari Nuseibeh and Ami Ayalon, Dan Bar On and Sami Adwan, Gabi Meyer and Ihab Balha, to

Najeeba Sirhan and Osnat Aram-Daphna, these relationships have created an impression that is unmatched in the Israeli–Palestinian context.

The impact of unusual pairs has been going on for a long time in history. For example, historical friends such as the legendary Jewish philosopher Abraham Joshua Heschel and Martin Luther King made an impression on an entire generation of Jews and African Americans in the 1960s. It made the American Civil Rights struggle into a universal cause, a cause beyond African Americans fighting for themselves. It made the struggle universally human as King was joined by nonblack admirers and fellow travelers. This is how it became unstoppable in the minds of hundreds of thousands of people, not just one ethnic group pitched against another with competing claims, but a universal drive that had to overtake and transform the American dream itself.[9]

Witnessing friendship across ethnic, racial, or religious lines makes a deep impression on the human psyche, and we have only begun to see its power in conflict resolution. In reality it should revolutionize the training that we do in diplomacy and conflict resolution. We need to not just be grateful for the accidental relationships of history, but rather cultivate and set a stage of opportunity for such partnerships to emerge.

We should shift our teaching and training to encourage these friendships to emerge, from the youngest of people to the oldest. Indeed, our current programs are poised for this already, in that they tend to bring together very special people from opposing ethnic groups. We educators need to be much more self-conscious, however, about making these friendships into something to be supported and cultivated over many years. We will see a greater elaboration of this theme in our case study on Syria in the next chapter.

INCREMENTALISM, RELIGION, AND THE NETWORK FOR GLOBAL CHANGE

Incremental acts of positive change have a special kinship to religious practices. The religious consciousness values the increment, the small acts of righteousness that add up to a way of life. Such increments are seen as inherently powerful and empowering.[10] A simple good deed is also transformed by religion into an irreducible expression of the sacred. Mystical Judaism, for example, embraced this experience over the centuries by hallowing the everyday deeds of spiritual practice as possessing cosmic and historic significance. Such deeds not only change history, they heal a wound in the very nature of God, claims mystical Judaism. The idea of the healing and even unification of God through increments of practice is a shocking but ancient Jewish idea.[11]

Healing history and healing God's very nature suggests the awesome level of empowerment offered to its practitioner. There is nothing that a beleaguered peacemaker, underfunded and suspected by his own group, needs more than a sense of efficacy and empowerment. Incrementalist approaches to conflict resolution can sometimes provide for the religious practitioner a way to rescue hope from the despair of outcome-based obsessions that often dominate secular conflict resolution. Such outcome-based approaches tend to hold good practices hostage to distant historical outcomes that are beyond the control of the individual practitioner. These outcome-based fixations constitute a utopian, unrealistic demand on one moral agent or, phrased professionally, the lone conflict resolution practitioner. The strain is unbearable, but the sacralization of the PIC can be emotionally transformative and more sustainable.

I am not arguing that *only* a religious consciousness can be empowered by incremental acts of conflict resolution. Rather, that the religious consciousness of increments and their power provide a better role model for empowering *all* practitioners of conflict resolution in new and heretofore unexplored ways. The model suggests that we should find a way back to *re-value* the secular peacemaker who has been buffeted not only by the trauma of day-to-day conflict and violence but also by the unrealistic expectations of this work on the part of donors and academic theoreticians; this has led many of my friends to despair that is unfair to them.

The religious sacralization of the increment can provide a precedent for a secular valuation of the increment in and of itself as an irreducible success. This requires not only a revolution in evaluation that we discussed above, but also a psychological shift in consciousness by secular practitioners but especially academic theoreticians and donors.

This also requires a revolution in conflict resolution training and education. More time must be consecrated to focus on the inherent value of each and every increment of this work, every successful encounter where adversaries are brought closer together (through encounter, film, networks, and other creative methods) in a way that some transformation of relationship and understanding is achieved and appreciated. This conscious focus on appreciation and valuation of individual increments should be a sine qua non of future training in conflict resolution.

This in no way discounts the need to be discriminating in evaluation of individual increments. I fully support critiques of superficial encounters, dialogues, and any deeds that just make one party to the conflict feel good at the expense of others. That is not the kind of deed I am seeking to validate or encourage. Rather, if individual increments of change pass the test of legitimacy that we have described above, they must be valued by the conflict resolution and diplomacy community as inherently exalted and valued, whether or not they are currently part of some "success story."

Some situations will not reach a successful stage for a hundred years. But if we neglect or denigrate the peacemakers who intervene in such places of intractability we are setting them up for failure.

SOCIAL NETWORK AND THE
WORLD OF RELIGIOUS PRACTITIONERS

Considering the high value that religion places on the individual deed, the study of religious peace practices should have some special place in the weaving of new approaches to citizen diplomacy and conflict resolution. Religious approaches to diplomacy should be included in the creation of new global commitments precisely because religion has been such a divider in the past. If there is to be a new global civilization there must be "buy-in" from millions of religious people who are not just spiritual but also quite traditional.

How can that happen? Not through intellectual conferences and policy negotiations alone, but through the networks of relationships that influence the attitudes of millions of people. This is why social network must play a pivotal role in the dissemination of conflict resolution in the future. This is the only way that will affect enough millions of people to create the necessary paradigm shifts at the centers of global civilizations.

We need buy-in from millions of people in every civilization for a paradigm shift to occur regarding a new global social contract and concept of community. That also means that there must be secular/religious coalitions, and a coalescence of some agreed upon set of values and practices that implicitly support global social contracts. This can happen, but due to mistrust on all sides it will have to happen initially in an indirect way of building trusting relationships through social networks.

Social Network Theory

Let us take a moment, therefore, to introduce briefly social network theory. Marc Granovetter, based on Gabriel Weiman, has argued that the greatest and most effective form of social change is through the weaving of loose or "weak ties" by special individuals, often referred to as "connectors," who make constant contact with concentrated clusters of "strong-ties" groups as well as loose ties across society or even across the globe.[12] "Strong-ties groups" refers to those groups that are more insular and closed, such as members of a particularly specialized academic discipline, a small village, or a devoutly religious group.

Strong ties and loose ties each have their own advantages for human beings. Loose ties have some distinct advantages because they are the means by which ideas and information spread the most quickly. People tied loosely are generally networked with more than one group, and so information passes through many groups. Weak ties provide the best way to find jobs, for example.

By contrast, strong ties can sometimes stand in the way of enough connections to improve yourself, to expand your horizons and opportunities. This is endemic in poor communities. Connections to loose networks, however, allow for the greatest mobility in access and influence. If you find yourself exclusively within a small, tight-knit group or neighborhood you may have less access to new opportunities.

On the other hand, communities of strong ties offer many advantages to people at the level of emotion and meaning. But this is not necessarily the best network to find scarce resources, such as educational advancement and job improvement, or new approaches to endemic problems such as war with other groups.

Penetrating Closed Networks of Traditionalists

The relationship between loose ties, connectors, and traditional strong-ties communities is the most interesting, in terms of opportunities for peacemaking. Conservative religious communities are often considered communities of strong ties. They are the communities that are the most resistant to change precisely because so much about them is inbred and self-referential. Changing the attitudes of such communities is thus the most challenging. But once new ideas *have* filtered in, there can be remarkable levels of communication and cross-fertilization.

The advantage of strong-ties communities is that once new ideas have infiltrated, then leadership within the community can effect and encourage transformation rather quickly. So that if, for example, the Catholic Church, or even the Vatican, were to become "carbon neutral" that would have a massive effect overnight on hundreds of millions of people. This is not because all Catholics would be coerced into carbon neutrality in today's age of relative religious freedom, but rather because that moral choice would now hold far greater weight in the eyes of hundreds of millions of traditionalists. The strength of such community ties can actually create a paradigm shift in thinking and behavior.

Weak ties provide the linkage to the outside world, indeed to many worlds and new visions. This in turn can induce a creative stimulus of paradigm shifts in thinking and working. But the strong ties of the religious community are critical also. Because once such a community is infused with a new approach to an adversary the closely knit nature of the community provides a powerful engine for lasting change.[13]

This is precisely why religious peace networkers with the greatest amount of talent are the ones who generate the greatest amount of loose ties. They appear often to have no boundaries to who they will see, talk to, and invite into ceremonies.[14] They establish bonds even with individuals and groups that others write off as "the problem," "the rejectionists," "the militants," "the terrorists." The traditional religious peace networkers' origins are in strong-ties communities, but what is extraordinary about them is their ability to generate loose ties within and between religious and secular worlds. It demonstrates a resilience of the human capacity for bonds, and the discovery of reasons to be connected to others.

For example, when one hundred conservative rabbis and imams from the Middle East actually gathered through the help of religious peace networkers, some interesting realities emerged. Very mainstream clerics, isolated in the center of clusters[15] in their own worlds, are usually surrounded by strong ties that tend to sustain a one-dimensional conception of enemies; they have very few ties connecting them to any other worlds. Sometimes they are utterly isolated by equally religious but separate sects in their own religion! This is true of some Hasidic sects, for example, and is one of the reasons there can be hostility from time to time between these remarkably similar groups.[16]

When the imams and rabbis gathered they discovered collective memories of their families' relationships before 1948 in a variety of Arab countries. They discovered that there were tight bonds between their fathers, also rabbis and imams, who used to cooperate in matters of jurisprudence, even helping each other with ritual and legal decisions, even knowing the same tunes![17]

In technical terms, these two disparate groups of clerics came from strong-ties communities that had critical loose-tie connections to clusters of each others' religious communities. In human terms, they discovered that despite all the obvious differences between their communities they were deeply connected by common values and a history of mutual respect that had been buried by the Arab–Israeli wars.

The amount of loose ties connecting very disparate religious communities may in fact be a critical marker of peaceful coexistence that needs further examination historically and globally. We may be able to predict which warring groups have the potential to reconcile based on an examination of the quality and nature of the old ties that used to exist. These clerics discovered the foundations of why they had coexisted in peace for so many centuries until the tragic Arab–Jewish split occurred.

When these imams and rabbis rediscovered each other it created an emotional sensation. This would not have happened without the creative work of the "connectors," extraordinarily networked people, with ties to all groups. These unusual people managed to create a bond between clerics of adversarial groups who are usually enclosed, but suddenly there was an opening up of ties between two tightly bonded worlds. All this occurred because the connectors smashed through the walls of the enemy system.[18] It also occurred because of the precedents among them of unusual friendships across enemy lines that became a symbol and a stimulus for the organizers and funders to follow as they decided to risk a gathering of Arab and Israeli clerics.

Here is the most important point then about religion and conflict resolution. A religious unit of strong ties represents a cluster of human interaction that is generally conservative and resistant to change, but that nevertheless is highly motivating in terms of its chosen and approved activities. Thus, people on the margins of such groups with many loose ties can act as a bridge between strangers, between adversarial groups. And once the world of strong ties has been entered, any nonviolent shifts of rhetoric or ethical practice that are generated by the shocking meeting of strangers will make a crucial difference. Even small shifts, with regard to the frame and understanding of "enemy," will have a significant impact. Large numbers of otherwise cloistered people who usually form the bedrock of enemy systems will now be bonded in a new way, through the efforts of the connectors among them. And it will be more difficult for their fellow group members to demonize the other group without qualifying their accusations and characterizations. Peace at its first stages requires a complex view of the enemy other.

Interfaith Relations as a Stimulus to Social Networking and Paradigm Shifts

Without social network analysis, comprehending the nature of religion and peacebuilding has been a difficult challenge. Most of the typical forms of conflict resolution interventions, such as formal dialogue and negotiation, do not easily apply to what is happening among religious peacebuilders.

In general, there are many obstacles to dialogue as an effective form of religious conflict resolution. In fact, it is abundantly clear from my field work that of all things that religious traditionalists are capable of doing in terms of peacebuilding, dialogue is not their best suit. I realize this may be jarring to the reader who naturally associates interfaith peace with the pervasive programs of dialogue. But there are at least three reasons for this. (1) Traditional religions tend to emphasize exclusive, often chauvinistic, rituals that do not encourage authentic dialogue. (2) There are dogmatic beliefs and teachings that do not generally allow for self-reflection, especially when outsiders are listening. (3) Authentic dialogue, were it to be honest, would be a threat to the hierarchical nature of many conservative religious communities, compromising notions of absolute authority. Thus, people-to-people conversations are either discouraged, or extremely artificial. This is especially true when it comes to women who are often disallowed from

dialogue altogether in very traditional contexts. This means that the interfaith dialogue that does exist is actually attended by relatively few people.

When high official religious representatives of different faiths do gather,
they tend to excel not in recognizing problems but in competing for who
has the most beautiful and peaceful religious tradition. Now this is not necessarily bad! In fact, it is a step up from mutual recrimination. Constructed
well, I have participated in and witnessed such events become an excellent
bridge of respect, honor, and mutual acceptance.[19]

This is a kind of theater, however, and it does not always lead to communication and negotiation that addresses fundamental problems of injustice,
violence, and war.[20] But theater does have its place, and it can lead to strong
impact on the networks of people in conflict. Theater's greatest impact is not
the event itself, but the stimulation of new relationships between acquain-
tances who are also enemies. This then expands the network of enemy relations to a very large network on both sides. There is then a kind of shock or
reaction of disbelief to these new connections by onlookers, witnesses, and
the religiously faithful; this in turn stimulates paradigm shifts in thinking.
This must be repeated often by religious leaders to create permanent paradigm shifts, until the day that what was once shocking is now "normal."[21]

Clearly this networking phenomenon would be magnified enormously
with the help of secular political leadership endorsement, considering the
power of leaders in regressed situations of violence,[22] as well as if the media
covered this broadly. As we will soon see, we were fortunate in Syria to have
wonderful media coverage, as well as senior religious leadership involved.

AN ACCOUNTING OF RELIGION,
CONFLICT RESOLUTION, AND THE NETWORK OF PEACE

The best way to characterize, from a methodological point of view, the
work of religion, peacebuilding, and conflict resolution is to see it in terms
of a complex social network of peace. There are a number of reasons to examine religious peacebuilding from the point of view of social network:

- Social network theory best explains the behavior of religious peacebuilders who, otherwise, appear to behave randomly and unprofes-
  sionally, when in fact they are continually creating connections between enemies who might never meet. This can appear to be erratic
  and disorganized activity to donors who prefer measurable conferences
  with presumptuous titles.
- The nodes of individual religious peace actors and the ties they appear
  to have across a very large spectrum of people in enemy camps is their
  greatest strength.

- The various expressions of religious peacebuilding are systematically unfunded or underfunded, due to prejudices in the system of peace funding globally, which favor rather isolated liberal events that feel safe and right to donors of a similar political persuasion.
- Paradoxically, this underfunding appears to have pushed impoverished but passionate religious peacemakers toward interventions that are network-based rather than programmatic. They don't have any money for conferences, or hardly any. Therefore the most interesting religious peace networkers will develop friendships with everyone, with police, military, radicals, visionaries, men, women, youth leaders, musicians, academics. Essentially they pursue anyone with whom they have some spiritual/cultural common link, and who they can pursue with relatively little funding. This fits well with the kind of socialization that is typical of the outgoing, evangelical spirit of many religions. But there is a twist because it is not about proselytizing to exclusive conversion but proselytizing subtly to coexistence, pluralism, or a spiritual commonality with all people.
- Paradoxically, this approach has given impoverished religious peace-builders a broader range of ties than program-based or conference-based intervention, which tends to service again and again the same liberal clientele or elite intellectual clientele. This means, for example, that people in police departments and armies, people with guns, may be included in this loose religious network, but never be caught dead at a "left-wing" peace conference. This is the genius of loose ties, or what we might call evangelical peacemaking.
- What is also remarkable is how much more challenging this methodology is to traditional comfort zones. What I mean is that conferences and dialogues often gather people of reasonably similar opinions. In a very real way those who are in the "dialogue business" are a more tightly knit unit with more predictability. But they generate less energy outflow toward change across clusters and groups.
- But social networkers, when they do gather their many loose ties, often throw together a wide cast of characters with unpredictable results. The synergy of such meetings has been remarkable, based on what I have witnessed.
- There is a secondary phenomenon now of somewhat more savvy brokers between the world of exemplary religious peacebuilders and the donors. This has created some interesting funding for conferences, such as between the imams and rabbis originating from Arab countries (under the auspices of Hommes de Parole), as previously mentioned.
- What remains the bedrock of the peaceful social network system is the individual religious peace networker, the driven relationship maker, the connector, who defies all boundaries of enemy systems. One sees

them on every continent and in every conflict. In fact, the more violent the conflict, the more one finds these driven individuals. They are the Rosetta Stone of peacemaking, and studying their ways of interaction will provide the key for understanding this special form of conflict resolution and citizen diplomacy. It may be the key to all of future peacemaking, and the primitive and early steps we take as humanity toward a global social contract that can include radically different constituencies. It is diplomacy without the constraints of state interests. It is citizen diplomacy that spans all barriers that stand in the way of creating a global community.

"THE SINGLE ONE," THE PEACEMAKER, AND THE BONDS OF NEW COMMUNITY

The connectors of religious peacemaking are a singular group of people on this planet. They occasionally bond with each other to create an Unusual Pair, referred to earlier, which makes them even more remarkable. In their personalities and choices of life they have embodied the place in between one human and another, the place where there is a radical choice between treating the other as an object to be ignored, used, or destroyed, or treating the other as a unique subject, as an individual with whom one has the deepest of bonds.

Martin Buber, the great existentialist philosopher, articulated more than any other thinker the place "in between," in between human and human, and in between God and the human being.

Buber's brilliant essay, "The Question to the Single One," can be seen also as a distinctive characterization of the life of the peacemaker. In this essay, Buber took on the challenge posed by Kierkegaard as to whether there was anything sacred to be found in the "crowd"—or in marriage.[23] Kierkegaard's answer was a decisive "No!" Kierkegaard was determined to remove these distractions from before the man who would address God.

Buber took on Kierkegaard, quite diplomatically, but knowing full well that he was arguing for the opposite of Kierkegaard's choice. Buber investigated the notion of a bonded community, how to be part of "the crowd," remain responsible ethically within the crowd but without being tyrannized by its demands. Buber insisted on responsibility to the crowd, but also not to be taken in by it. The parallel to his own dialogic philosophy is the constant choice of how and when to manage relationships as I–it versus I–You, where the other is either an object or a subject. We cannot help as part of "crowds," or civilization and society, to see each other bureaucratically as part of a numerical count of citizens, for example. But I–You is the only moment of true meaning in relationship, where all objectification of the other ceases. This is the moment sought after by every brilliant religious peacemaker I encounter.

It should be noted that Buber was writing this precisely at the same time, the 1940s in Palestine, when he was choosing to participate in this grand Jewish experiment of returning to the Holy Land after two thousand years. He stood apart from "the crowd," the Jewish Zionist crowd in this case, by insisting on a binational state with absolute equality of Jew and Arab. So much blood has been spilled in the name of nationalism on that land since the 1940s. Buber, however, argued endlessly for the rest of his life for the essential holiness of the Other, the holy human being standing right before us, even when we disagree with him, even when we are from distinctive and opposed political communities.[24]

Buber was not a liberal Western Jew, living in the comfort of upper-class Jewish life when he wrote this. He was right at the heart of the most fateful and desperate choices that both Jews and Palestinian Arabs were facing in the 1940s. He was a "Single One" in a desert of understandable fears, searching for a bonded community of Jews who could meet the Other with courage, generosity, vision, and empathy. Alas, his spiritual heirs are still striving to create the bridges that his generation failed to do.

The most interesting moment in the essay is when Buber declared that the essential challenge of being human is the confrontation with difference, embracing the other as other, but also leaving space for principled disagreement. This is in many ways the sacred translation of conflict resolution.

The Single One, as Buber describes her, is the networker par excellence. She bonds all others in an authentic relationship of love and care. But she does not allow herself to be swallowed by the crowd and its tendency to confuse the ethical moment with the moment of loyalty. The Single One is a paradigm of the religious peacemaker who endlessly seeks the bonding of humanity through single relationships, one at a time, that redeem humanity from its dark face as "crowd." This is the answer to Kierkegaard's despair of human relationship per se, and especially the ultimate relationship with the crowd. Kierkegaard did not see the hard work that turns the crowd into humanity, from time to time.

The Dalai Lama, in a spiritual move strikingly parallel to Buber's, has asked repeatedly for everyone to practice a simple meditation every day.[25] He has asked in recent times that everyone across the globe:

- Spend five minutes at the beginning of each day remembering we all want the same thing (to be happy and loved) and we are all connected.
- Spend five minutes cherishing yourself and others. Let go of judgments. Breathe in cherishing yourself, and breathe out cherishing oth-

ers. If the faces of people you are having difficulty with appear, cherish them as well.
- During the day extend that attitude to everyone you meet—we are all the same.
- Stay in the practice, no matter what happens.

It is true that the Dalai Lama's epistemological position on the nature of the self is fundamentally different from Buber's conceptualization of self and other, or I and You. Nevertheless, both sacralize the moment of relationship with the other, and our conception of that. The Dalai Lama's meditation is meant to habituate the mind and the heart to the fundamental elements of Buber's philosophy of dialogue. Both of them, I am proposing, implicitly embrace the singular peacemaker who every day seeks to set this philosophy and mental practice right down into the hardest space in between humans, the space of conflict and violence.

CONCLUSION

In sum, the phenomenon of religious peace networking and the thread of its results may constitute a new way to evaluate change in conflict situations. A version of network theory may be devised in the future that demonstrates why religious actors, and, in fact, any actors who specialize in extensive cross-cutting ties, are effective far beyond their numbers in generating change, whereas negotiations conceived in highly specialized environments of political elites may be hampered from generating serious change due to the closed circle of their very impressive but ineffective ties.

It may emerge from further study that the early networks of religious and cultural network and transformation must lay the groundwork for path-breaking political negotiation. Perhaps only when the two dynamic processes of change, social network and formal negotiation, work together with greater mutual respect will we begin to witness the birth of forms of diplomacy and conflict resolution that are more irresistible, more attractive to critical masses of people in conflict situations around the globe. Perhaps it is their unity and collaboration that will be the key to the creation of authentic global community.

Many people crave to act in this world as Buber and the Dalai Lama suggest, but they have had precious little guidance on how to do this in the in-between place of destructive conflict and violence. For this they may need to study more the behavior of singular individuals and Unusual Pairs, who seem to be weaving together a different fabric of humanity, right beneath the radar screen of organized violence. It is a fabric that intimates the beginnings of an ethical and political contract of humanity with itself.

We must begin in the coming chapters of the book to think about a global social contract and the kind of citizen diplomacy that is capable of weaving together the early workings of that contract.

NOTES

1. For a thorough introduction to the integration of social network theory and conflict resolution practice, see Susan Allen Nan, "Conflict Resolution in a Network Society," *Negotiation Journal* 13 (2008): 111–31.

2. There are, however, some positive developments in that area, including the work of Mary Anderson and CDA. See the Collaborative Learning Projects, *Reflecting on Peace Practice Project* (Cambridge, MA: CDA, 2004), found online at cdainc. com/publications/cda_books.php; also see the manual by Chayenne Church and Mark Rogers, *Designing for Results: Integrating, Monitoring and Evaluation in Conflict Transformation Programs* (Washington, DC: Search for Common Ground, 2006), and found online at sfcg.org/programmes/ilr/ilt_manualpage.html. See also the Peace and Conflict Impact Assessment by Kenneth Bush and Robert Opp, idrc.ca/en/ev-27981-201-1-DO_TOPIC.html.

3. See Johan Galtung, "Twenty-Five Years of Peace Research: Ten Challenges and Some Responses," *Journal of Peace Research* 22, no. 2: 146–47. Also, see Edward Azar's work on protracted social conflicts, and on the need to restructure significant portions of society and its institutions in order to overturn repressive structures: Edward Azar and Renee Marlin, "The Costs of Protracted Social Conflicts in the Middle East: The Case of Lebanon," in *Conflict Management in the Middle East*, ed. Gabriel Ben-Dor and David B. Dewitt (Lanham, MD: Lexington Books, 1987), 29–44.

4. The goal of donor communities to encourage collaboration is an excellent one, especially because there is so much replication and waste on the ground of interventions in many places, such as in Israel/Palestine. But making that the responsibility of the beleaguered peace innovators who are already savaged by underpay and overwork is to simply evade the responsibilities of the rest of us. Any agency, government or otherwise, that wants to see collaboration has to invest a portion of its own budget on "collaboration specialists" who could work with various groups *and* invest the funds necessary to make the collaborations workable for everyone.

5. See the story of John Snow, an amazing father of epidemiology in the nineteenth century who figured out the true source of cholera in London. He was an integrative thinker, possessing what E. O. Wilson refers to as "consilience," the ability to combine several disciplines to figure out a revolutionary approach to a problem. In this case it was sewage treatment that saved London, saved countless victims, and made way for the modern city. See Steven Johnson, *The Ghost Map: The Story of London's Most Terrifying Epidemic, and How it Changed Science, Cities, and the Modern World* (New York: Riverhead, 2006). Note what a hard time Snow had gaining acceptance for his ingenious discovery from any number of establishments that stood in the way of his discovery and its implementation as a strategy for saving lives. The field of conflict resolution integrates several areas of human knowledge, from political science and sociology to anthropology and psychology. And this is precisely why

these intellectual fiefdoms give conflict resolution as an academic discipline such a tough time, not unlike the travails of John Snow. Even conflict resolution theory gives my field, religion, a hard time. Consilience is hard but it is the only way to create real paradigm shifts in human thinking and social change.

6. *New York Review of Books*, July 19, 2007.

7. Ad loc.

8. This truth about nonlinear approaches to change and persuasion is finally seeping into military strategy regarding terrorism, "the government is seeking ways to amplify the voices of respected religious leaders who warn that suicide bombers will not enjoy the heavenly delights promised by terrorist literature, and that their families will be dishonored by such attacks. Those efforts are aimed at undermining a terrorist's will." See Eric Schmitt and Thom Shanker, "U.S. Adapts Cold-War Idea to Fight Terrorists," *New York Times*, March 18, 2008. The U.S. government, in other words, finally acknowledged what so many of us had been arguing for years with no one listening in the White House, namely that nonviolent religious persuasion matters, even in terms of deterrence of hardened militants. It took five thousand American soldiers dead, twenty thousand wounded, two thousand trying to commit suicide, four and one-half million Iraqi refugees, and ninety thousand dead Iraqis to utterly discredit the "bomb only" school of American diplomacy and strategic deterrence of the Bush years. Now there is an admission that the soft power of promoting religiously moderate voices has a detectable impact on the will of religious people, even extremists.

9. See, for example, shalomctr.org/node/122. There was a picture of Heschel and King walking together arm in arm at the front row of the Selma March on March 21, 1965. This picture alone leaves thousands of Jews deeply emotional to this day. It is reprinted many times in Jewish textbooks and many other interfaith publications. A simple Google search of Heschel and King, under search subheading "images," yields dozens of shots of this photograph, *forty years* after the Selma March. See, for example, dartmouth.edu/~religion/faculty/heschel-photos.html. Why? Because friendship across boundaries has an hypnotic effect on the human imagination. Many of us naturally crave intimacy beyond the isolating boundaries of group antagonisms and alienation. We want a world that is more intimate, and we long to see evidence, some hard evidence, that it is possible, that it can be real. That is why even just a mere picture of a singular friendship of a white and a black visionary together, arm in arm, can be an increment of powerful change, an icon of visionary possibility.

10. See, for example, the Buddhist practice of Tonglen, which involves accepting one's own suffering and that of others in a way that is transformative, that channels it into something that enhances compassion and happiness. Contemporary articulations of this can be found at shambhala.org/teachers/pema/tonglen1.php and spcare.org/practices/tonglen-practices.html. On compassion practices of the Dalai Lama, see this recommended practice that he asked to be spread globally, salsa. net/peace/article22.html. See also, the Dalai Lama with Victor Chan, *The Wisdom of Forgiveness* (New York: Riverhead Trade, 2005), 166.

11. See, for example, Yehuda Liebes, *Studies in the Zohar* (New York: SUNY, 1993), 140. Throughout the book Liebes addresses the expansive and cosmic significance of acts of unification of the Divine Name, such as in the recitation of the Shema,

the classical expression of Jewish faith. Unification of the Divine Name is a pivotal theme of everyday mystical experience of prayer as well as practice, but also many other forms of unification that involve a messianic transformation of the world in its entirety. See, for example, Liebes, *Studies in the Zohar*, 2, 159. This is encapsulated in the pervasive expression utilized in Jewish mystical practice before the performance of any *mitzvah*, or deed of practice: *le'shem yihud kudsha brikh hu u'shekhinteh*, which translates roughly as, "for the sake of the unification of the Holy One, blessed be He, and His Divine Presence." The individual deed of concentration and unification is not only efficacious in itself but has an historical and cosmic impact. Part of the despair that often plagues conflict resolution work is a lack of a sense of global impact, frustration with unfulfilled goals, and therefore a lack of significance to what one is doing; this is a direct assault on one's sense of self. This may be why there is pervasive cynicism about this work among bystanders, namely a fear of investing in work that appears to bear little impact. Faith communities that see increments of deeds as having cosmic impact have a distinct advantage in motivation of the individual actor who believes that what she or he is doing is not only effective but as *cosmically* effective.

12. See Granovetter, "The Strength of Weak Ties."

13. See Granovetter, "The Strength of Weak Ties." This *change* can take place at the individual level, as Granovetter argues in *Getting a Job: A Study of Contacts and Careers* (Cambridge, MA: Harvard University Press, 1974), but it can also take place at the social level. One must take into account the influence of loose ties in social movements and community mobilization efforts, where loose ties between individuals serve as communication vehicles for social action, taking the movement beyond the limited clique to a broader segment of the population (p. 202). I am arguing further that, although conservative religious communities are tightly woven, once an idea does manage to seep in through connectors and boundary spanners, it can be spread very quickly.

14. Who but Eliayhu Mclean would have an event in Jerusalem on nonviolence with five people sitting next to each other in conversation: a Hasid in full black garb, a Deputy Mufti of Jerusalem, a head of a Zionist Yeshiva, a veiled Palestinian woman, and a veiled Jewish woman? This is a common occurrence for him. See flickr.com/photos/jerusalem_peacemakers/sets (accessed May 16, 2008).

15. In social network theory a "cluster" is mainly understood as the group of individuals (themselves connectors, hubs, or nodes in other clusters) who are connected by strong ties to a single node or connector. In some sense, the schematic of this relationship is akin to a core-periphery relationship where the core and periphery are connected through strong ties and together form a particularly dense social network that sets it apart from other adjacent clusters. While common wisdom inclines us to value the degree of centrality inside the cluster (the hub) on the basis that "the more connections, the better," this is not always the case. What matters is where those connections lead to. For a schematic and discussion of these basic social network analysis principles, see orgnet.com/sna.html.

16. See, for example, Menahem Friedman, "Haredi Violence in Contemporary Israeli Society," in *Studies in Contemporary Jewry*, vol. 18, ed. P. Medding (New York: Oxford University Press, 2002), 186–97.

17. Interview with Eliyahu Mclean September 10, 2008, at my Center for World Religions, Diplomacy and Conflict Resolution. Eliyahu reported on his and Sheikh

Bukhari's intervention at the meeting of imams and rabbis that helped lead to the shared memories and music. See more at imamsrabbis.org (accessed November 30, 2008).

18. They were acting as "brokers" and "boundary spanners." See Valdis Krebs and June Holley, 4.

19. See the work of Yehuda Stolov and the Interfaith Encounter Association (IEA), which brings together Jews, Christians, and Muslims in activities dedicated to "promoting peace in the Middle East through interfaith dialogue and cross-cultural study." Sometimes this involves clerics but mostly not. Their retreats and conferences provide opportunities for intensive and intimate encounters in which members of the three faiths spend time expressing views, their fears, and hopes, while having time to witness the prayers of the "other" and celebrate this diversity. Other projects of the IEA include cross-cultural study tours to sacred locations with the purpose of "educating the public about the meaning and significance of the land, and its value to each of the monotheistic traditions." See interfaith-encounter. org/projects.htm.

20. Much dialogue suffers as well from what I term "overrepresentation," that is, the tendency of all dialogue to be theater in which parties to the dialogue instinctively feel themselves to be ambassadors of their group, with the safety of the group's future dependent upon their "defense work" in the dialogue! It is a theater of defense. This behavior often seems comical because so little is actually at stake, but at the same time it is tragic. There is a desperate need to put the best face on their group, defending it, glorifying it in ways that they would never do in private, as if their lives depended on it. I have witnessed this dichotomy of public false face and private authenticity, sometimes within minutes, from the same person. Most of us as practitioners see this continually in secular dialogue as well. Thus, religious "overrepresentation" is not unique, but it seems to be exaggerated by the strong group ties generated by many faith communities that actually *obligate* their members to witness, or put the best face possible on their religion in public. There are principles in all three Abrahamic traditions, Jewish, Christian, and Muslim, that seem to require this rather duplicitous approach to the public. Of course, it is always framed in righteous terms as something done for the greater glory of God, or the sanctification of God's name, or to prevent *God's* humiliation. But it in fact is often simple duplicity. This aggravates the already problematic nature of public dialogue as conflict resolution.

21. Unfortunately, these events are rare due to funding constraints and the refusal of foundations and governments to see the long-term value of repeated exposure of religious enemy populations to each other as a critical ingredient of confidence building. Religious people are the single most underserviced population of traditional peace funding.

22. See Vamik Volkan, *Killing in the Name of Identity: A Study of Bloody Conflicts* (Charlottesville, VA: Pitchstone Publishing, 2006), 69–70; for a broad overview of this leader-group interaction and violence, see Vamik Volkan, *Blind Trust: Large Groups and Their Leaders in Times of Crisis and Terror* (Charlottesville, VA: Pitchstone Publishing, 2004).

23. Martin Buber, "The Question to the Single One," in *Between Man and Man*, trans. Robert Gregor Smith (New York: Routledge, 2002), 48ff.

24. Martin Buber, *A Land of Two Peoples: Martin Buber on Jews and Arabs* (Chicago: University of Chicago Press, 2005).

25. The practice was suggested by the Dalai Lama in response to the following questions. The exchange is worth citing in its entirety:

> A group met with the Dalai Lama for several days to dialogue on what they believed were the five most important questions to be considered moving into the new millennium. The group was asked to come up with five questions before meeting with the Dalai Lama. They asked: How do we address the widening gap between rich and poor? How do we protect the earth? How do we educate our children? How do we help Tibet and other oppressed countries/peoples? How do we bring spirituality—deep caring for each other—through all disciplines? The Dalai Lama said all the questions fall under the last one. If we have true compassion, our children will be educated, we will care for the earth, and for those who "have not." He asked the group: Do you think loving on the planet is increasing or staying the same? His own response was, "My experience leads me to believe that love IS increasing." He shared a practice with the group that will increase loving and compassion in the world, and asked everyone attending to go home and share it with as many people as possible (accessed at circlesoflight.com/articles/dalai-practice.shtml and salsa.net/peace/article22.html).

In a later chapter I will directly address the question of the pragmatic impact of the Dalai Lama's wisdom and insight-based approach to global problems.

Section II

CITIZEN DIPLOMACY AND INCREMENTAL CHANGE: A NEW APPROACH TO PEACEMAKING

4

On the Road between Damascus and Jerusalem: A Case Study of Citizen Diplomacy

CITIZEN DIPLOMACY AND THE ART OF INTERVENTION

Until now I have introduced the state of religion, conflict, conflict resolution, and peacebuilding in today's world. I have proposed a blueprint for the steps that need to be taken to create a global social contract that will include religious traditionalists. I have also challenged the way in which we have evaluated religion and conflict resolution and its role in building global community, and I have suggested at the theoretical level some rather new approaches to measurement of success in terms of social network theory.

I would like now to shift toward an exploration of a very specific form of religion and conflict resolution that is citizen diplomacy, focusing on one concrete case study.[1]

It is to the art of citizen diplomacy that I want to turn in the second half of the book, with a special emphasis on what my colleagues and I have learned about it. I will examine citizen diplomacy initially by an in-depth look at the Syria case study in the next two chapters. The Syria case study will serve as an example of building global community in even the most difficult circumstances.

Citizen diplomacy is an activity that is much larger than merely religion and conflict resolution. It refers to a whole variety of ways in which individual citizens across the planet are engaged in efforts to reach out to civilizations and countries that may be in conflict with their own. The case study that I will explore is a combination of my own experiments with religion, conflict resolution, and citizen diplomacy.

I have engaged in two major citizen diplomacy experiments that have taken me decades. The long and ongoing experiment of five years that is described below is specifically in Syria. But I have always intended from the beginning that the Syria work would provide a diplomatic key to unlock the larger Arab–Israeli conflict, my other lifelong obsession. I also hoped that it would uncover a way to reverse the Western conflict with radical states in the Middle East. Due to the unusually tolerant form of Islam that is state-sanctioned in Syria, I also hoped that our work could provide some new possibilities for Islam's relationship to the rest of the world.

My approach to this middle section of the book is to switch styles and explore the case study with personal narrative.[2] I will explore with in-depth narrative and personal experience the approach to intervention in conflict that has been proposed in the first three chapters, but that is encapsulated by the words "citizen diplomacy." As such I will be proposing that the pre-eminent and most hopeful form of social networking, conflict resolution, and religious peacebuilding of the future will be variations of the work of citizen diplomacy.

I will also introduce the moral ambiguity inherent in citizen diplomacy work, which therefore requires experimentation, humility, and ethical reflection. Citizen diplomacy requires a constant effort to draw upon human wisdom wherever one can find it. This will become the basis of reflections and analysis in the final chapters on ethical dilemmas raised by intervention in human conflict, especially deadly conflict, which a citizen diplomat will confront. We will examine how and to what degree ethical reflection, self-examination, and spiritual wisdom traditions can be helpful in tough interventions.

My aim is to tell a story of citizen diplomacy that will suggest by its example a new way of thinking about war, conflict, and "enemies," as well as how to pursue *increments* of peace and reconciliation. As I have indicated earlier, I am a firm believer in the importance of attempting to create positive increments of change, especially where they have never been tried before. I am looking for diplomatic innovations that can become triggers of larger movements and paradigm shifts.

Citizen diplomacy is distinct from conflict resolution interventions involving workshops, conferences, training, or unofficial negotiations. It can *lead* to those things, but citizen diplomacy is characterized more by networks of informal relationships, as I described in earlier chapters, that lead, rather unpredictably, to new opportunities for public events, for real breakthroughs in relationships, both public and private. It can lead to a steady increase of a network of relationships, or it can sometimes have a dramatic impact overnight through the media or through exposure to high-level actors.

Citizen diplomacy is far more experimental and unpredictable than standard interventions. That is why it is rarely supported by funders. It is deeply relational and also highly flexible, adjusting itself constantly to what is possible in each radical situation. Its flexibility is exactly what makes it less fundable, but it is also what gives it an advantage in utterly intractable situations.

Citizen diplomacy is often at the frontier of exposing radicalized and cloistered populations to the idea of a global community. The more sealed off a citizenry is from the rest of the world due to an authoritarian regime, the more potential do citizen diplomats have to make a difference where no one else can. A good citizen diplomat with the right connections can often enter into situations where NGOs and formal international projects are uninvited; as such they are often the pioneers of building an alternative to war when war could be imminent. We will keep coming back therefore to the theme of citizen diplomacy as a cornerstone of the new global social contract, a path to weaving together a new human civilization, even in the hardest places on earth.

I am also suggesting, through the moral ambiguities[3] raised in the stories I will soon tell, that the weaving together of a global civilization, and the effort to make the earth whole, is an art and a science all at once. It is both intuition and experimentation, creativity and rational learning, intuitive discovery and hard-nosed trial and error. It entails sublime moments and terrible falls. Neither scientific discovery nor artistic creation is linear, and the outbreak of peace is altogether enigmatic. But the peaceful bridge to others when it does happen, the moment of bond to enemy others, is blissful and sublime.

This truth is at the heart of my story. Such moments intimate, in their rare manifestations, both the best experience of human discovery, as well as a hint of the transcendent aspect of this noble work. It is those times, looking into the eyes of enemies who are now beloved friends in whose hands I place my life, that even a wounded peacemaker like me finds faith and hope.

For the earth to become more whole, more of a global community, thousands of people need to take this step, take these risks, and consider the virtues of citizen diplomacy in their own lives. Citizens of all ages need to draw upon the best skills of their minds and hearts to reach out individually and creatively to the alien other.

The paradigm that I am suggesting involves relatively little institutional support; it requires the personal investment of no more than a couple of thousand dollars a year for travel, lodging, and communications, a great deal of time artfully lifted from other jobs (or from retirement), and the willingness to engage in the experimentation, risks, and heartbreak of this work. It entails taking the kind of journeys that I describe below—journeys across civilizations and especially journeys toward your most terrifying enemies.

Citizen diplomacy is what policy makers, diplomats, flawed leaders, and military men need more than anything else from the rest of us. I have met with such officials many times, always showing great respect for them. And I have come to be amazed at how much I was expecting *their* leadership, while they were actually anticipating *mine*! They actually can do surprisingly little to promote positive change, given the confines of their mandates. Their jobs, from the lowest to the highest, are about the status quo, whereas the mandate of citizen diplomacy and peacebuilding is steady, positive change.

Leaders and those "in power," ironic as that phrase is, need a path to be cleared for them. They need a new example to point to and to tentatively follow if and when the timing is right. In a word, they are more followers than leaders, and it is only my age and experience that appear to be convincing me reluctantly of this truth.

I have grown up in a very traditional culture, always expecting and perhaps anticipating leadership from elders, and that "someone else" knows best what is to be done. It has taken me time to accept the fact that we, the citizens of the world, are far more responsible than our leaders for what does and does not occur in human relations, for the opportunities gained and the opportunities lost for peace.

It has been amazing to me just how much of an impression journeys of peace across enemy lines make on everyone. Carrying on in this work is far more difficult emotionally and physically than I ever could have imagined, but the impact on power is far easier than I expected. Perhaps it is because there is such a vacuum in the dangerous void between enemies that it does not take much to fill it.

Citizen diplomacy is required most especially in confronting the "gray" areas of human ethics and relationships. You are always confronting behavior of states that varies from poor to abominable, but with many good people stuck in systems that are beyond their control. It entails facing just how many basically decent people can be part of systems resulting in horrific human behavior, and figuring out where and how and when you have the capacity to nudge forward relationships across these deep divides. It entails a constant balancing act of acceptance and challenge, silence and truth-telling, red lines and crossing lines. And it is tailor-made for the imperfection that is at the heart of the human condition.

FRIENDSHIP AND THE NEW DIPLOMACY

The story I am about to tell is also a tale of friendship and unusual partnership, across the lines of enemy systems and civilizations, for there is no true citizen diplomacy without deep friendship. I have had many partnerships, and I have witnessed many. I have worked with settler rabbis who held the opposite religious philosophy from mine, with Islamic Sufi masters far more oriented to mysticism than the kind of science that is the bedrock of my reality. I have worked with Christian fundamentalists who need me to think well of Jesus and believe only in earth's creation five thousand years ago, and I have worked with military men who have a past of killing my fellow Jews. I have witnessed mystical Jews and Muslims, beloved of each other, praying together for the health and well-being of sick people in their communities, and I have seen warriors weep helplessly before the ravages of battle. I have watched these same warriors exchange greetings of love with each other across enemy lines.

All of them are united by one thing: their driven desire to reach across the human divide of ugly war, in search of authentic friendship, care, and loyalty. These are the heroes of citizen diplomacy—ever-present, clandestine, and the best hope of the earth.

Always I have been stunned by friendship, by the power of love across enemy lines, and the astonishing thing that two adversaries can do when they join their worlds and establish a whole range of new relationships through the bridge that they have created. The consequences of persistently built and maintained bridges are far-reaching, and the number of connections they create just seems to grow on its own.[4]

It is as if war is a mighty river passing at the bottom of a deep fissure of the earth, dividing the banks from each other, and then there are bridges over these dangerous waters. Mostly in war bridges are destroyed and bridges are built, again and again, for traffic to go only one way, the way of conquest and victory.

But when two people from opposite banks build a bridge that meets in the middle, and when the traffic goes in two directions, the amount of positive shifts in relationships spreading in all directions seems to multiply geometrically. New roads start to spring up everywhere on both sides of the river in ways that the original bridge builders could not possibly have imagined.

I spent so many of my best years, my stronger years, trying to build bridges in Israel and Palestine. I remain convinced that equal coexistence is doable and inevitable. But I did despair over the amount of suffering that so many people are enduring while this inevitable direction becomes a reality.

WHY SYRIA?

It was in one of those years of despair that I discovered Syria. I also had been keenly aware that, as in many other conflicts, the two major parties' extremists were unnaturally strong due to outside interests in pursuing or perpetuating the conflict. I knew that comprehensive peace is the only peace that realistically undermines spoilers. I sensed therefore that Syria, as well as the other Arab states and Iran, must be partners on the road to any Israeli–Palestinian peace if we are truly to undermine a minority of spoilers. This is self-evident but often lost on political leaders whose need to appear tough and violent for their constituencies consistently outweighs their rational choices about violence. Israeli and American leaders ignore Syrians one year and focus on Palestinians, then they ignore Palestinians and focus on Syrians the next year. Maybe this is rational for survival in politics but it makes no sense in terms of survival of states and civilizations. It does not address the root causes of the cycle of conflict, and it shows little respect for parties to a serious conflict with real grievances on all sides.

But there are other questions about Syria that the reader should be asking. Why build an approach to peacemaking inside a police state? Why go to Syria, of all places, a question I was asked endlessly in 2005. The answer is simple. I have always believed that it is wrong to construct an approach to intervention, to peacebuilding, that cannot work in the most difficult situations. We need a *global* social contract on many issues much sooner than democracy will be firmly established in every country. We need ways to communicate, listen, negotiate, and persuade, even in the most difficult political environments. Of course, in the context of all-out war or ruthless dictatorship, such as Saddam's Iraq where anyone could have been shot at any moment, there were moral impediments to any serious citizen diplomacy. History clearly showed, however, that military intervention was no less a failure!

An authoritarian regime such as Syria's is different. There are many abuses and hazards, but deciding whether or not one can effectively intervene and reach more people to build a better future is a calculation that must be adjusted to every situation and time. (Indeed, this also reflects a sophisticated form of ethical decision making.) There are countless human rights abuses in the world's dozens of evolving democracies and countries at risk; weak minorities and human rights activists are abused everywhere. But serious global diplomacy cannot write off the hundreds of millions of people in all these countries. Rather, peacemaking requires engagement, but also a constant moral calculus of silence and activism, "pushing the envelope" and maintaining relationships.

Furthermore, I came to realize that the "evolved democracies" are not doing well of late either in the human rights departments. There is an arrogance of judgment in the West that decides which countries are worthy of engagement and which are not. Citizen diplomacy can know no such boundaries and cannot be as quick to moral arrogance and judgment. The fact, for example, that the United States was failing so miserably in human rights in the middle of the first decade of the twenty-first century made it much easier for me to suspend judgment on Syria and its people.

With these ambiguities as a background I will address moral calculations of the citizen diplomat in great detail in the last chapters. Nondemocracies are the best test of our ability to weave a new social contract with the mostly nonfree world. At the same time, the moral dilemmas around any appearance of support for repressive actions of governments was and is a constant concern, and I will address this below. Finally, there is a vast difference between working respectfully and diplomatically in a police state as cautious citizen diplomats, and the kind of right-wing—and left-wing—global actors who jet in and jet out of such states, blithely offering blessings to the powers that be. This is not what we did, not at all, but I will let the reader judge.

The religion and conflict resolution interventions that occurred in Syria have taken place over a period of several years and are still ongoing. I will therefore recount this story chronologically, with some attention to how my reactions and thinking evolved over time.

BEGINNINGS IN 2005

Provincial Origins of a Global Journey

In 2005 I was in a period of intensive reflection on what was and was not accomplished by my interventions in the Middle East. I have been taking stock of my life in recent years, especially as I edged against my will toward fifty, and I often wonder at this late date how I ended up spending my life flirting with war zones. It certainly was not how my life began; at least that is what I like to tell myself.

I knew my parents had a kind of war zone going on in the house, but actual war, any kind of violence with guns, was as distant as the North Pole. I think of my childhood in Boston as safe and comfortable, at least in terms of the backdrop of my middle- to upper-class society. It was very stable physically, and it also involved a steady immersion in a world of hopeful ideas and religious experiences.

I dream sometimes of my walks on sunny winter days in New England, arm in arm with my frail, old rabbi, a teacher to thousands, a wellspring of intellectual worlds spanning Talmudic law and ancient Greek philosophy, worlds that he shared with me and countless others. We called him "the Rav," "Master," and he truly was that to me. I was thirteen in 1970, he was sixty-seven and recently widowed, and he spoke at my Bar Mitsvah of a love affair between us. I did not understand it then, and I do not understand it now. I just know we met on a spiritual and intellectual plane of friendship that was a lifeline to me in a very bewildering world.

It was 1995, I recall, two years after he died at the age of ninety. On a cold starless night I sat on a freezing cement step of Rawson Path in Brookline, Massachusetts. It was the same path that I had helped him on year after year of my teenage years, up and down the steep path, back and forth to synagogue on the Sabbath, as he struggled with his vision, with his old age, and with the ice and snow of winter. I had felt such a clear mission as a boy, to serve him, and through him to discover the infinite worlds of the human mind and spirit.

I sat there on the cold stones in 1995 for an hour and a half, trying to keep my fingers warm, peering down into the darkness of the path, more lonely than I had ever felt in my life. I thought I caught a glimpse of him turning the corner, his long white beard, his black hat, his eyes intense, lost in thought, his breath crystallizing in the cold night air, the same crystallized breath that always mingled with mine as we huffed and puffed our way up the hills for so many years. But it was not my master; it was a phantom.

One thing I knew for sure, something that was more certain to me than anything I could figure out about war or peace or politics. My teacher had an amazing flare for the dramatic. He loved life intensely and especially the intensity of human drama, both its exhilarating and its tragic moments. Philosophically he was an existentialist, and nothing matters more to an existentialist than the revelatory intensity of the moment of human drama—and the fateful choices we make in those moments.

The memories and shadows of my teacher made me believe at the time that everything right now, whatever that "now" is, is dramatic; everything matters, every place, every person, every time in history. I believed at the time that at every moment there is some kind of Compassionate Intelligence to the complex character of the world, and that the choices we face are momentous. I believed that the journey of the human being through those moments is tragic, filled with flaws and mistakes, but also filled with the majesty of being the hand of the Divine on earth.

There was no time for foolish pursuits in the master's world, only for contributing to the unfolding of the Divine/human drama, with all the intellectual and existential intensity that it requires. I came to believe through his teaching—and through the experience of losing him—that if there is any presence or power to God on this earth it expresses itself through the momentous impact of the single human being.

I thought on those steps that night, "God, help the people who don't understand their own power, who don't see that at every moment they are the hand of God on earth, for better or for worse, depending on how they use their power."

I was dreaming of that dark, haunting night of revelation in 1995 when ten years later I found myself in very different nighttime circumstances. As an American Jewish rabbi who had spent a lifetime since my youth both loving and fighting with my people over Israel's policies, I now found myself on the border in between two Arab countries in the Middle East at midnight. It was this master who had shown me, at least in private conversations, the way to stand up to my people's flaws, to think independently of "the crowd" (a phrase from Buber, who he avidly read), to strive for vision in the most difficult situations, especially when it came to the complex tragedy of Israel's experience and behavior.

I was now a professor of conflict resolution, and I found myself slipping into dreams of that night on the lonely steps of Rawson Path when I thought I had seen the master. The night in Syria was black, and there I was: surrounded by Jordanian security a few hundred feet behind me, Syrian security ahead of me, not knowing a word of Arabic, in the dead of the winter of 2005 at the age of forty-seven.

I felt like I was watching, from the outside, a drama unfolding that was at once terrifying, awesome, worth living for, worth getting sick over, and even worth dying for. I could not believe that I had put myself in this position without any knowledge of the language of the police forces and little knowledge of the culture; I was entering into a land that had sent major armies against my cousins to the south, a land that was still in a state of war with Israel, not to mention the United States, and I was completely at the mercy of Syrians in the car who were taking me forward into the darkness. I had taken risks in Palestine before but always a few miles from my cousins. Nothing like this.

I heard the master's voice on that border in that darkened car, as I waited for security to interview me. Late nights often remind me of him. He used to lecture every Saturday night on philosophy and Torah, the Hebrew Bible, and sacred commentaries, and I could still hear the cavernous sound of his aging but dignified voice resounding through the lecture hall. I was in that lecture hall late on Saturday nights from the time I was ten. My earliest memory of the lectures was not the lecture itself, but finding a corner of the lecture hall, lying down, and falling asleep on the benches to the sound of his voice.

On one of those nights I heard him talking about someone mysterious looking over his shoulder when he studied, an elusive companion in the dark of night, a shadow, a phantom, a tormentor, a companion. It was a face of the Divine for him, a shadow-companion accompanying him on his strangest journeys and discoveries of the unknown. It was just like the Jewish patriarch Jacob, according to biblical narrative, who had been accompanied in his wanderings in this very Middle Eastern region by a mysterious being who followed him, a being who fought with him at night—but also protected him.[5]

I felt something behind me on that international border between Amman and Damascus, on the flat plains near Dar'a, no city lights or lampposts for miles, with the moon's light bathing the rolling hills and thousands of stars above. I felt a phantom, guiding, protecting, taunting, goading, looking down at me with a bemused, wizened smile, as if to say, "I have seen your type so often. I have seen people like you come and go for thousands of years, always dreaming, always hoping, always seeking. Let's see how you do."

I looked at those plains and rolling hills, and understood for the first time how flat the terrain and astonishingly short the distances were between Amman, Jerusalem, and Damascus, between ancient Moab, Canaan, and Aram. Peering out of the car windows into the shadows created by starlight, I saw thousands of years of armies traipsing back and forth between these lands. I at once understood why it was so tempting for empires to go back and forth in the endless exchanges of armies through these plains, the land of Aram, with Judea and Samaria to the south, and Babylonia and Persia not far off to the West.

I have always envied the Dalai Lama, his ancient home a completely landlocked roof of the world, utterly impossible to reach for centuries, so hard for arrogant men to pass through with their vast armies. His tragedies are more recent. But we who came from this small part of the Middle East, saddled with these long shorelines and flat plains, were fated for thousands of years to entertain an infinite procession of military men acting as gods, raping the land, determining the fate of millions on a whim, always framed as in the empire's strategic interest—and always with a god on their side.

I felt I had a job to do, to respond to these darkened plains and their wars, just as surely as ancient Jewish philosophers and poets had tried to do. I also knew, sitting in the dark car at night on that border, how utterly unprepared I was in that role, how absurd it was to think that a man like me with my weaknesses could actually do something constructive in Syria, something that the diplomats and negotiators had failed to do. It was arrogant and shameless, but something drove me on like a cannon ball. I could not fathom my own will to persist in the face of such inadequacy because I knew things about myself that no one knew.

I knew, for example, that I have a tendency to internalize every illness I can get my hands on when I am nervous. Place me in the same room as a dog with rabies and I am sure I would develop the urge to howl. Despite my love of psychology, I thank God I never became a psychiatrist because I am sure I would be in an asylum by the end of my first set of rounds as a resident. My empathetic tendencies have helped me since I was young to quickly absorb the human dramas around me, but they have also been a curse. I cry when a pope dies with whom I completely disagreed on numerous issues, and I feel the Nuremberg rallies when I see them on television as if I was there; I feel its lure for Aryan Nazis and its terror for Jews.

Not exactly a prescription for tough persistence in Syria, or through borders dividing warring countries! But there I was forging ahead as if I were General Patton. The cowardly and the impulsively reckless combine seamlessly in me as I march through life, and I have no idea why.

As I was waiting in the car at the border I tried to retrace how I had gotten there. I had been invited to speak and teach at two separate seminars in Israel in January of 2005. Months before, as I contemplated the trip, I realized that I had a total of eight days free in between the seminars. I found myself in crisis because I might have a vacation, and workaholics tend to have an inverted set of fears and pleasures. At the same time, something else was developing that was strange, to say the least.

HIND KABAWAT AND THE EVOLUTION OF PARTNERSHIP

I happened to sit near the front row of a session at the World Economic Forum at the Dead Sea in Jordan in May of 2004. I found myself next to an extraordinary person who seemed itching to jump out of her seat in response to things being said. She was tall and striking in appearance, and when the question/answer period was announced she practically jumped out of her seat, hand raised higher than the sky, like in high school. Then she spoke out clearly and confidently, and I was stunned by her unique combination of self-conscious Syrian pride and bold commitment to a new Middle East, a place of human rights and democracy that *every country*, including Israel, had to observe!

She was a Syrian-Canadian attorney by the name of Hind Kabawat. Coincidentally she was a recent graduate of the Fletcher School for Law and Diplomacy, where I had just finished five years of teaching in my hometown of Boston. Her vision was powerful and optimistic, yet demanding and hardheaded. She did not hesitate to criticize Israel, as would be expected of her from fellow Syrians at the conference, but she clearly expected the same high standards from *every* Arab country in the Middle East; and that was new to me.

This was not the standard, rehearsed political game of singling out Israel and hiding from Arab problems. This was new; this was an authentic voice, and it was a mostly unique voice at the conference that year. I think that half my life I was waiting for a partner from Arab radical states. I was looking for someone just like Hind, somone who could be a critic of Israel's approach to the Palestinians, but who also could combine that critique with a democratic vision of the whole region, and a call for Arab cultural renewal. To me this combination of messages from the Arab world that Hind was articulating would be the true key to the long-term survival of Jewish people in Israel. Israel's fate is wrapped up in the fate of the oil-drenched Middle

East, and I knew that Jewish Israel had to share the land equally with the Palestinians. But I also knew that Israel would never be really safe in doing so until evolving democracies began to emerge around it. This encounter with Hind seemed to me to be an interesting opening, at least for a one-to-one partnership. But that is all that ever changes history.

As I got friendly with Hind at the conference I started to wonder if she was a spy. At the conference you were either opulent, or an invited intellectual who could barely afford the hotel and airfare, let alone the $10,000 registration fee, or you were someone just a tad shadowy, with no apparent affiliation, but who could afford the registration fee. I met all three types in this Middle Eastern conference, but Hind just didn't fit. She seemed part of a privileged elite in Syria, and yet not a part of it at all. That intrigued me because it is just such people who often change history.

Agents of Change and Citizen Diplomacy

Change agents are unique people who are born into positions of some power over the fate of a civilization. They also have skills and values that set them apart. Hind's father, a member of an old and distinguished Christian family, was one of the highest placed Ba'ath party members until 1963, and also a key military man. On the other hand, Hind is absolutely not a Ba'athist.

There is an intimate love/hate affair among those who presently lead and those who have led Syria in the past, all part of a very uncomfortable team. Many are never completely thrust out, but everyone is always nervous. They have gone to the same schools and are often classmates.

My interest was precisely in an insider/outsider. People who are both inside and outside power groups are the ones who can effect the most change. They can make connections across the greatest number of people both in and out of power, wealthy and poor, privileged and underprivileged.

Then there is also the issue of character, and here the work that Malcolm Gladwell has collected in *The Tipping Point* demonstrates the centrality for civilizational change of people with new ideas or approaches who seem to know everyone, connect everyone—*and relish the experience of doing so*. These are the "connectors" who often hold history in the palm of their hands, as we saw in the previous chapter. That is Hind.

But then there is one more ingredient, and this is what finally persuaded me to trust her. (I do everything based on trust that emerges after a period of skeptical inquiry.) Hind's website and her public statements strongly suggested a person of great moral commitments to the future of humanity and to the just and compassionate conduct of countries. She combined a rare blend of national pride, power, charisma, and global values. I gravitate to people like that, whether I want to or not, whether it is prudent or not.

I knew that a serious and empathetic journey into the culture of Syria would take me on a left turn away from my work in Israel. I suspected many would view this move on its face as an abandonment of the Palestinians—and also as an object of suspicion by the Jewish community. Indeed, I got all of those reactions eventually. But something said to me that my world might change through Hind's world, and that I might change her world. That was dramatic, and I have a penchant for dramatic possibilities.

We continued to speak by e-mail, and I studied further her work and affiliations. Then one day, out of the blue, after hearing that I was coming to Israel—which I did not mention by name even though it was understood—she invited me to Syria to give public lectures, meet a large range of officials, and participate in a full array of media interviews, but all under the banner of interfaith diplomacy.

I was in shock, and I remember receiving the simple e-mail and my heart stopping. Many Arabs had invited me to their countries, but it was usually a diplomatic gesture, with no intention of or capacity for follow through. But every time I raised an objection, a challenge, Hind wrote that it had been taken care of. Then I really worried that she was a spy!

How could she make arrangements like this? How could she arrange for officials to meet me at the border to ensure the ease of my travel, and how could she get me from Israel to Syria through Jordan without it causing major problems for her and for me? But it turns out she was part of an elite culture in the throes of change and struggle, and there were a few windows available to the clever and connected for bold public experiments. It was completely different from what officials in the United States or Israel or the global media even begin to understand about Syria.

Everyone in the Israel–United States axis that I was familiar with in Washington and Jerusalem had written off Syria, but I soon discovered that this was based on very poor human intelligence. They did not understand the dynamic nature of changes that were possible in the early part of the decade, before the Lebanon War, before the Harriri assassination, and before the White House started pushing hard for regime change, for a coup in Syria. More importantly, they failed to see our own responsibility when we condemn such societies and claim they cannot change. Our very inflexibility becomes part of the reason that new openings are killed at birth. I was determined to never be such a reactionary.

The many European and Asian ambassadors I met, by contrast to the Americans in Washington and the Israelis, knew it was more complicated in Syria, more fluid, more open to peace and change among some of the ruling factions. I saw an opportunity to create an opening. This gap in human intelligence, this fluidity in struggles for change, gave me an opportunity with Hind.

Partnership in Citizen Diplomacy

I would eventually discover how much of the so-called "Old Guard," the diehard Ba'athists in Syria, were vigorously opposed to interfaith and intercivilizational diplomacy. But they were not in a position apparently to punish prominent citizens for this kind of activity, especially if it was approved by the president, which our work was. If, on the other hand, I had turned out to be rude when I came, if I had gone out of my way to insult the regime, the whole experiment may very well have backfired. No one ever told me this, but I understood this by implication.

It was on this basis that we were allowed to hold an unprecedented public dialogue with hundreds of people on peace, right in front of all of Syria's state cameras at its most prestigious public location, the Asad Library in the heart of Damascus. The forward-thinking Syrians who partnered in this undertaking were taking a big risk with me, and I with them, though the price I could pay was minimal by comparison to them. They had no idea what I would say, and their stress showed.

I had always been attracted to citizen diplomacy as a key to global change. Private citizens, unhampered by governments or by NGOs, beholden to no one, have the greatest flexibility to maneuver impossible political situations. And it is the impossible that attracts me (perhaps a vestige of my religious/scientific fascination with the deeper meaning of the concept of "miracle").

Citizen diplomats can adjust themselves with great resilience, and I sensed that Hind and I were both consummate pragmatists, willing and able to adjust our strategies to confront and avoid every possible obstacle. As her trusty driver Ali dodged cars at high speeds every day in the infamous circles of Damascus traffic, I watched in awe, holding on for dear life in the passenger seat, as Hind in the back seat simultaneously dodged one political obstacle after another as she negotiated every detail on the cell phone. He was speeding like a wild man, she was speed dialing and fast talking like a wild political virtuoso, and I sat in a jet lag stupor wondering what I was doing there. It was all nerve-wracking to the core, with no missteps possible, but God, I felt alive for the first time in years! This was high drama.

Citizen diplomacy would make Hind and I both somewhat more poor, being unsupported by any government or nonprofit. But we would have the maximum freedom to confront many spoilers and simply work around them. We would seize every opportunity for relationship and connection that furthered the progress of our work.

Hind was also no spy, it turns out. The only way she got to the World Economic Forum in the spring of 2005 was by working for the Bank of Oman as a consultant for a short time. The Syrian government never would have sent her, but neither would they stop a prominent citizen like her from going to the conference, at least in 2005.

Apparently then fate was offering me an opportunity to play a role as a citizen diplomat, in a political drama unfolding in Syria—a real struggle, a game of quiet push and shove that was being carried out on a very subtle level. It turns out that much of this subtle push and shove was within the government as well, even within the Ba'ath party, and that intrigued me even more as a conflict analyst.

The twentieth century is littered with millions dead due to overt and highly adversarial confrontations with oppressive, old power structures, going right back to the beginning of the century in czarist Russia. Those revolutions and wars were sometimes carried out as noble struggles for human rights, but the struggles killed and maimed countless millions, and they often provoked counterrevolutions even more tyrannical than what they had sought to uproot. This was the essential tragedy of most liberal and communist revolutions, from France to Russia.

That is why what has always been more intriguing to me is *evolution* rather than *revolution*, the irritating push and pull of nonviolent movements. They too can create violent responses, but not as violent as revolution and war. I wanted to experiment more with how authoritarian systems can change from within, and how we could stimulate that nonviolent change as citizen diplomats and networks of friends. As an American, as a Jewish rabbi, as a professor, as a naïve peacemaker, as a lover of the Palestinian people, I wanted to be to the Ba'athists a very friendly, respectful, and sympathetic irritant; a fly that might be shooed but not swatted.[6] The safety and security of my new friends may have also depended upon it.

We were searching for ways to make change but avoid pressure that could lead to violence or repression. What few realize is that there is high drama in evolutionary change as well, and it too is dangerous, but it often bears more fruit that is less liable to rot. I cannot resist its drama.

The Long Path to the Border of Syria

Before I go more deeply into the Syria experiment, I want to take a step back and explain exactly how I transitioned that winter from an Israel-centered reality to a Syria-centered reality. This is important to a better understanding of the nature of the Syria experiment.

This then is the story of how I came to the border of Syria and Jordan on January 2, 2005. In between the two seminars in Israel in December and January of 2004 and 2005, I slipped out of the troubled country of Israel that is the home now of so many of my cousins, the original home of millions of Palestinians. I left my work behind there for a time, crossed the Allenby Bridge into Jordan, and then into Syria. I did not tell anyone except my immediate family and one Israeli colleague whose help I needed at the last minute to get me across the border.

It was a difficult crossing for a few reasons, including the fact that I was suffering the effects of an interminable sinus infection, and therefore my ears were injured by the overseas flight to Israel. I was really sick, already having taken two courses of antibiotics, could not fly to Amman and then Damascus, and I had to therefore take a complicated land route between Israel and Syria with two passports, one for Israeli eyes and one for Syrian eyes.

I kept both passports in my wallet, perpetually in terror that I would mix them up. The Syrians would reject me outright with the Israeli stamps, and if the Israelis saw that I had a Syrian visa stamped into the other passport they might try to dissuade me from going or cause some other problem. I was new at this and I had no idea who might discourage me from going or sabotage my trip, the United States, Syria, or Israel. And so I informed almost no one.

I ask myself to this day how I could have even started the trip. I knew getting on the plane in Washington that I was not shaking the illness. For a week I took every drug to reduce the stress on my ears, but I failed, and I must have been much sicker than I wanted to admit. As the plane descended toward Tel Aviv I went into a state of agony. Down on the ground I could hear very little but I managed to get to my first hotel bed, one of thirteen beds I would stay in over five weeks of illness in four countries, Israel, Jordan, Syria, Israel again, and Switzerland. My final destination before returning home was the World Economic Forum (WEF) where I was to run a session. The Syria experience would exhaust me so much that I would do pretty poorly at WEF at a critical session to which Richard Gere came. I felt like I was risking so many of my networks to persist in the Syria journey, but I could not be deterred. I have abused my body many times in my life, but this trip surpassed all previous escapades; I was downing cortisone everywhere to keep going.

Something said to me if I don't go now to Syria, the land of the enemies of my people, it may never be possible ever again. I felt that Hind had put much at stake planning all of this for a skeptical group in Damascus that could never imagine that this could be pulled off, a national event with an American Jewish rabbi. I went, barely able to do my first seminar in Israel—in fact I royally screwed it up—took enough antibiotics and cortisone to get somewhat better, and then undertook the land journey from Jerusalem to Damascus.

Mistakes on the Israeli–Jordanian Border

I decided to go over the Allenby Bridge to Jordan. It was the closest exit point from Jerusalem where I was based, it was easy for me to tell Hind where to meet me on the other side, and I liked the name of the bridge and its history. I think I wanted to pass over the Jordan River like ancient Jews did.

I needed help on all fronts because on the other side of the bridge in Jordan I would have to be careful to not talk about a trip to Syria. I did not realize until after the trip just how intensely the Jordanians resented the Syrian regime, and I did not know of the attempts of the Old Guard in Syria to destabilize Jordan. I did not realize just how much Syria had housed the virulently anti-Jordanian factions of the PLO. Hind knew this but she had a habit of not wanting to tell me too much "bad news," as she put it.

Hind said she could not meet me directly in the terminal on the Jordanian side but would not say why as a Syrian national she might have a problem. So an American friend in Jordan stepped in at this point to help this hapless, sick rabbi get through. I swear I felt like Gene Wilder in *The Frisco Kid* playing an East European rabbi in the Wild West. But I felt safe with the cell phone number of a wonderful American official waiting for me on the Jordanian side who had informed the police that I would be coming over, and he had the right credentials to be taken seriously.

The problem was that the one entrance to Jordan that required a visa from Israel was the Allenby Bridge because it was not a recognized international border, being a part of the disputed territory between Israel, Jordan, and the Palestinians. This caused the first crisis due to my stupidity, but I was so proud of myself getting to the bridge from Jerusalem! Most cab drivers from West Jerusalem—the Jewish part—never go to the Allenby Bridge, and I could not understand why until I realized I needed the visa. It turns out that the Allenby Bridge was a mostly Arab crossing where Israel pushes Palestinians to do all of their border crossings.

Before the bridge there is an isolated outpost in the middle of a no-man's land where the Israeli police had a booth on the road. They stopped me and asked me for my Jordanian visa before proceeding to the Allenby Bridge terminal. When I did not have it the soldier curtly waived me back, explaining that I will make a big mess going onward, that it was getting to the end of the time when buses go through anyway, that the Jordanians would charge me a great deal of money to send me back from Jordan, and I would lose all my money. So my second mistake was not realizing how early the bridge closes, and that I had come at the last possible time period.

I said to the soldiers that I had people waiting for me on the other side, and assured them that they would get me through without a visa. There were two Israeli soldiers at the checkpoint with oversized guns, and one of the soldiers was Russian. The Russian one started screaming at me and telling me I was an idiot. Of course, I agreed with him, but asked him if I could go on anyway. He shouted no, kept on waiving his hands and his gun and holding his head in disgust because I was such an idiot. Finally he shouted, "Listen, I will make a call. Watch!" He lifted up the receiver of an old phone with a ridiculously long, ancient cord in his security booth, "Can this jerk go over without a visa?" he hollered into the line in Hebrew, slammed down the phone in two seconds, and barked in English, "You see, No!"

While all this was going on I was still seated in the back of the taxi, window opened, shuddering. The middle-aged Jewish taxi driver from Jerusalem—wonderful man—was waiting patiently (unlike most of my other Jewish and Palestinian cabdrivers), offering consolation. He was the first Israeli of many who, when I told them where I was headed and why, seemed in awe and helped me in various ways. I let private people know more of what I was doing than officials, which always seems to help me.

I started offering the cabdriver more money for his time, terrified that he would leave me alone with the two lovely soldiers. We sat on the side of the road for an hour because if I lost the cabdriver I would be alone in the West Bank with no one around for miles. It was a completely deserted location, with only the two soldiers to taunt me, and I thank God this wonderful Israeli stayed with me.

It was at this point that I realized that I needed help. If I did not get over that day I was not sure I would ever make it over. I could not reach the cell phone of my Jordanian friend a half-mile away on the other side of the bridge to see if he could do anything because my brother-in-law's Jerusalem cell phone—which he thankfully lent me—was on a different operating system than Jordanian cell phones. The wonders of "cold peace." So I called Rabbi Ron Kronish, whose seminar I had badly attended, in Jerusalem, and he called Hind's Jordanian friend who was sitting on his cell phone on the other side of the bridge; Allenby Bridge, Israel, to Jerusalem land-line to Allenby Bridge, Jordan side. And that is how the conversations went for half an hour. You would think it was the Paris peace talks. Jerusalem rabbis, Israeli cab drivers, Jordanian Americans, and the Syrian Hind, were all in conversation trying to get me past the angry Russian soldier representing the State of Israel in the West Bank. I had not even begun the journey to face the Syrian television cameras and I was already causing an international incident.

I started needing to urinate every five minutes for some strange reason. That happens to me when I am a tad nervous, but it came on so suddenly at the bridge that I marveled at the timing. So I kept passing the same guards asking them for the bathroom. I passed the guards to pass water, at least seven times in one hour. They must have thought I was nuts. Finally, my bladder empty, my body sufficiently dehydrated, we rolled the taxi up to the guards once again, and I said that I am happy to pay all the money it will take to try to go over, and to please let me waste my money.

It was so interesting to me that this Russian guy was abusing me because I was going to waste my money. It was such a Jewish encounter! The greatest crime was not peacemaking with Arabs or cavorting with the enemy, but "*haval al ha zeman,*" a waste of time and money that he could not bear to let me perpetrate. He did not threaten me, did not say no without any reason, but he berated me for getting a bad bargain on my trip to Jordan! I wanted to thank him for caring about my finances more than anyone I had ever met, but I was too frightened of him. Finally, his partner, who had always been nicer, turned to the Russian and, in Hebrew—which they thought I could not understand—said, "If the idiot wants to waste his money, let him." So he let me through on three conditions: on condition that I understood that I was an idiot, that I would not be permitted to enter Jordan and that, most importantly it seems, that I would lose a great deal of money.

The Allenby Bridge Terminal: A World unto Itself

And so I journeyed on with my wonderful Israeli taxi driver into the universe of the Allenby Bridge terminal, a place of passage that was for me a place suspended between worlds. The terminal was a place that was neither Jewish nor Arab, or perhaps it was both. There were quiet Israeli soldiers, mostly young women, Arab travelers, European offbeat travelers, mixed families of Arab descent, everyone mostly on the poor side, and ailing me. We sat and waited, and we waited. We waited for a bus to come and take us a few hundred yards, over to the Arab world.

For the first time since I had arrived in Israel I suddenly felt that I was a suspected minority. No one really talked to me, and I seemed out of place. Here in the waiting room there was no more Hebrew at all, but I was comfortable with that, and I still felt safe with the Israeli soldiers.

In my heart of hearts I am terrified of the Arab world, I do not speak any Arabic, and I felt that I was just like the twentysomething thrill seekers who jump off cliffs with a flimsy bungee cord—except they get to be filmed by American videomakers doing the macho American frontier thing, but nobody understood or cared why I was doing what I was doing. So there I was, doing something I thought heroic, that everyone else couldn't care less about. It was a good lesson in humility.

The lonely terminal was also a good liminal space for me, where I was able to experience different worlds without being in an alien environment. Language means a great deal to our sense of safety, and I was still in a safe place of both Hebrew and English, but I knew that this was the last time I would feel that. Such spaces are so critical for peace and so rare. Most people never leave their safety zones where they are the majority, and yet it is so basic to our work that there is no change without experiencing the fear of being a minority, of being different, and above all of being across "enemy lines."

I remember dozing for a long time, waiting for an eternity for the bus to come to take us over the bridge, and I remember dreaming of twilight on Saturday night in the Brookline synagogue when I was a child deeply immersed in listening to my master as he responded to our religious questions. We were waiting for the Sabbath to end, a time of both trepidation and hope, a time to end rest and begin the work of building the world, not knowing what was to come but rejuvenated by rest.

Saturday evening is a magical time in Jewish tradition. It is neither here nor there, neither in the redeemed world of the Sabbath nor the unredeemed world of hard work. It is a time of hope that perhaps the Messiah will suddenly arrive and the world will continue with only the Sabbath, no more work, no more striving, no more want, no more war, no more fear.

I was in a space that was neither Israel nor the Arab world, a place of passage and of unknowns, and it felt more comfortable and more hopeful than the false certainties of strident national identities and official boundaries. Ethnically I feel safer in Israel in an immediate sense as a member of a majority, but not really. In fact, I feel like a big target. But as a solitary human being I felt more comfortable in the terminal, in between majority worlds. All I had to do there was wait, anticipate, daydream, hope, and then pass on. Maybe this is a necessary part of life's journey and life's end.

I have to say at this point that something else was happening to me, something I did not want to tell anyone else. I do not know if it was the illness or something else, but I was so sick that I felt that something was trying to kill me, to get me to stop, and that I may not come back alive to Israel once I left. It was completely irrational but it was a very strong feeling. I knew I wanted to immerse myself in the land of my people's enemies and that I needed to learn and teach, and I had to go, but I felt my life was in danger. The Russian screaming at me while holding a big gun did not help negate the feeling that someone was trying to kill me. It was the second time in my life that a nervous Israeli soldier yelled at me while holding a big gun. I knew both times that, unlike what Palestinians go through, he would not shoot me, but the experience itself put me on edge. It was as if he was warning me that something bad was about to happen.

It was in that spirit that I boarded the bus with the other passengers who were not talking to me, some of whom seemed angry that I was there. I was clearly in a place where my Jewish looks counted against me. Everyone there either had relatives on the West Bank, lived there, or were Europeans who made a point of visiting there and not Israel. Unlike the other crossings to Jordan, the Allenby Bridge is a very Palestinian crossing, and I could feel the resentment given the situation.

We finally boarded the bus to take us to the Jordanian side, and I was not the only one who seemed nervous. I got flustered on the bus when the Jordanian soldier started asking me questions, and another passenger graciously intervened as I explained the situation. Fortunately everything was clarified on the other side with the help of friends, and I was allowed to proceed into Jordan without a visa after the soldier on the bus made a few phone calls.

From Jordan to Damascus

Hind was waiting on the other side with our American friend. It was a wonderful moment for all three of us because we knew it was the beginning of a life-changing journey. The car ride to Amman would have been uneventful except for a powerful rain and thunder storm that made the rocky climb on winding narrow roads a bit daunting. We finally arrived at the wonderful home of our friend in Amman, where I would switch to a Syrian car and driver. The home was like a museum, with beautiful pieces of art from all over the Middle East, and I felt that I had truly crossed over into another world.

After tea, we started on the late evening journey toward the Syrian border. I tried hard to fight off an anxiety attack. As we arrived we moved forward slowly past the Syrian border police, and then they proceeded to escort me, the driver, and Hind to a mysteriously large, ornate, and uninhabited building right at the border crossing on the side of the road.

Constructing My Enemy

Anything uninhabited in Syria gave me the willies as a Jew because I was ready at any minute for a brutal interrogation. I don't know if it was my paranoia, a healthy dose of fear of a police state, or a sense of humor that made me expect the whole enterprise to end in being beaten up by a security officer with a Saddam-like moustache. Maybe due to the fact that Talmudic rabbis tortured by the Romans, and more recently Gandhi and King, had been my heroes growing up, I was now ready for a thrashing. But the opposite happened, for which my body is eternally grateful—even as it left my mind perplexed. My prejudices about Syrians came into full view for me, and it began the first of many reflections even as I was walking through the experience.

Cognitive psychology has made the point in recent decades that our mental constructs determine our emotional states quite often. And the brain's amazing plasticity is increasingly offering an explanation for how we construct our emotional health resiliently or, conversely, how we construct emotional illness through our thoughts. Memory and emotional and physical experience all seem to determine our thoughts, depending on how we frame them in our thinking. But it is also true that our thoughts, and how we construct them, seem to lead to our most emotionally intense experiences.

Unalterable enemy systems make sense to me in the shadow of the Holocaust; they are a central part of my mental construct of the world. More importantly, brutal police are a given of the way I see the world, or *expect it to proceed*. Nazi SS men are always before my eyes. But when police officials act differently from how you expect them to, it chips away at the familiar and the comfortable, and it prevents you from passing judgment on whole civilizations. It is not that I was ignoring what police were doing to others. It is rather that my own prejudices and worldviews were being exposed.

How else could I exist without passing judgment on police states? How else could I organize my world? But I guess the whole point of going to Syria was to be shocked, one way or the other. I did not expect, however, to be shocked, frightened, and welcomed all at the same time at the border! I did not expect to feel tension, fear, and friendship merge so seamlessly as I crossed the border. But borders are by definition places of great tension and transition.

I frankly did not think much about what to expect or what to feel. Cannonballs don't expect anything, they just fly, and I had been flying ever since I got the strange notion in my head that I was responsible to history, ever since my master teacher convinced me years ago that history was in our hands.

Life as a Cannonball

Unlike my master teacher who lived a life completely dedicated to religious law, I had mostly one law that I was following as I flew like a cannonball through life, and that was the law that one must be driven to pursue peace and save human beings from horrific misery. The Psalmist said three thousand years ago, "Seek peace and pursue it." The rabbis of the Talmud added two thousand years ago, "Seek it in your own place, and pursue it to other places," which I guess I understood to mean, "pursue it to other places that are the most risky that you can imagine." I have no idea why I favor this interpretation. This law, of all ancient Jewish laws, resonated most with me because I understood being driven and impatient; it fit my personality well, and it seemed to sit well with a Gopin tendency to march forward like a bull.

Max Gopin, my grandfather, strode forward in life, in building family, wealth, and community, like a bull, with no impediments allowed to slow his determined gait. I can still see him in a picture I hung up for years on my wall. It was 1945, and the picture shows him following a frail old European rabbi holding on for dear life to a Torah scroll. Not just any scroll; it was a scroll wrenched from the clutches of the Nazis, brought to Chelsea, Massachusetts, to be rededicated and to stand in, somewhat feebly, for millions of murdered families.

The weathered, old rabbi in the photograph is frail and frightened, but my grandfather walks behind him with a look of serious, impatient determination that would frighten anyone in his way. Still further behind him, his face barely visible, is my great-grandfather, the one I am named after, Hatskel—a Yiddish name referring to the prophet Ezekiel. This was the prophet who declared a few miles from Damascus, over two thousand years ago, that each person should be judged for his own actions, and that there should be no revenge on children or clans or tribes for the mistakes of their fathers; Ezekiel had boldly announced the very foundation of liberal justice.[7] In the picture my great-grandfather looks somber, gentle, quiet, almost cowering behind his powerful son Max; fathers and sons, burying the dead, saving the Torah scroll from the fires of a hell on earth in Europe, walking forward no matter what.

I really got that scene; I got walking forward no matter what, staring defiantly at the face of hell, and it became a part of who I am. Some images and memories in life become a part of your essence, a part of your mental construct. But another side of me had always taken along on that vigorous walk a full complement of psychosomatic disturbances unknown to my grandfather—stress-related illnesses. This is otherwise known as being a little nuts.

I tried to contain my incredible stress at the border and simply comprehend what was happening around me. Thank God I only needed the bathroom twice. Everyone was a little tense but also somehow exhilarated.

Shocking Reception at the Border

I never understood the boundaries of what was official and what was unofficial in much of my visit to Syria. For example, I was greeted at the border by a representative of the Ministry of Information, who gave me what seemed like an official talk, summed up by the words, "our president has offered a full peace to Israel and normalization of relations, based on negotiations, and we are waiting to hear from Prime Minister Sharon." It was as if I was supposed to respond to that in some official way! The discourse was strangely formal for an informal event, and yet it was accompanied by a sense of warmth and hospitality that never ceased for the entire eight days that I was in Syria. In hindsight I realize that this young official was trying to negotiate the boundaries of citizen diplomacy as it bumps up against official diplomacy. He did remarkably well.

Excessive hospitality was the defining and most hopeful characteristic of the Syrian people that I believe could form a basis for a thaw in relations with traditional adversaries. Despite the problematic reputation of their security apparatus, the fact is that I felt Syrians had much to teach Americans and Israelis about generosity of spirit and hospitality. This would remain a constant lesson.

My mouth dropped upon hearing the words of this ministry official because I was hardly coming as an official. These were also the last words I expected to hear from a Syrian governmental representative. I was just hoping to be tolerated in Damascus, and yet I was being treated like a king after having great difficulty getting over the Israeli border. We sat at the border in a massive single room building set up for VIPs, surrounded by high walls and ornate couches and chairs, presented with the requisite bitter coffee (at midnight), which I had to drink, despite my sleep issues, and two massive side-by-side portraits of Hafez and Bashar Asad, approximately fifteen feet high, staring me in the face.

One rather cynical former American diplomat told me before I left the United States, "Take in Old Damascus, it is quite a sight, but the Syrians will bore you." I remember burning inside when I heard those foolish words, because I could not comprehend how someone could dismiss an entire people just because the officials that *he* worked with were boring. Besides, "boring" may be another word for frightened. Did he ever stop to think about the pressure that those men were under coming from a police state as to what they could and could not say? This makes many a Syrian man unusually silent.

For me this was already turning out to be the most intriguing cultural odyssey of my life, and I immediately sensed why American diplomacy had failed to penetrate this extraordinary, intricate, if troubled civilization. I could sense right away the ancientness of this culture, the diversity of its people, the arrested glory of so many past civilizations, and the embarrassing hints of poverty adjacent to past grandeur. I sensed from this official's speech, and many other things that I would learn in eight days of private talks, that President Asad was looking to extricate Syria from the burdens of recent history and to recapture ancient glories. He was looking to reenter history after the Cold War's devastating isolation of his country. He was searching as a leader of an ancient culture, trying to open up his country to the modern world.

The question was how to do this given entrenched interests standing in the way, and the predictable desire of elites to hold on to as much power as possible over the Syrian economy, its people, and its neighbors. How many politicians in any system easily relinquish power? But that does not mean Asad was not interested in change the year I came, and the interest in change is the most important thing you build upon in conflict resolution.

At the VIP lounge we exchanged cordial smiles and small conversations, I said what I had to say about conveying to Israel and to the United States their president's desire to open up a new chapter in history, and then we left, sometime after midnight. Finally we reached the Old City of Damascus, the very Old City of Damascus, dating back some thirty thousand years of primordial human habitation. It is quite a sight.

My New Home in Old Damascus

Every time I go to Syria I stay in the Kabawat House in Old Damascus, which is hundreds of years old and a classic example of the great Arab house inside walled cities, replete with the extravagant courtyard and a beautiful sitting room. I felt like I was living inside Fatima Mernissi's memories,[8] but this was no harem! This was the home of a woman who would become in a few short years a symbol of Arab feminism and peaceful change in her country, a powerful agent of change in the most difficult of circumstances.

Hind's family and assistants treated me with incredible respect and wonder. Her husband, Sam, was a constant presence of quiet serenity amidst the storm of our work and efforts. He provided calm precisely when Hind needed it most. His hospitality toward me and acceptance of me knew no bounds, and he was consistently there as a supportive presence when the work got difficult. This old house was his ancestral home, and he opened it to me as if I were part of the family. The same went for their amazing children, John and Nousha, for whom I developed deep affection. They have a set of workers that include members of different ethnic minorities in Syria, and a whole cast of characters as friends. Suddenly I was swimming in a new world.

Especially the first time I arrived, people just seemed amazed that I was actually there, and that I was real. We were really breaking boundaries that had never been crossed. Everyone knew where I had travelled from, but the country's name was never uttered. Change in some ways is a game of cat and mouse.

Hind planned an unprecedented private and public set of formal dinners across Damascus in homes of various prominent citizens, all dear friends, of course. We were raising publicly, in various venues for the first time in forty years, the subject of peace in the Middle East with Syria's immediate neighbors. But this is the most important point. We raised these issues indirectly and only through the lens of culture and religion, a less threatening approach than pure political discourse. I would also raise these issues as a scholar of conflict resolution with a cultural background as a religious American Jew.

Whatever my abilities may be in public speaking and private dialogues, the fact is that this effort was so politically complicated that only a person of political and networking talent like Hind could have pulled this off. She displayed a fascinating combination of intense national pride, deep commitment to peace, political savvy, and public relations know-how, which really should be studied. It is a textbook example of how to open up a dialogue of civilizations through dinners, private meetings, and public events, when there has been only war for generations.

We were building on the strengths of Syria, including their obsession with hospitality, especially when the guest has made enormous efforts to come. We were building on a self-conscious tradition of interreligious tolerance that has had its ups and downs in practice, but is very important to the Syrian cultural psyche. I cannot tell you how many people came over to me speaking mournfully about Jewish neighbors and friends who they grew up with, who moved to the United States, and whose absence they felt as a personal loss for the culture of Syria. The anger at Israel would be aired often, but there was real love for Jews here also, and this astonished me.

We were breaking boundaries and taboos on public discourse in this political environment. At the same time, the discourse was from a cultural and religious perspective that allowed for a broad ethical discussion on shared values and an attempt at a shared vision of the future. Most important of all, everything was approved at the highest levels, even though all the engagements remained officially unofficial.

Turning Point at the Asad Library

The main public dialogue on Thursday night, January 6, 2005—excerpts of which were nationally televised—was attended by three hundred distinguished guests, government officials, artists, professors, and professionals. First Hind spoke, then I spoke, and then there was a long question-and-answer period between me and the audience.

This all took place in the most prestigious building of Damascus, the Asad Library, and guests included the American, Canadian, and Swiss ambassadors, the Syrian ambassador to the United States, assistants to President Asad, and representatives of various ministries, especially the Ministry of Information and the Ministry of Expatriates, in addition to many professors, professionals, and officials from Lebanon. It was preceded and followed by television, newspaper, and radio interviews, and it was done from the beginning with the approval of President Asad. Several people joked, perhaps half-seriously, that someone probably had an open cell phone so that he could listen to the proceedings. Nothing of this sensitive a nature would have proceeded without his approval. In fact, his aides asked some of the pointed questions after the talk, and Hind went out of her way to send the president's wife, as well as about fifteen other officials whom I met that week, a copy of my book on the role of religion and culture in the future of peace in the Middle East.

Naturally, being me, I became exceedingly nervous in the library, and I had to retreat several times to the bathrooms before we began. Here too I discovered the same paradox as at the border. The Asad Library hall itself was beautiful and stately; the bathrooms, however, seemed unfinished, and there was no place to sit. I sensed again a culture trying to regain its dignity but struggling with a level of poverty that it did not want to admit to the world. This made me quite sympathetic, for it is the subtle efforts of human beings to preserve and increase their dignity that make them so precious, so human. And so the image of "enemy" was slowly wilting away for me.

The atmosphere of the public dialogue, simultaneously translated between English and Arabic, was electric in many ways, with great anticipation of how a public dialogue would proceed with three hundred people on the most sensitive issues of war and peace. This is not an easy task anywhere in the world, let alone in this unprecedented Syrian public encounter. But I tend to relish such encounters with large groups.

I was treated with immense respect, but, at the same time, some in the audience had the opportunity to vent a great deal of anger at what they saw as the victimization of Syria and the Palestinians. Others expressed deep appreciation for my willingness to come and listen. I expected this diversity of reaction and wanted it to happen.

We had a great, tough dialogue. I knew I was setting myself up for some anger because I made it clear to the audience that I was a religious Jew, and I quoted several times from the Bible and Talmud. Elie Cohen had succeeded in becoming the most damaging Israeli spy in Syrian history, and I was well aware that since the time of his discovery Jews were broadly suspected of always being spies for Israel. The Elie Cohen Affair had been a devastating humiliation for Syrians, and its effects last to this day.

Those two hours of questioning in front of cameras and three hundred Damascenes were among the hardest of my life in terms of dealing constructively with adversarial politics, and with a delicate balance of agreement, sympathy, solidarity, honest confrontation, and positive vision. I withheld many things I had to say in response to some of the more angry statements. I knew the political leadership was watching every word to see if this experiment of public dialogue between civilizations would fly and be a precedent, and I knew the American ambassador was watching too. As if the pressure was not great enough, the host and everyone else expressed through word and deeds their sense of astonishment, nervous fear, and hope that something utterly new was happening.

The words that Hind Kabawat said publicly by way of introducing me were far more important than mine because she is an insider/outsider/reformer to the culture. She is the kind of catalyst that can change history nonviolently because she is from within the privileged group that leads the country, and yet she is an agent of change. The question hovering over the entire trip was: Would the West listen to her words? Would the West engage a complicated Syria and support its best reformers, or would it ignore her and others? Would it see the side of President Asad that is trying to make change, or would it focus instead on the Syrian supporters of Hezbollah and other violent incursions in the region?

I was troubled all along by the way in which the West has two types of countries, those countries who tend to intimidate other cultures into compliance and submission, and those who simply take advantage of other cultures while pursuing selfish objectives. There are those foreigners in

Damascus who are preoccupied with how to take advantage of corruption, and then there are those who keep the place in a state of quarantine. But where is the place in statecraft for nonviolently and respectfully strengthening official and unofficial reformers in such societies, without undermining them? This is the question that preoccupied me for years to come.

Doubts about Intervention

I was amazed to watch history unfold there on that Thursday night. For me, speaking there was a very tough assignment, but I do not prepare too much in advance for momentous occasions because it would negatively affect my ability to be spontaneous. I had absolutely no notes as I spoke for forty-five minutes and then responded for another hour and a half to questions. I was nervous enough about just being in Syria; I could not on top of that memorize a speech. I never do, actually. I just looked forward to the spontaneity of the exchange, because spontaneity opens up my heart the most, which in turn makes my mind work the best.

It was my friends and hosts, however, who made me feel the trepidation, the historic weight of the event, and it started to terrify me by the middle of that night. They also were taking an enormous risk with me, not knowing what would come out of my mouth.

What right do any of us have to interfere this way in another culture, I asked myself as the trepidation grew. What right do we have to put people at risk this way? Ever since the talk on that Thursday night, this question became my number one preoccupation: would everyone who made this event possible be safe, or would they incur the wrath of some people who did not want change? Before the talk I was driven to move forward as if by a magnet drawing me in, but immediately afterward it was as if I awoke to what I had done, and who I may have put at risk.

WINDS OF CHANGE IN SYRIA

Despite the fears, I am convinced of what I saw in Syria in the course of so many private meetings. I saw some winds of change at the heart of this extraordinary culture, winds that the West was missing or failing to take advantage of in 2004. In fact, my biggest problem since I left Syria was that no one in Israel believed that the event actually took place, nor that a religious Jew would be treated this way in the capital of Israel's fiercest foe. Fortunately we made a videotape, and yet the sense of disbelief among outsiders remained palpable. I said this to one Syrian and she took it in stride, with typical generosity of spirit, remarking, "It's OK, we could hardly believe it ourselves; how could we expect others to believe it?"

A number of people, both during the session and afterward, expressed enormous gratitude to us for stimulating this first-ever public debate and discussion. Almost as important were at least six or seven beautiful dinners in the following week, hosted by prominent families throughout the city, including one at Hind's house, attended by officials, reformers, many doctors—and some problematic wealthy individuals whom I actually had the audacity to try to befriend.

This lasted over the course of eight days in which many discussions ensued on the most vital topics regarding the future of Syria and the region. We had an interesting time managing my Kosher needs, all the while ordering vegetarian food wherever possible. My greatest challenge was not any anti-Jewish prejudice but rather how secular the elite culture of Damascus is; rituals of religious practice were not easily explained. It reminded me very much of Tel Aviv and Manhattan, and I found it humorous and strangely gratifying as a religious scholar to be opening up a bridge between secular civilizations in Syria, Israel, and the United States. I kept thinking how similar Damascenes were to many in Tel Aviv, and that they might get along very well. Both like to party and eat late at night, and have little patience for religious conservatism. Bohemian that I am, despite my dietary restrictions, I liked them all the more for the way they relish the freedom to party.

We also visited over a period of days with more traditional religious representatives, Sunni and Shi'ite leaders as well as Christian leaders. The hospitality and friendliness was absolutely astounding, and I did not feel a single hint of anti-Judaism the entire time, only a feeling of sadness from many people that most of Syria's Jews were no longer there. I knew well the history of Jewish tragedies there in the recent past, but these were people who knew the old Jewish families, and several had kept up with those families in Brooklyn and elsewhere. This was a diverse culture that had been torn asunder and drained by the Arab–Israeli wars, as well as by the international divides of the Cold War.

A Shi'a Encounter

The Shi'ite leader, Sheikh Shehadi, was a paragon of religious pluralism and tolerance, describing to me a life and a set of writings committed completely to peace. After a long meeting in which he examined me and I him, I admitted to him upon leaving that I was a rabbi. (Few people in Syria were told about this initially, even though the officials all knew.) He was astonished; he smiled so broadly, and said that peace is only achieved when a rabbi (*hakham*) participates in the deliberations.

I have attended hundreds of interfaith events in my life; it is my business as it were, and my academic specialty. No one ever said that to me, and the last place I expected to hear that was in Syria, and yet there it was. I know that I have come to take the attacks on Judaism personally in the Arab–Israeli conflict. I have always felt as an analyst that the Arab–Israeli wars had triggered a great deal of anti-Judaism, but that it was thin, a political weapon to hurt Jewish supporters of Israel, not a foundation of Arab culture. But attacks hurt, even as I try to understand this endless conflict. I could not help but be affected by this deep compliment from the Sheikh that helped give me some pride in my identity.

There was not an idea I expressed that Sheikh Shahadi was not saying at the same time. Hind was translating between us, and at one point she was brought to tears, because she could not believe that I said something in English and the Sheikh said something in Arabic at the same time—and it was the same spiritual idea from Islam and from Judaism.

None of these Syrian religious encounters touched overtly on political matters, and I was keenly aware that everyone I was with was viscerally opposed to Israeli policies regarding the Palestinians. Yet, I sensed how much everyone wanted an end to war and the beginning of normal relations with Jews, with neighbors, and even normalization of relations with Israel. This was said explicitly on many occasions.

All of this touched me deeply, but I was always fully aware that Hamas and Islamic Jihad offices were somewhere nearby in Damascus. I knew that I was breaking new ground in relations, but that the sentiments of almost a century of warfare with Israel were deeply embedded in this city. It always made me nervous and uncertain. I did not find any resistance to a vision of peace and coexistence, neither in Damascus nor in Jerusalem. It is the comfort with extreme violence that plagues both realities, Israel's and Syria's, and that is what keeps wars going even when no one wants them. A suicide bomb is the embodiment of extreme violence, but so is a cluster bomb.

I lived with paradox at every moment. I was always conscious of intense generosity, sincere respect, and especially gratitude for making this effort to tell the world about Syrians and Syrian life. In many conversations we were struggling for friendship, solidarity, even unity of purpose. I sensed their passion for a new, free, prosperous Syria, and it is that yearning that I addressed in my speeches and talks. For me these were legitimate moral and spiritual yearnings of an ancient and proud people who had blessed the world thousands of years ago with its first languages and arts.

But Hezbollah was popular all over Old Damascus, despite its penchant for suicide bombs and religion by force. I was never blind to the paradoxical reality in which even the most hopeful and courageous people, religious and secular, civilians and officials alike, live and function in this society. In most cultures in the world, including my own, I continue to be astonished by the gap between visionary values that most people have and the political positions and parties that they feel compelled to support.

Opportunities for Constructive Engagement

Syria has system-wide problems with entrenched interests keeping reformers from moving forward. At the same time, and after extensive interviews with key figures, I was convinced in 2005 that Bashar Asad was serious about reform, even if his methods of proceeding forward were agonizingly slow. Since then it has become more complicated, with many steps backward in Syria's internal relations with its people, as well as its neighbors. But in the first half-decade since 2000, Washington had completely missed the subtle openings to new possibilities. The White House was apparently so wrapped up in the desire for revenge for 9/11 that there was no space to analyze new political openings in the region, opportunities that would not last for long. Openings in war and peace rarely last for long, and that is why flexibility is the key to resilience in de-escalation from states of war.

We were missing the key signals, and also not thinking through the ways to quietly help move things forward. Instead of pursuing regime change, which ultimately beat back many openings in Syria and damaged severely their reformers, the United States could have seized the opportunity at this time in history to support reform in Syria constructively, not through instigating coups. They should have learned from human intelligence who to support in the government and the military, who not to support, and who to try to pressure through negotiations into change. It was the same foolish American approach in those years that destroyed Gaza and handed it to Hamas, supporting the wrong people in Gaza to dominate and control by brutal force and corruption rather than to encourage positive change from within.

Ironically, some of the worst criminal offenders in Syria were clever enough, I learned, to get American contracts in Iraq, even as Congress was slapping the whole of Syria and its economy with sanctions! This flabbergasted me in its stupidity, in its clear American message to the Syrian people that corruption pays. By contrast, blanket condemnations and boycotts of a society of eighteen million people are useless, immoral, and just create solidarity with the hardliners in their midst. We have seen this time and time again globally.

We should have learned this in grade school: collective punishment creates solidarity with and even admiration for people who would otherwise be considered bullies or criminals. How sad that one government after another in Israel has not learned this in their war of attrition with Palestinians. It reaffirms the truism in our work that bad policy in war is often the product of a poverty of alternative thinking. Collective punishment has to be the stupidest human military reaction ever conceived in history. It is the single most effective creator of undefeatable local insurgencies. And yet the most impoverished military minds have been repeating this mistake since the dawn of time.

The enormous power of American economic might should be used judiciously and skillfully, not as a blunt instrument. No matter how busy U.S. congressmen may be getting reelected, serving local constituencies, and doling out funds that affect the lives of their constituents—and I respect the challenge they face—confronting any foreign society with a blunt instrument is foolish and always backfires. A subtle, informed, and morally defensible approach to confrontation is called for with regard to Syria, not blunt instruments of boycott. This remains as true now in many places globally as it did in 2005.

Men with Guns

I also came to understand after years of experience in Israel, Palestine, and Syria that there should also be a secret channel created to military and security services of any problematic country, not to deal with them corruptly, as we have done in South America, but to provide a way out for hardened warriors and criminals. Those with guns are the ones who need to have nonviolent options in the future, to increase the chances that they will support a transition away from militarized societies.

I had several conversations about these issues in all three countries, Syria, the United States, and Israel. Today we stand at a progressive stage of relationship between Jordan and Israel, for example, in which there is actually a society of former generals from both countries who meet regularly and who have done so for many years now. Almost all of those generals are now leading peacemakers who have the unique political cache of being able to influence military and security thinking. What a perfect model for the future of Palestinian–Israeli relations or Syrian–Israeli relations. It seems impossible now but it needs to begin with just one friendship, as it did in Jordan.

There is no way to move forward in opening up relations between states in conflict without some in the military starting to buy into the startling, utterly radical notion that you can have a strong military that is also in good conversation with adversaries. And in terms of democracy building, it is of the utmost importance that military men on all sides deepen their conversations about democratic safeguards and civilian control. That is the essence of democratization, and yet we never think creatively about how to quietly cultivate this stance within militaries and police forces that need to change.

We cannot expect President Asad to go it alone, to magically and single-handedly move entrenched economic/military interests forward. We need to help this along in quiet ways, in economic ways, in political ways of creating strong incentives and rewards, but also in a military way. The evolution of military and police forces is essential to any substantive change that moves toward liberalization. The same is true in Israel and Palestine where military and industrial interests need to be prepared to invest in peace.

To Conquer Borders through Tourism

Another missing ingredient between the United States, Israel, and Syria is imagination and vision. So many people in Syria, and in the Middle East in general, feel stuck, with no way out, no way out of poverty for average people and no way to escape an impoverishment of their culture. So many in America and Israel are plagued by fear of terror, of the nightmares of what the world can do to them, but these nightmares can stifle the very tools of finding a way forward.

In our public and private discourse in Syria we promoted a vision that emphasized the future, one in which an open Middle East would be an economic and cultural boon for Syria in particular but also for the whole region, as well as for Muslims, Jews, and Christians across the world.

The country is just waiting for millions of tourists to discover the origins of several civilizations, and I spoke about this at length in the Asad Library. This was a way for me to both compliment their civilization but challenge it at the same time. Old Damascus, for example, is a goldmine of multiple ancient civilizations and yet it is rather empty of tourists. I believe in our lifetimes that this will change radically, but it must be a vision that everyone, East and West, embraces. In fact, since we raised these issues in 2005 the Syrians are spending a fortune completely renovating Old Damascus.

There is something about tourism that addresses human needs at a much deeper level than we imagine. Tourism addresses our need to wander, to find more than one home, and to return to places of ancient origin. I sensed a longing in Syria, for example, for the land of Palestine, a romantic recollection of a previous century in which Syrians freely roamed east and south. Some will call this imperialism and a wish to conquer Israel, and for some in the Old Guard that is an accurate read. But it is also a longing for home and belonging which most people want to fulfill nonviolently—if we find a creative way.

Tourism and open borders are deeply human, ancient, nonviolent forms of conquest and ownership. There is a way in which people around the Middle East, including Israelis, long for that openness and wandering to ancient homes. We need a nonmilitary imagination of how everyone can do just that, how everyone can reach Jerusalem and the ancient Holy Land without violence or conquest, how Jews, Muslims, and Christians can visit ancient roots across the region. And we need to devise a way that Palestinians can rediscover a real home in this world, which they so deserve.

This was the vision that we shared that night in Damascus at the Asad Library, and it is a vision that is both spiritual and also profoundly material, a way to generate new prosperity and dignity for populations that might otherwise be carried away by the false promises of ultra-nationalism and religious fascism. There is no peaceful future for tribalism and nationalism in the Middle East, but there are new ways for nations to live in peace and share their space.

The Uses of Political Religion

One of several mistakes I made in Syria was speaking too much about religious conflict. They are proud of the fact that there is more freedom of religion in Syria than most places in the Middle East, and that it is a place in which secular people and women have equality of opportunity. In fact, a refrain from many Arabs over the last few years is the fact that the United States and the West have attacked the two places in the Middle East that had the most freedom of religion and the most equality for women, Iraq and Syria, while siding with Saudi Arabia, where women have the least freedom and where there is the least religious pluralism, and whose citizens, including members of the royal family, have invested billions of dollars radicalizing Islam across the region and the world.

Many Syrians saw in the Bush years an ultraconservative, religious American administration, aligned with conservative Christian efforts to militantly spread the Gospel globally, also making an alliance with Saudi Arabia, the most aggressive state in the region that proselytizes for reactionary Islam. Then America attacked the two places that are secular as the axis of evil! Educated Syrians wondered what kind of collusion of religious extremisms is at work here. I have wondered about this as well, especially since everywhere I turn in the Muslim world, the greatest complaint from moderates and reformers is how under assault they are from Wahabi funds originating in the Gulf.

Now I know the readers will be astonished and say to themselves that these folks are just ignoring Saddam's genocides, Syria's human rights record, and the support for key terrorists groups. But it is worth hearing this perspective from educated people who live in the Middle East.

But you will respond that they also support religiously extremist Hamas and Hezbollah, so how can Syrians explain this? Well, they do not. Those are dismissed as political alliances, and it is generally not encouraged to question Syria's political alliances. There are taboo subjects, and this is one of them, because it involves Arab states in conflict, and the political use of religion in the war against Israel. All this must be acknowledged.

But what also must be acknowledged is what Syrians see as America's hypocrisy. Syrian citizens cannot fathom an American society championing democracy and freedom that would side with those Arab states who are ushering Islamic extremism into the Middle East. They are itching for the United States to be a *consistent* champion of human rights so that *their* chances of attaining these rights at home could increase.

No one is naïve about the power of oil and therefore why America would coddle some states and not others, but the outrage among Syrians at this hypocrisy is palpable; really it was an anger beyond words in 2005—and I am speaking about the rage of Syrian liberals and democrats. One senses how many of their democrats want the United States to be a compelling and consistent model for them, and how disappointed they are that America is failing to be that model.

Many states indirectly and directly support religious extremism, its incitement, its imperialism, and its terrorism. Syria coddles and allies itself with religious extremists, but so does the United States. Meanwhile Islam has become a political football globally, and it is no wonder that so many young, poor Muslims are bewildered.

The Syrians I met tended to underestimate the danger in their own midst of Islamic extremism, and did not admit that it may only be extreme state control that is holding it back. In 2005 we heard reports while I was there of clerics in the countryside urging young Syrians to go and kill any foreigners in Iraq, and some there quietly confided worry about massive outside funds pouring in for the building of new and radical mosques; always Gulf money was implicated.

It seems that most secular policy makers, East and West, are still trying to ignore the power of religious passions, and the vital strategic importance of redirecting those religious passions toward democracy, equality of opportunity, and human rights. There is no escaping the power of religion to either promote or destroy the democracy that so many yearn for in this region. The United States in Afghanistan, Israel on the West Bank, and Syria in Lebanon have all used religious passions for their state interests. But they have all underestimated the devastating price that all states are paying for using religious passions—Muslim, Jewish, and Christian—when it is convenient. They are surprised and horrified when those unleashed passions backfire on states.

American and Saudi support for extremism in Afghanistan and Pakistan led directly to the development of a sea of *jihadis*, some of whom trained for and executed 9/11 and many other anti-American attacks. Syria cannot support extremism across its borders and then expect it not to boomerang into Syria. And Israel cannot stimulate and encourage religious zeal to hold onto the West Bank for forty years and then be surprised when they lose one of their greatest political icons, Yitshak Rabin, to assassination by a religious Zionist; and lately they are embarrassed by a continually renascent minority of Jewish fascists. Israel is now pigeonholed in its political options because it created a monstrosity of the settlements right in the heart of a future Palestinian state, in addition to encouraging Hamas' growth at its inception as a way to undermine Fatah. These are patterns and hard lessons about religion that are emerging throughout the world.

It was hard to argue with the moral outrage felt in Syria by those who had heard from 1.5 million Iraqi refugees streaming across their borders with tales of rampant abuse by American soldiers. This unfortunately tempered any sense there that the Syrian clerical extremists advocating war by any means in Iraq needed to be confronted.

On a certain level my friends in Syria are absolutely right: Syria really has a remarkable level of religious pluralism and equality for women. At another level, however, they will need to confront the use and abuse of political religion in much the same way that every state in the world needs to. They will need to wholeheartedly support moderate Islam in Syria, and not cynically use Islam as a weapon across its borders when convenient. The Middle East can no longer tolerate the rampant use of the Abrahamic religions for political and military gain. It is devastating the region, and it must be reversed.

Israel and Palestine at the Center

Democratic reform is yearned for in Syria by many people, and there is eagerness for normalization of relations with Israel, let alone the United States. But I found that the decent people only want this if the historic wrongs to the Palestinian people are addressed. They hope for a new era of dignity and equality to emerge in which the Syrian people themselves are actually freed to live a new life. The one compelling excuse for holding back reform and supporting hardliners and corrupt individuals is the ongoing hostilities with Israel. Thus we are left as always with the chicken and the egg, reform needing peace and peace needing reform.

We stand at a dangerous crossroads in the course of the Palestinian–Israeli conflict. In 2005, it was felt increasingly that Israel could, for the first time in its history, experience a Jewish civil conflict due to the withdrawal from Gaza. Many observers felt that it would be political suicide for Sharon to also open a Syrian–Israeli peace track, specifically involving giving back the Golan. Yet I questioned many whether the Palestinian–Israeli track can proceed with Hezbollah and Hamas, clients of Syria and Iran, doing everything to disrupt the peace process.

I argued that what Asad, Sharon, Abbas, and the United States needed most was not the immediate start of Syrian–American–Israeli negotiations but a palpable thaw in relations. They all needed a firm direction away from belligerence by proxies. They needed in 2005 gestures of political and economic improvement that could set the stage for a new relationship between Syria and the West, as well as a new relationship between Israel and the Arab world.

Unfortunately the powers that be were only to realize this two years later, when Gaza was lost to Hamas, Lebanon was devastated by another war, and radical Iranian influence was on the ascendancy throughout the region. Thus one disaster after another, costing many lives, led at the Annapolis meeting at the end of 2007 to what could have occurred in 2005. The only real incentive, however, that led the Americans and the Saudis to the table with Syria was not the desire for peace in the region, not concern for the people of the region, but fear of Iran's successes in Iraq, Gaza, and Lebanon.

But everything I saw and heard in Syria in 2005 suggested to me that, despite oppression at home, there was an address in Syria for serious negotiations on a new construct of the Middle East. But it was a beleaguered partner, a partner that was still muddled in old political and military structures, in addition to facing a population with widespread anti-American and anti-Israeli popular feelings. Asad was keenly aware of those sentiments, and as a politician he could not afford to ignore those popular sentiments. And he certainly could not afford to alienate his main patron, Iran, without a very clear set of alternatives and a complete cessation of American hostilities against Syria.

If Asad was to undertake even the most limited international steps of peace he needed the people with him. But they would not be with him, and still will not be with him to this day, if a rapprochement with Israel is unpopular. But it will be unpopular until the Syrian people sense a real change in treatment of Palestinians by Israel, in addition to a sense that the dignity of Syria can be restored by the return of the Golan. In some ways, I hardly heard about the Golan on my visits, but I heard endlessly about how wrong Zionism had been from the beginning in what it stimulated in the region. A Syrian–Israeli rapprochement will take a profound shift in understanding between these two peoples about coexistence, equality, and a completely new Jewish–Arab relationship.

The same lesson comes up again and again in this region. Each side has rational thinkers who can see a peaceful future, but very few see the consequences of their violent behavior and how it prevents adversaries politically from moving toward peace. The Arab world has yet to understand the devastating emotional and political impact of killing or trying to kill Jewish women and children on the streets of Jerusalem by funding Hamas or any other group that believes that killing women and children is a military success. The Israeli electorate has yet to understand the devastating impact on the Arab world of their daily theft from and mistreatment of Palestinians, both inside Israel and beyond the Green Line.

What was needed in 2005 was a conscious Western effort to demonstrate a new set of rules for engagement between Israel and Arab populations, and between America and Arab populations, especially in Iraq. What the United

States and Israel rightly should have expected in return was a steady about-face on the Arab use of terror by proxies—Hamas, Hezbollah, and Islamic Jihad—as a pressure tactic against the West. The much needed bargaining between the sides on these issues is self-evident, but only actions of trust-building with Syria's Asad could set the stage for this. The next step then in an impending thaw, I argued, was working out what those bilateral actions would be.

I had discussions on these issues very privately in Syria, and made indirect allusions to many of these positions in my public talks and interviews on television and radio. I had to avoid any criticism of Syria or its government, but I found indirect ways to raise all of the above points. This was appreciated by many.

There were other extraordinary experiences in Syria, including meeting an amazing artist, Moustapha Ali, who, in a few years, would develop a small artist colony in Old Damascus. I have wanted his work to be known to the world ever since because his themes express all that is noble, ancient, and tragic in Syria's culture today.

I also was profoundly moved by a trip to the Christian city of Miloula, one of the only places left on earth where Aramaic is the spoken language. This had special meaning for me after spending half my life studying the Talmud in Aramaic. Of course, I could not understand their dialect but just seeing the letters and recognizing a few words reminded me just how tightly woven my culture is to this region. I love indulging the past as a way of understanding the present. I left Syria exhilarated and exhausted.

A COMPLICATED RETURN TO ISRAELI REALITY

The return trip to Israel by way of Jordan was eventful as usual. I remember two weeks before seeing Israel from Jordan as I travelled toward the Allenby Bridge, and feeling that I was truly in Exile, out of Israel. I always feel Moses in my bones (I am named after him) looking out over Israel from beyond the Jordan River. But I would cross over the river back to Israel feeling that I deserved to return this time, that I had done my utmost in this land for peace, and that I had tried to set a good example for my people to follow.

There was a rude awakening at the border, however. On the bus with me going over were many Palestinians returning from a Muslim holiday. There were hundreds of people at the terminal. The situation was insanely chaotic, the organization of the system of retrieval of luggage absurdly humiliating. Everyone had to push and shove; there was no other form of organization that the Israelis had created. In addition, the metal detector that we all had to go through was the most extremely sensitive I had ever passed through in any airport. Old women had to go through again and again and again.

I was the last in line, of course, and when my turn came I went through and failed. I took more out of my pockets, failed, took more off, then failed. At this point the Arabs in line were getting a kick out of this scene. They seemed to know I was Jewish but the Israeli guards did not. Further disrobing I pulled out a Jewish head covering, a *kippah*, from my pocket because it had a metal pin in it. The Israeli guard looked at it and exclaimed in Hebrew, "You are Jewish?!" I said in Hebrew, "I am a rabbi!" He said, "What are you doing in this line?" I had not realized that this was an Arab-only line. So I looked at him intently, contained my anger, and said to him quietly and deliberately, "One line for everyone." He scowled at me, and I continued to strip. By now I had to hold up my pants with one hand, my passport with the other and walk through. Everyone was laughing, but I enjoyed it too. Finally, I passed. This was a good lesson for me in the reality of the situation, the so-called *status quo*.

As I emerged from the terminal, after climbing over dozens of pieces of everyone's luggage strewn everywhere in the dust, I found my way to a shared bus/taxi to Jerusalem. Here too I got strange looks, because apparently this was an Arab-only bus without anyone really saying so. I did not appear to be welcome. I would soon discover yet another side of Israel along the trip to Jerusalem. We were stopped at a check point right on the road up to Jerusalem, at a spot I had never noticed before, a spot I had passed dozens of times entering the city by Jewish taxi from the airport in Tel Aviv. There had apparently been a terror alert, which increases Jewish tension in Israel astronomically.

We waited in the bus next to the highway, cars racing past right next to us. We were shouted at to show our papers by a very young soldier who was clearly terrified as he entered the bus. Some foolish person had trained him that the best way to conquer his own fear and take command was to shout. I took out my papers nervously and waived them. We were ordered to stay seated.

Then, coming toward the bus, was a German shepherd barking ferociously and struggling to be free. A soldier was holding on for dear life to the dog. I could not understand the presence of such a wild dog. German shepherds have a special meaning for me as a Jew of European origin, and my imagination is sometimes too powerful to bear. The only time I ever see those dogs is in Holocaust films.

In the bus there was a lovely five-year-old Arab boy playing at the front near the door, wanting to go out, and my mind kept picturing what would happen if this five-year-old wandered off the bus and his father ran after him. I imagined the fast cars, the scared soldiers, the shouting, and the wild dog being set loose, and the mangled child, and the Arab father's rage, and the shots, and then I felt sick, and I hid my tears from the Arabs. I was back in reality, at the heart of the Arab–Jewish war that had scorched this land and damaged all these people for most of the twentieth century. I sat frozen in the bus, and I have nightmares about that moment to this day. I still see the child dancing at the front of the bus, with the wild dog dancing right in front of the bus outside, trying to get free, both of them perfectly aligned in my line of sight.

I could not do anything about that checkpoint in Israel, but I felt intuitively that my Syria work was getting somewhere, that somehow it was all connected by a chain of causality. If I could make breakthroughs in my work in Syria it would begin to break down the assumptions of the enemy system in the region on all sides. And *that* would impact the longevity of those cursed checkpoints that save Jewish lives but also make Palestinian lives into hell on their own ancestral land.

I woke up the next day in Jerusalem, fresh from dreams and nightmares of the previous days, and knew that this mission still demanded of me that I persist. And so I determined that I would continue to come back to Syria, no matter the cost to my health.

NOTES

1. On organizations dedicated to citizen diplomacy, see coalitionforcitizendiplomacy.org; uscenterforcitizendiplomacy.org. See also Paul Sharp, "Making Sense of Citizen Diplomats: The People of Duluth, Minnesota, as International Actors," *International Studies Perspectives* 2, no. 2 (2001): 131–50.

2. Narrative is an important new approach to both conflict resolution theory and practice. See, for example, John Winsdale and Gerald Monk, *Narrative Mediation: A New Approach to Conflict Resolution* (San Francisco: Jossey Bass, 2000). On narrative and conflict resolution, see Stephanie Stobbe, "Using Narrative to Understand Conflict and Conflict Resolution among Laotian Refugees," paper presented at the annual meeting of the International Studies Association, Hilton Hawaiian Village, Honolulu, Hawaii, March 05, 2005, allacademic.com/meta/p71806_index.html (accessed May 16, 2008); Sara Cobb, "A Narrative Perspective on Mediation: Towards the Materialization of the 'Storytelling' Metaphor," in *New Directions in Mediation: Communication Research and Perspectives*, ed. J. Folger and T. Jones (Newbury Park, CA: Sage, 1994), 48–66.

3. See Simone de Beauvoir, *The Ethics of Ambiguity* (Secaucus, NJ: Citadel Press, 1948). While I disagree with some of her positions, especially an altogether coddling approach to communist-rooted violence, she is one of the few philosophers of the twentieth century to enter deeply into the impossible moral ambiguities of war and peace. She confronts openly the outrageous choices involved when operating in dangerous and unfree environments, the attempt to anticipate consequences, and weighing bad and worse choices in the balance. Her shades of grey and black reflect the true reality that is constantly shoved under the rug by professionals and ethicists alike.

4. See Susan Allen Nan, "Conflict Resolution in a Network Society," 111–13. Nan argues that networks can either reinforce conflict or generate new possibilities of conflict resolution. But there are also inclusive and exclusive networks. Inclusive networks, she argues, are the most likely to generate conflict resolution. "Inclusive networks are more suitable for supporting meaningful participation in conflict resolution processes, while exclusive networks entrench conflict" (p. 111). Building on Nan, my experience demonstrates that deep friendship between citizen diplomats who come from enemy communities tends to expand vastly and inclusively the network of people who would otherwise be utterly cut off from each other. This dramatically opens many new doors of a new conflict resolution network. We will demonstrate this below. It is also undoubtedly true that the friendship across enemy lines between two people who are classic "connectors" may cut them off from some people in their own community. Often citizen diplomacy and friendship across enemy lines vastly expands new networks but curtails or cuts off others. It all depends on the capacities and mental stamina of the citizen diplomat. That is why the investigation in the coming chapters of self-reflection rooted in ethics and wisdom traditions is essential to the practice of citizen diplomacy. This work is risky, for it can be wrenching to the social self whose network of relationships forms a basic part of a stable identity.

5. Genesis 32:23–34.

6. As is well known in Tibetan Buddhism there is a reverence expressed for all sentient life, such as worms. In the movie *Seven Years in Tibet*, the young Dalai Lama at one point turns to one of his most venerable teachers in search of advice, and his teacher smiles mischievously and responds, "I am a bug." The Dalai smiles mischievously right back as their minds and heart meet. But I thought as I watched that scene many times what kind of confidence and belief in oneself, in the worth of every living being, it must take to make such a statement. I have tried to live by this psychology since then, but it is hard. On the other hand, once in a while it has helped me endure insults with some degree of enjoyment. I am also finding that the most effective change agents belittle their own work, and it seems to be a way to "get away" with change while the guardians of the status quo don't take you seriously and are therefore not looking. I knew such "guardians" who worried me from Washington, to Jerusalem, to Damascus. I was determined to fly under their radar screens until what we were doing was unstoppable. That has worked as a strategy many times. I believe it helped in our efforts to generate a rapprochement between Syria, the United States, and Israel.

7. Ezekiel 18:20.

8. Fatima Mernissi, *The Harem Within* (New York: Doubleday, 1994).

5

Syria 2006–2008: The Transformation of Relationship

I spent seven days in Syria at the end of May of 2006, concentrated on encounters and presentations in Damascus and Aleppo. This was part of my ongoing partnership with Hind Kabawat and her friends. It was also a culmination of experimentation with techniques of citizen diplomacy, relationship building, and networking. The appalling turn of events in the Middle East in the months immediately following our work in May 2006, including the Israel–Lebanon War, cannot diminish the revolutionary moments of conciliatory human encounters that we managed to create. My relationship with the people of Syria that May, and with some Iraqi refugees that they house, was transformed. Moments like those I am about to describe are sometimes the only positive things that exist in the unpredictable environment of violent conflict. In the mind of witnesses they stand out as a symbolic allusion to a different reality, to alternatives to extremism, war, and solutions of force. The bridge of religion and the networks of religious figures were central to the astonishing moments of reconciliation that I will soon describe.

A CHANGED SYRIA

I flew to Syria knowing that I was walking into a place that was under considerably more stress than when I had first started coming in 2004. The Damascus Spring (a period of optimism regarding Syrian domestic reform that began in 2000) was turning into the Damascus Fall without even the benefit of a summer. Key events had overarching significance: the Hariri assassination in Lebanon and the world's subsequent condemnation of

Syria, the humiliating withdrawal of Syria's troops and security personnel to the heart of Syria, the UN investigations, the radical determination of the U.S. White House to push regime change everywhere, and the alliance of Khadam (a former leading Ba'athist) and the Muslim Brotherhood for regime change. There was almost a panic about possible invasion or a coup among government personnel and there was an intention to clamp down hard. This fear and aggressive response of repression continued until 2009.

The Syrian government, despite its behavior in Lebanon, had been sending out clear messages to the U.S. government that it wanted to negotiate regarding disputes concerning Iraq and other matters, only to be continually rebuffed by the White House. After certain humiliating disappointments with rejection of costly Syrian gestures to the U.S. government that I will not elaborate on here, the Syrian government made it clear that it would veer away from the West and toward Iran and militant groups, where it had had old and longstanding financial and military relationships. This was music to the ears of the President of Iran, who seized on America's diplomatic failure with Syria just as surely as he seized on American failures in Iraq.

Security has been the number one Ba'athist concern considering the threat of regime change from the United States and others, and this translated directly into a level of repression of opposition and reform voices that became a deep disappointment to the people of Syria. Dozens of reformers and writers were arrested, and everyone was afraid and frustrated. The oppression continued through 2008 with invasions of privacy as absurd as cancelling Facebook, hundreds of other websites blocked, very moderate democrats jailed, and the continued censorship of all e-mails. A pall has been cast over civil life.

REFLECTIONS ON POSITIVE PEACEBUILDING

I was not deterred in 2006, and neither was Hind Kabawat. We remained committed to the people of Syria, to the people of the region, and their long-term prosperity, and we held that in our gun sights (excuse the expression). Despite the atmosphere in Syria, we were determined to focus on an approach to peacebuilding that is a unique blend of networking and positive peacebuilding.

I mean by this a strategy of eliciting, through numerous relationships and networks, whatever is positive or hopeful to move cultures and peoples in conflict in a better direction than current stalemates. This approach builds on strengths of civilizations and subcultures, and networks of trusted relationships. It resists attacking anyone or anything, and it is especially attuned for work in very difficult political constraints. It is a way to build on the best of what is and take it further.

In very difficult circumstances, that is precisely what we did in Syria, and we knew it would elicit criticism from some who rightly point out all of the gross injustices in plain view. Hind Kabawat, one of the wisest citizen diplomats today, helped devise this approach despite the enormous pressures on Syrian citizens now. Everyone is sad about those who are suffering and who live in fear, both in Lebanon and Syria.

We continue to dance between those who want us to be more pro-government and those who want us to be more antigovernment. We focus instead on the good will of people—in or out of government—and because we focus on a positive approach to religion and patriotism alike, we seem to keep building surprisingly good relationships with a wide range of people and institutions.

Western approaches focused exclusively on human rights can easily stimulate confrontation in such places and put lives at risk. Often Western approaches force democratization because people in free, more prosperous societies do not understand the complexities of the atmosphere where others have to continue to live. Crass forms of forceful democratization have been discredited of late because they can easily empower antidemocrats, such as what happened in Rwanda right before the genocide of 1994, or in Gaza in 2007.

There is such a fine line between the stimulation of courage and recklessness, between encouragement of others and endangerment of their lives, between aid and imposition. There are careers, families, and lives at stake in places like Syria, and this must be constantly kept in mind as one tries to stimulate authentic change.

Balance is the key to wisdom in both short-term and long-term approaches to citizen diplomacy and conflict resolution. Often efforts at social change by privileged outsiders are unbalanced. By contrast, the best practitioners of religion and conflict resolution constantly weigh in the balance social and political objectives on the one side and, on the other, permanent values such as protecting human life, respect, compassion, and patience. This allows them to exist in less than ideal environments, and that is why Kabawat and I got along so well with a variety of visionary religious leaders in Syria.

Sheikh Shehadeh and Mufti Hassoun and their allies were especially instrumental in conceiving of ways to inch forward in creating positive human relations across the deadly boundaries of the Middle East. They trusted our intentions but also our behavior because it was attuned to their cautious approach to nonviolent social change.

We have discovered our own balance in Syria by suspending assumptions and generalizations, by exercising patience, and above all, through flexibility. After my experience I will never again generalize about Shi'ites, Sunnis, Ba'athists, Alewites, Christians, or government officials. I will never again

listen to any Washington insider who blithely makes sweeping generalizations about Syrians or any other Arab cultures, because it is the generaliza-
tion that has become anathema to me as a field worker.

In addition and in reaction to my cultural and ethnic roots, I have to
admit that my extraordinary level of fear as a religious Jew was unjustified.
I have never seen a single objective reason to be fearful for my life in Syria,
despite the fact that everyone outside Syria assumes that I should be fearful.
On the contrary, I was made to feel extremely safe, welcome, and honored;
this came as a shock to me. There have been extensive *political* uses of anti-
Judaism by a few elements in Syria at various points, but it is not essential
to the culture.

On the other hand, at every moment I was painfully aware of *other*
people's fears in Syria, the fragile relationships between groups who have
been battered by the winds of history and politics. There are old memories
of strife and civil conflict that haunt deeply and remain unaddressed.

Some of the more oppressive people in Syria are actually living in real
fear for their own future due to the many enemies that they have created,
but their victims are more justifiably fearful. No one is certain what the
future may bring. One thing everyone shares in common: even some of
the most militant people there are searching for safety and security. History
has not given the Syrian people an easy way to trust each other enough to
open up to democracy.

When you think about it, democracy is an outrageous idea; it requires
incredible trust of one's neighbors. And in places of the world where many
minorities have lived side by side for centuries without equality, it is an
enormous transition to nonviolent democratic struggle, as opposed to violent nondemocratic struggle.

Wisdom would suggest that understanding and acknowledging this reality, dealing with it patiently but persistently, presents an opportunity as we
citizen diplomats network for conflict resolution. Understanding all the
narratives of Syria is a way to discover needs that people share in common,
a way to open up discussions of the future of civil society without threat,
without arrogance, and with the deepest respect for age-old accomplish-
ments of Syrian civilization.

Late at night as I would reflect on all these complexities of the culture, I
would be reminded of the Dalai's Lama's meditation that we are all connected, that we all have the same needs, that we all want to escape suffering
and be happy. And then I would be further reminded of the foundations
of my field of conflict resolution in human needs theory. Social science,
spiritual wisdom, and the lessons of the field work started to merge seamlessly into a strategy of including everyone's needs in peacebuilding. Late
at night, exhausted by the work, this seemed to me intellectually clear but

emotionally very difficult. It is not easy to consider the emotional needs of oppressive people when you know their victims.

Syrians are battered by many forces, and those Americans who emphasize the virtue of threats, punishment, and regime change may be well intentioned in their desire to foster a democratic alternative, but all the evidence of what I witnessed is that they are truly ignorant of how constructive change occurs; they are doing more harm than good.

In always focusing on threats and punishments, without any respect for or investment in the Syrian people, they mirror what they claim is the threatening behavior of those who are oppressive and corrupt. Effectively these Americans are not facing the violence in themselves. I became convinced by hundreds of conversations that the replacement of traditional diplomacy with a cult of threats by the United States has made things dramatically worse.

I can also see from conversations and networks created in Syria that if there were proof of a different set of American intentions, intentions that were markedly different than occupation and destruction, such as in Iraq, there would be a major shift toward Western institutions. All that Syrians saw coming out of the Iraqi invasion in 2006, and what they heard from the 1.5 million refugees who came to the mosques, was about abuse, destruction, and civil war. They know the role of Arabs in these tragedies, but they were astonished by a liberal democracy that seemed to deliberately provoke the destruction of an Arab country and its culture.

Dinner Diplomacy

As the week in Damascus continued, Hind Kabawat created an amazing dinner that brought together numerous ambassadors, writers, professors, and others, many friends of mine from previous trips. The dinner culture in Syria, when done by a skilled strategist, is a crucial way in which positive elements in society are weaved together. Hind has created a hopeful network of relations that, despite all the troubles, continues to offer leadership, good advice, and vision.

I was very impressed in 2006 with the brilliant Swiss Ambassador Jacques Watteville, now at the European Union, as well as the retiring Canadian ambassador. And I later learned that even as he was encouraging our public diplomacy, the Swiss ambassador was facilitating secret diplomacy between Syrians and Israelis. Thus they were orchestrating simultaneously public and private pressures for transformations in relationships. This too should be studied as a model of official behavior that allows for unofficial participation in shaping the historical and psychological pressures for positive change.

Through the role model of these diplomats I have come to see the enormous potential that ambassadors have to generate their own increments of positive change in the world, even in the most difficult circumstances. They are constantly networking, linking people, providing openings at various levels of culture, religion, and economics, and trying to devise new ways out of an impasse. I cannot imagine our work in Syria without their quiet, moral support. The American Deputy Chief of Mission who retired to teach in San Diego, Steve Seche, had been nothing less than graceful and supportive in many ways as well, though it would have been far better had he had a White House that understood the realism of their kind of diplomacy. Official diplomacy at its best is a central key to positive global change.

From Abu Ghraib to Forgiveness: Four Hours in an Aleppo Mosque

The most difficult but awe-inspiring part of the 2006 trip was what happened in Aleppo, and this is where the combination of networking, religious relationships, and symbols triggered a major turning point in our years of work in Syria. The journey to Aleppo where I was accompanied by the able and wonderful Nizar Mayoub, head of the Syrian Public Relations Association, took me through the hills, the countryside, and a variety of terrains for almost four hours.

Nizar explained to me everything we saw on the road to Aleppo, and made me feel honored and informed at every stage of my trip. I passed tens of thousands of newly planted trees that have been part of a national campaign to reforest Syria. Two million trees are being planted, and it gave me hope that even in this place which has been under such duress, one can see the positive effects of an emerging global consensus on trying to improve the earth's absorption of carbon dioxide. Every common concern globally is an opportunity for weaving new relationships and positive change.

As we arrived in Aleppo I realized that we were in a city of great culture going back thousands of years. This was one of the most important centers in the history of Arab culture, as well as of Islamic and Jewish learning. Some of the very foundations of the Hebrew biblical texts were analyzed and gathered here millennia ago.

The Grand Mufti of Syria, Sheikh Ahmed Hassoun, had been on a panel together with me the previous year, and we had exchanged warm greetings through third parties since then, all due to Hind's relationships. Upon hearing about his courageous stands for tolerance and coexistence with Christians and other minorities I had invited him to our Center for World Religions, Diplomacy, and Conflict Resolution at George Mason University to receive an award. Due to complicated reasons that we will not elaborate on here Sheikh Hassoun could not come, and this made him deeply frustrated. He, like us, saw the opportunity to come to Washington as a way to further dialogue and provide an alternative to conflict between America and Syria, as well as to present a different image of Syria to the world.

Sheikh Hassoun invited me to Aleppo on Friday, in a reprise of a previous invitation from a previous trip. I did not know for sure that I would be invited to the mosque but I knew that I wanted to honor him by traveling all the way to see him. When we spoke for half an hour before the Friday prayers the sheer weight of his concerns and frustrations were apparent; it was the height of the burgeoning Shi'ite–Sunni civil war in Iraq.

I was not going to talk at all about the Washington visit, but he went on at some length about politics and religious leaders, and how dangerous they can be to world peace. He was angry, and later in his sermon he was almost apocalyptic in his sense that extremists in *both* politics and religion were destroying the world. The Iraqi refugees, whom he was trying to feed, were uppermost on his mind. I was worried for him.

When we went to the central Aleppo mosque, we first went into a beautiful private antechamber where about seventy people were gathered. There were two seats in front at some distance from everyone else, everything set up very formally, and I realized I was supposed to sit next to the mufti in front. This made me nervous as I have grown unused to formal religious situations where I am the center of attention. I used to do this all the time, but I have grown shy of religious ceremonial moments. I was not asked to speak at this point, for this was simply a more intimate session with the mufti before the main service.

Then something happened. In the course of giving a long discourse, the mufti introduced someone on my right who was tall and young, maybe in his late twenties. He was dressed in white from head to toe with a traditional coat and cap. The mufti told the story of this young man, and he said it in very few words. "He is Iraqi; he was in Abu Ghraib for eight months and then released without charge. His two brothers were also picked up and have never been heard from since. This young man also spent twenty-two days living in a coffin in Abu Ghraib. The American soldiers would take him out at meal times and then shackle him back inside the coffin." I have to presume from what the mufti said that the coffin was also his bathroom. Then the mufti continued with his discourse.

But when I heard about the young man my heart began to pound hard and I began to breathe heavily. My hands trembled, and I increasingly felt the need to get up from my seat, but I did not. I needed to get out of my seat; I was dying in my seat because I needed to do something, but I could not know what.

No one knew how strongly I have reacted in my life to recent American torture, and how much it has simply changed me. It had begun to change me at least two years before in 2003, well before Abu Ghraib, on my way back from Jordan on a plane. I was coming back from the most rewarding peacemaking of my life in Damascus that I described in the previous chapter. Sitting right next to me on the plane was a "consultant" to the American military in Iraq. This man described to me in detail how he has "taken care of trouble" both in South Africa, his native country, and now in Iraq.

At first the conversation went well, both of us sharing how the standard institutions of government do not know how to solve violent problems. Then there was a moment on the plane, with his hand touching my bare arm, and earnestly looking into my eyes up close, that this man working for my United States government proudly described cutting off the thumbs of a recalcitrant black worker in South Africa; he chuckled as he told me that the man's name changed to mean, "man with no thumbs." I then got a good picture of this employee, being paid with my tax dollars, and I now understood what he meant by taking care of problems in Iraqi villages.

This man was so different than some of the wonderful people I encounter at the State Department or the United States Institute of Peace, or even at the intelligence agencies, believe it or not. But this is the complex reality of my country, indeed the complex reality of human sin when it is perpetrated by an entire culture through uncontrolled wars. I would think about this man for years to come, but the encounter on the plane changed me, for it changed my understanding of my American citizenship. He appeared before my eyes again, in Aleppo, just at the moment when the mufti was describing the life of the young man dressed in white shrouds of purity, shrouds of death.

The mufti went on speaking about other things, but I started to hear nothing of what he was saying. I was staring at the young man from Abu Ghraib, and he at me, and I could not take my eyes off of him. He had an intense look on his face—of pain—and also a curious kind of shame; but I did not feel any hatred coming from him. He looked as if he was concentrating on some puzzle that he could not figure out; he did not avert his eyes from me.

I remember the moment that his face was becoming seared into my memory, like a burning feeling. I have forgotten so many things and so many situations in my lifetime. I am terrible with names back home, in school; even in the halls of power I forget the names of congressmen all the time. But this name and this image and this young man's face were burrowing into my lifetime memory. Sometimes in life you feel you are living through a moment that is being burned into a new construct of your reality, and I felt a burning brand on my heart and on my eyes.

I could not sit anymore. I broke decorum and I got up in the middle of the mufti speaking with hundreds of people following my movement, and I walked across the hall to the young man. The interpreter followed nervously not knowing what I could possibly be thinking. The mufti stopped speaking, and all eyes turned toward the side of the room. I moved up close to the young man and spoke to him quietly. I told him how deeply sorry I was for what had happened to him, and I apologized in the name of the American people. Then I held his arm, and then I embraced him. My eyes were blurry and burning as he stood there close to me with a look on his face of confusion, as if he were searching hard for an answer from me. It was not an angry look but exceedingly pained. I knew the question. Of course I knew the question, but I could not answer it. The question was as old as the biblical Book of Job: "Why me?"

I went back to my seat after a time and there was some commotion. I kept looking at the young twenty-eight-year-old man. The mufti was moved by what happened but in a strange way. It was as if he had expected this from me even though we never spoke. He looked as if he was sighing with a re-signed look on his face. Every time I did something that resonated exactly in his tradition in the last couple of encounters he has seemed strangely resigned, sad, almost as if he could have predicted what I would do. It made him sad, I think, because he knew in his heart that this is the way it could be between our peoples if only we were allowed to teach this way to the world, to the political leaders.

But the world does not recognize repentance, apologies, or the impulsive embrace of enemies who suffer. It does not recognize emulation of a mythic figure called Abraham in his way of love for total strangers, nor in Abraham's ways of compassion and generosity, according to both Hebrew biblical and koranic stories. Not the hard world of politics, and not the hard world of today's organized religions, as a matter of fact. The mufti and I are just as spurned by our fanatics as we are by hardened politicians; it is what drove me out of being a congregational rabbi.

There is only a hearing for the mufti's way in the rarefied universe of those committed to the heart, and they are always overshadowed and cen-sored when religious ethnic groupings, mobilized for war, insist on being drenched in righteous anger. Emulating the mythic Abraham in the world of Abrahamic religions today is like holding your finger to a hole in a win-dow with a flood on the other side.

I let the Syrians accompanying me know that I wanted the names and exact information about the missing brothers of the young man from Abu Ghraib in the hopes that perhaps this family could be reunited someday. And I sent out this information on the Internet to all my readers in the hopes that someone reading it in the government agencies would give this to someone else in the halls of power who might look into the case. The brothers' names are Hamed abdul Hafez al-Kubaysi, born 1981, and Ayman abdul Hafez al-Kubaysi, born 1983. They were taken on June 22, 2005, from the city of Basra, and went, as far as the family knows, to Buka prison. Passing on this information was all I could do for them in 2006; and it felt like I did nothing at all.

Before a Sea of Iraqi Refugees

This was not the end of the episode, however. The session ended and then the mufti and everyone else promptly and quickly went into the larger chamber of the mosque where the worshippers awaited. Our group of guests, including myself and Nizar, were brought to the back of the mosque on the balcony. There were no less than three thousand Muslims on all the floors and flowing to the outside on that hot sunny day. Then the official prayer ceremonies began and they went on for a while until the sermon. Then, at a single moment in his sermon, the Grand Mufti of Syria began to weep.

I came to attention at that moment, straightened my back, to bear witness to this Muslim leader of Syria as he wept over violence, extremism, and war before three thousand worshipers. I later would learn how many people in the audience were refugees from Iraq, and how unspeakably difficult their situation was. I sensed that day that he was quite agitated and nervous about the situation. There was clearly tension at work in the social and political situation that I was not privy to. It was at a time when Shi'ite/Sunni killings were reaching unprecedented heights in Iraq. He spoke again and again about how Islam forbids the killing of civilians, and also the love that he has for Christians.

Then the mufti announced after the services before these three thousand people that there was "a man of religion" from America and invited me to come forward and say something as a guest, not as part of the service. Only later would he let it be known in Aleppo that I was a rabbi. He is a smart man when it comes to dealing with difficult emotions and enemy systems, and there is a reason why the people in that mosque are so fiercely devoted to him. As a former cleric myself, I understand how the mufti was trying to both comfort, lead, cajole, and also challenge his flock.

To get through the mosque and the crowd I was escorted quickly through various doors outside and then inside, each time putting on my shoes and taking them off, having absolutely no skills at what is standard practice in maneuvering around a mosque. I was trembling badly as it was very difficult to stare at so many people who were not smiling at me. I would later learn how many of them were poor and Iraqi.

I went to join the mufti down with the people, his senior sheikhs who seemed to be engaged in subtle forms of crowd control, and the young man from Abu Ghraib was there as well, placed right next to me! I elected to cite many of my religious traditions that paralleled the mufti's lecture, but without citing them as Jewish sources. I cited biblical teachings on love of neighbor (Leviticus 19:17), on the sin of hatred in the heart, on avoiding doing to others what is hateful to you (*Talmud Bavli* Sabbath 31a), a quote from Psalms that those who love life and want to be God fearing should keep their mouths from speaking against others, and that they should pursue peace (Psalms 34:14). I spoke of true heroism being the changing of enemies into friends (*Avot of Rabbi Nathan* 16:1), and how humbled I was to have the chance in my life to learn spiritual truths from such a heroic figure as their mufti. I talked for three minutes.

Then the mufti told them what I had done with the young man from Abu Ghraib, and this created quite a stir. I believe he said, "He apologized; how can we not respond to this?" He also rebuked them and mentioned how rare it is that they apologize, meaning the Muslim world, when they do something wrong. Then some commotion occurred at the front. Some members were saying things to the mufti, and I asked what was going on. They said that people were objecting to his bringing me here. There was a degree of agitation emerging in the crowd. They said, "He elected George Bush." Quickly, I took the microphone, and with my voice trembling, I responded, "We did not elect torture." That seemed to create stillness.

Then the mufti put me together with the young man to face the crowd. And he said to his followers, "Show the world what we have done here today." Immediately ten or twenty people in the front rows took out their cell phones and began videotaping our group standing with the mufti and the young man. They put me next to the young man from Abu Ghraib and filmed us. Afterward, as I was walking out through the crowd, which dispersed with amazing speed, a young man smiled at me broadly and meekly held my hands, bowed slightly, and gave me a small set of Islamic prayer beads made of green plastic. I still have these beads, and I have draped them around an award my father once got that I keep in my bedroom.

Gems of Indigenous Religious Culture

We left the main hall and proceeded into another beautiful reception hall where about fifty people were gathered. Again, I sat in front with the mufti. We were treated to a wonderful visit of a contingent of Ismaili Muslims from a village in Syria who were paying their respects to the mufti. Such minority groups are deeply grateful to this mufti because his tolerance for all sects keeps them safe from the extremists.

In addition there was a remarkable lecture given by a five-year-old who came up to my knee. He proceeded to hold forth for almost twenty minutes repeating the mufti's lecture, it seems word for word, complete with dramatic gestures, pauses, passion, and sighs! I could not believe what I was seeing. The father was at the far end, and I noticed him wiping his eye a few times. The child's blind teacher was there as well. I thought to myself about what a rich and ancient culture there is here, and how vital it will be to engage it with care and respect at every level. Never in my travels have I ever seen a child that young perform this way. Of course he was a prodigy, but it was the investment of the Islamic culture in him that was astonishing.

My hosts and I left the mosque, but not before the mufti gave me a beautiful piece of religious art and a Koran as a gift. I sensed strongly that he wanted more time together but it seemed not to be possible politically at that moment. The truth is that I also had to get back to Damascus before sunset as I did not want to travel by car on the Sabbath. We went to get some humus, zatar, and pita, sat right next to the ancient Citadel in the heart of Aleppo, and then went home to Damascus.

Unexpected Outcomes of Religious Diplomacy

What happened in the mosque was apparently broadcast in various venues and it became a news story inside Syria. I subsequently heard from a certain person who said that President Asad said to him personally that what happened at the mosque "was worth more to me than a hundred speeches by the American president." This was said in private, not for commercial consumption or political purpose, and that made it very interesting.

It is hard to know exactly what Asad meant. Was it because Syria had hosted a public apology from an American for what happened at Abu Ghraib? Was it the honor of Islam and Syria by an American, or was it the interfaith encounter itself? It certainly seems to have something to do with the deeds that we did in terms of apology and reconciliation. And why was it so meaningful to Asad, or important to him, or valuable politically?

I put together these cryptic comments with the knowledge I gained about other appointed muftis in Syria who are hard line or even jihadist, and I concluded that for just one day the grand mufti shifted the balance a little. The mufti was able to show to his followers, and therefore to Asad, that you can get further politically through honoring guests, receiving apologies and acknowledgments, even with the hated Americans. For just one weekend he was able to demonstrate to his people as well as to the ruling power structures that there are ways to deal with America that do not include brinksmanship or flirtations with religious radicalism that is virulently anti-American.

What I learned from this experience, as well as what we in the field have observed and written about, is that culture and religion provide unique avenues of diplomacy and conflict resolution that are both elusive and powerful. These avenues are so unique for each circumstance that it is challenging to come up with set formulas about how to pursue this work. It seems then that the flexible role of the citizen diplomat, ready to seize moments of reconciliation, is indispensable.

And so what becomes pertinent to the future of this work is enlisting the efforts of many more citizens who can reach into themselves and prepare for these kinds of encounters. That will take not only training in conflict resolution, but also a kind of ethical and spiritual training, preparing for impossibly challenging circumstances of being between enemies while maintaining a positive spirit of wisdom, friendship, caution, and cleverness. It will take a great deal of reflection on the dilemmas of this work that we will address in the next chapters. But first we should continue the story.

2007: REACHING FARTHER AND DEEPER WITH INTERFAITH DIPLOMACY

The year 2007 brought an opportunity to do something that I had always dreamed of but had never realized before. We discovered the opportunity to show the media a living demonstration of interfaith dialogue on timely issues that would demonstrate a more constructive role for religion in the Middle East.

Hind Kabawat and I continued to develop our wonderful relationship with the courageous Nizar Mayoub, who had recently changed his work and set of priorities. Taking a great gamble, he set up his dream of a center on public relations and diplomacy and invested in a building in Damascus.

Hind Kabawat, based on her excellent relations with a variety of clergy, developed the idea of a televised debate/conversation between clerics representing the three Abrahamic faiths. Unlike other presentations, however, this one would be moderated in a very intensive way, like a press interview. Hind would present a series of questions to the clergy, and the answers would be limited to two minutes apiece.

We debated which questions to ask, and finally came up with questions that would focus on the ways in which religion could play a positive role in the future of civil society building in Syria. This released some fascinating energy on the panel and in the audience.

In general, traditional religions in the Middle East are not in the business of discussing how they can work together to improve the lot of the poor or the environment, for example, or for peace. There is a lot of nice rhetoric, but the realm of religion is secondary to the state or kingdom which is supposed to order everything. We were breaking new ground in the conception of civic responsibility and religious civic responsibility. We were pushing the envelope not only on interfaith dialogue but also on interfaith cooperation in the building of civil society that would not be dependent on the state—Ba'athist or otherwise. In many ways, we were looking for utterly nonthreatening, nonviolent ways to empower average citizens to build their society together, on their own.

In addition, Hind's role as moderator was a fascinating development. I had been frustrated the year before that Hind as a woman could not come to the event at the mosque in Aleppo. It did not seem fair to me that she had set everything up but that I was the center of attention.

This was one of those moments when I struggled with multiple moral and conflict resolution agendas: interfaith bridges in the Middle East, a subtle shift in Arab–Jewish relations, an alliance with the mufti, a shift in the role of Americans in the Middle East. But Hind and I also shared a feminist agenda. So in our usual fashion, we juggled, reacted with flexibility, put the feminist agenda aside a few times, but then continued to seize opportunities.

What happened on television is that there was a complete gender role reversal. All the clerics, including me, were male. And yet Hind was completely in charge, rigorously—very rigorously—enforcing the rules, engaging the debate, pressing the clerics on firm answers. This was remarkable and empowering. There was also a powerful woman on the panel, also named Hind, who spoke for Shi'ites, in addition to Sheikh Shehadeh.

Nizar's Center was packed back to the walls, and to my shock the audience remained involved and rapt with attention for three hours! But the most astonishing development was the coalescence of another trend with our own initiative, and that is the privatization of media. It turns out there was a new satellite station that one of the wealthiest men in Syria set up, and he played this program over and over again for days. By the end of a couple of weeks everyone in Syria had seen this interfaith event. Nothing comparable in interfaith work could have happened on American commercial television, ironic as that may be, because profit margins would not permit it.

The program was deepening our work, pressing forward on the liberal agenda of civil society building, adding a feminist element, and reaching a far larger audience than we had ever done before. Remarkably, I was asked almost nothing about Israel this time. It was as if the audience was captivated by an earnest concern to deal with Syria's problems first.

Expanding Networks

As a result of our Syria work our networks kept expanding. Hind received increasing international attention for her pioneering work. Increasingly her expertise in conflict resolution, women's empowerment, and civil society-building was being sought after. Therefore she was invited to speak in Washington institutions, such as the World Bank, more often, which in turn helped our collaboration.

Hind also received an award for her work from the Tanenbaum Center for Interfaith Understanding at a ceremony in Bosnia. This increased her reputation as a peacemaker. In Canada, where she lives part time, Hind was honored as well, and her work became increasingly sought out by the Jewish community of Canada, a wonderful and unexpected network development. She in turn promoted my work to them, ironic as that may be, but network loops are filled with exciting ironies.

The networks that we connected began with us as an unusual pair working for peace, then an award for courageous peacemaking to Hind from the mostly Jewish-funded Tanenbaum Center, which then led to a Jewish community becoming more open to a Syrian–Jewish relationship. All this happened without Hind censoring anything of her vision for a just solution to the Palestinian–Israeli conflict.

Such is the power of network and peacemaking that the network that we created has indirectly given Hind a better chance of influencing Jewish attitudes than have all of my books in the last decade. *Her* words of respect and appreciation as a Syrian to Jews, *her* explanations of Arab worldviews, have a much greater impact than my words in terms of breaking down enemy systems. Similarly there is my embrace of the people and culture of Syria that has affected *her* friends and associates in Damascus in an unprecedented way precisely because of who I am. Thus, identity can be made to work for peace rather than against it when the bridges of networks are solid and deep.

Networks create amazing loops of influence. For example, the chair of the board of the Center of World Religions, Diplomacy, and Conflict Resolution (CRDC) has been Joseph Montville since 2006. I am the founding director of CRDC, and Joe is one of my important mentors. He, in turn, has been passionate about preventing war with Iran, and spent a huge amount of time promoting Shi'ite approaches to democracy and pluralism.

CRDC is housed at George Mason University's Institute for Conflict Analysis and Resolution. George Mason University also has a distinguished professor by the name of Shaul Bakash whose wife Hala Efsanderi is a very important American Iranian promoting democracy and civil society. She is also Iranian, and when she was arrested by the Iranians many people went into high gear trying to save her from prison. Joe was deeply involved, but unbeknownst to him Hind is a good friend of Hala and of the Wilson Center. Everyone was working at once for her release, loosely connected by a network. But Hind also had the advantage of being a citizen of one of the only countries allied with Iran at the time. Here was a network of good will that eventually led to Hala Efsanderi's release.

Another surprising network development was the relationship between the Baptist minister on the panel of the interfaith debate in Damascus, who is also Hind's pastor in Syria. He is also a graduate of Wheaton College in the United States. I, in turn, met with a group from Wheaton in recent years as I was creating a quiet alliance of Christian evangelicals and Baptists for a just peace in Israel. Due to that work I took this Syrian minister quite seriously, even though years ago I might have avoided him because I have such radically opposed views to most evangelicals on church/state separation and political religion. I was impressed by this Syrian Baptist pastor, however, and in fact I think he had the most creative things to say on that panel that we shared at Nizar's center. And so Hind arranged for us to meet at her house and deepen the relationship.

But the biggest surprise is that Hind got to know Friar Ivo Markovic in Bosnia, a Croatian hero of peacemaking who I also know. Hind somehow connected her pastor with Friar Ivo and they are now trading writings. So now there is a parallel Christian network to our work. This is further evidence of the limitless power of networks between people of good will, especially when there are ingenious "connectors" like Hind who see opportunities for expansion of the network everywhere.

Support for Individual Networkers: A Missing Piece

The success of "the connector" requires a moral quality as well, and that is a combination of personal confidence and generosity. But it also requires a level of humility that encourages network expansion that is NOT self-centered or narcissistic. This is the key to Hind's success, Joe Montville's work, and Eliyahu Mclean's as well, in terms of their lasting contribution to social change and peacebuilding. We will speak more in later chapters on ethics and ethical dilemmas, but for now I wanted to highlight these indispensable moral qualities that are crucial to what I have seen these people accomplish, with no staff and hardly any resources.

Well-funded social change agencies the world over that lack these qualities but instead engage the world with the aim of empire building cannot hold a candle to these people in terms of the social change potential. The beauty and power of limitless networks require a level of humility and self-surrender that is essentially a spiritual quality.

This strengthens the argument I have been making that we need today a radical restructuring of our support systems in favor of individuals, citizen diplomats, entrepreneurs, who create the cutting edge of change. The Nobel Prize committee has always understood the centrality of individual genius in human progress, but the philanthropic community has always underestimated or even stifled this in terms of positive social change and peacemaking. There is a nasty tendency, from education of young children all the way to funding of social change, to stifle individual genius and entrepreneurship. This in no way is meant to undervalue cooperative learning, planning, and execution of social change that is embodied by the concept of the NGO. Rather my critique is meant to tip the scale back from a rather extreme neglect of the individual pioneer that is often due to the prejudice of modern society toward bureaucracy and complexity, as well as to the overly cautious nature of donors.

Foundations need to tip the scale back to individual entrepreneurs in its support structure and to not overly rely upon NGOs to always be at the cutting edge of social change. After all, patronage of individuals as a way of advancing culture has a much longer history than grant making to NGOs, going all the way back to ancient Greece. Patronage of individuals has been essential to the flourishing of human genius for thousands of years. Donors and foundations need to reflect on this more carefully. What I have seen social geniuses have to do to make a living is simply criminal.

2008: THE INNOVATIONS CONTINUE

The year 2008 brought unprecedented opportunities to engage in conflict resolution training in places that we had only dreamed it possible a few years before. What we had done inside Syria until now was focused always on religion, but we had been frustrated with difficulties in setting up professional and academic foundations for teaching conflict resolution and social change. To directly address issues of diplomacy and conflict resolution was more daring in terms of Syrian culture.

It has been my experience and the experience of my fellow professors that the institutionalization itself of conflict resolution programs introduces a kind of paradigm shift in thinking about political and military problems. It becomes an avenue through which one can engage eventually the political, military, and security realms—the folks with guns—about alternative approaches to the toughest contests and conflicts. Thus, I was simply looking to get citizens used to the idea of a day of training in conflict resolution. Certainly Hind and I would emphasize cultural and religious approaches to issues, but we also knew that the implications of the methods would resonate with the deeper issues that Syrians, and everyone else in the region, had to face about interethnic tensions, gender conflict, human rights conflicts, conflicts with neighboring states, and conflicts over the distribution of resources and wealth in the society. We managed in 2008 to cement a relationship with Nizar Mayoub's new International Diplomacy Institute, and we formalized that relationship in a press conference in January of 2008 in Damascus.

The questions from the journalists present were most interesting, and they pointed to the subtleties of what we are trying to accomplish. They asked whether courses in diplomacy or public relations in academia could lead to evolution of the politics of the region. I responded that it is our experience that the study of these matters in terms of the language of conflict analysis and resolution could lead to new and previously untried approaches to diplomacy, and that this is what we were anticipating.

As of the winter of 2008, Hind Kabawat had evolved an international reputation and identity as the kind of Syrian that is working aggressively on matters of civil society. One article referred to her "reinvention" in the last several years.[1] She is also being sought out more by women entrepreneurs in her own and neighboring countries such as Jordan, and on interfaith matters in countries such as Qatar.

This is very exciting for me because I am convinced, based on my experience, that the single greatest change agent regarding all the issues around war, race, class, and religion in the Middle East will be an emerging network of empowered women. Women have always been the essential change agents of history when male-dominated cultures become stuck in their own structures of violence. The resilience of women in regard to conflict resolution in difficult circumstances is legendary,[2] but it will become essential to the future of citizen diplomacy, as it already has become essential to the mechanics of child survival and development.[3]

Five Days in Freezing Damascus

The winter of 2008 in Damascus and Jerusalem was the coldest on record since 1964. I had the privilege of freezing in these two cities, one week after another, trying to struggle at the same time with bronchitis and a touch of pneumonia. This made the trip between the two cities particularly difficult. I am not sure that the land route is working for me anymore between these two biblical towns, despite the emotional lure of doing it. There is so much stress and tension in creating a bridge between them when there is not supposed to be one. In any case, I made it over the Allenby Bridge without incident and proceeded to Damascus. Being sick limited my schedule this time. We did manage to have a wonderful meeting with Grand Mufti Hassoun, and it was once again a memorable experience. His combination of political savvy and antiviolent spirituality continues to impress me. I am amazed by his intellectual boldness. This time he was quite explicit that the best home for religion is in secular states, and I am hearing this increasingly from Muslim thinkers who are tired of extremist politics in the name of Islam.

We encountered some difficulties in our public conference this time. Highlights were aired on Al Jazeera and Dunya TV, and this was a good accomplishment. Our theme was a bit diffuse and we had too many speakers. We also did not have a good mechanism for dealing with those who had a political agenda. At the same time, I was at my worst. I was sick and weak, and I really got frustrated this time with a few people who railed against the West, against Zionists, but who failed to show any familiarity with or interest in the Palestinian people. I was the one who repeatedly brought up the Palestinians. I failed to model patience.

Sometimes I feel like I am living in a fantasy world of a small number of Jews and Arabs who can roughly be described as pro-Palestinian and pro-Israel. Not in the sense of being "pro" the behavior of governments or militaries, but in the sense of being in an orbit of people, from Jerusalem to the United States, who are earnestly working to free these two peoples from a century-long conflict. Then I move outside this circle and realize how few people really care about the welfare of Israeli Jews or Palestinians.

This is frustrating, and I did not handle it well this time. I realized that I should not go into challenging public encounters when sick. Nevertheless, we also deepened the relationship with Nizar Mayoub and his launching of an academy dedicated to diplomacy and public relations.

I am very blessed to have so many Syrian friends, from clerics to secular activists. We all know the politics and we all know the difficulties with every government. None of it has to be said or should be said. We just continue to work, to educate the public, to promote nonviolent approaches to building new relationships. Despite the test I was put to this time, despite my illness, I miss Damascus.

This time I was determined to indulge my physical needs more since I was so sick. I insisted on finding a place to "sweat," what Arabs call a *hamam* and what my ancestors called a *shvitz*. Unfortunately my lack of Arabic still plagues me. I apparently went at first to a very working-class *hamam* in the Old City, near the Christian Quarter.

There was a group of young men hanging out in the *hamam*, and they just could not understand that I did not understand Arabic. I think they thought I was mentally challenged. It did not occur to them that I was foreign. In any case, they played games with me, poured water over my head again and again, shampooed my hair, though I never asked for it, then sang songs and insisted on dancing with me. I was holding on to my towel for dear life, and doing Arabic dances with the other hand, and I could barely see anybody due to the vapor. This was an interesting experience.

In the United States no one talks to you in the steam shower of the health club; it is a very private affair. Not in this *hamam*, at least not for me. The next day I went to a *hamam* that was a bit more "upper class," near the Great Umayyad Mosque in the Old City. It had been built originally in the sixteenth century, and had a more professional air to it. I continue to lament my lack of Arabic and the situations it puts me into.

Speaking of which, on my way home, I took a cab from Damascus to Amman, and the driver did not speak a word of English, but he was a very industrious fellow. I had no idea why he asked for my passport as he stopped in strange broken-down shops along the side of the road, disappeared in the back, and then came out with "packages."

This made me nervous. I was even more nervous when once across the border, he pulled down his window and started negotiating at red lights with strangers in other cars. He made a few sales of what I hope were Marlborough cigarettes. I got even more nervous when we were stopped at a Jordanian checkpoint, and he slipped whatever it was underneath his seat.

I started to have visions of prison in the Middle East, and then I started to have visions of Brad Davis in *Midnight Express*, circling endlessly and mindlessly in a dark prison basement. Then I wondered whether the fact that I had hosted King Abdullah in Washington a few years back, in a reconciliation dinner with a hundred rabbis, might help my case in Jordanian court. In any case, the cab driver sweet-talked the Jordanian police, who never checked the car. Visions of *Midnight Express* faded as I left his cab, and switched to a much nicer person. Of course this was all my fault because I went with a much cheaper taxi in Damascus, and I could have spared myself a great deal of anxiety with another $100.

Once in Amman I missed the last bus at the King Hussein Bridge and slept over in Amman. Both Hind and I learned from mistakes we made. I have also learned that if I do not place my physical health front and center I will not be able to continue this work. We are also trying to cope with various pressures of an ever more stressful regional environment and we hope to persist one way or another in this work. One of the reasons it was so difficult on that particular trip is that citizens of Damascus were under ever greater stress from security services looking for any infiltrations of those who would create a coup in Syria at the behest of the American administration.

PEACE PROSPECTS AS OF 2008

I should say a word about the prospects of peace between Syria, Israel, and the United States as of this writing. In the course of my work in Syria many things have become clear. Bashar Asad is moving ahead with a bold plan to modernize the economy and to expand the amount of people who benefit from that economy. With each passing year Syria is moving a little bit away from an Old Guard, a small group of families, that controls all the money of the country.

At the same time, Syria resembles many modern economies that have unfair monopolies everywhere, just as in the West, only worse because there are still so few opportunities. Capitalism is hardly a panacea for economic injustice, but there is a concerted effort to reform and modernize in a way that would distribute wealth in a more pronounced way than what currently exists. This is tempting at least some expatriates to return.

This positive development has decidedly been decoupled from political reform or liberalization of any sort. Perhaps one can blame this to some extent on outside pressure from a right-wing American administration in the last decade, but much of the repression is hard to understand or justify. My sense, from what I have heard, is that as Bashar Asad steps on some toes economically he will not step on the toes of the security services as well. But that is assuming that he does not agree with the imprisonment of political liberals, and I have no evidence of that.

I do know that when it comes to Israel, he will be hard pressed to liberalize the economy *and* make a separate peace with Israel as some Israelis would hope for. He cannot make a separate peace with Israel without losing the people. He is, in fact, popular and he needs the people with him to liberalize anything or move the economy away from the Old Guard stranglehold.

I have witnessed myself the vestiges of Stalinist and Ba'athist thinking in Syria. But it is unpopular, it is old, and associated with old people inside and outside government. If Asad is to move away from that approach—which sees absolutely no possibility of a comprehensive peace plan for the Middle East without the destruction of Israel—he will need the people with him all the way. As of now they are with Sheikh Nasrallah of Hezbollah, for example. They want a good fight with Israel for as long as they see pictures of Israeli Jewish soldiers attacking Arabs for whatever reason.

This is a difficult straightjacket to overcome. Israel has legitimate rights to defense against rocket attacks and suicide bombs. But this is all a game of chicken and egg, and most Arabs, especially in Syria, see Israel as mostly to blame for the cycles of revenge. Their widely held belief is that Israel uses only military options, excessive force, humiliation, and collective punishment because there is a fundamental lack of respect for the Arab as an equal. They see an implicit disrespect or hatred of the Arab and the Muslim at the root of those tactics.

As can be seen from my narrative I am quite convinced that aggressive steps by Israel and the United States to engage Syria, as well as efforts to demonstrate progressive change in treatment of Arabs inside and outside of Israel, will significantly improve Asad's interest in continuing the overtures that he has made to Israel in the last few years. If Israel and the United States play a smart, moderate game they can stimulate a cycle of rapprochement rather than a cycle of brinksmanship currently underway. But Israel and the United States must be aggressively prompted to do so by third parties that want to see a stabilization of the Middle East.

It must be kept in mind that Arab Israeli politicians have frequently visited Syria, and their opinions matter in Syria. Of course they are a tough group and most Israeli Jews dislike them intensely. Nevertheless I think this is a moment of truth for Israel. If it is serious about wanting to live in peace in the region then it must take seriously the openings for peace. All of those openings depend upon treatment of Arabs as equals and demonstrating this change in every way both inside Israel and even with its Palestinian enemies.

You fight an enemy in this region, but you do not humiliate him, and you do not destroy more than is necessary to destroy in self-defense. It is essential that Israel desists from excessive force, collective punishment, or humiliation, and that, on the contrary, it clearly demonstrates honor and respect for Arabs, Muslims, and Palestinians. Remorse over past crimes would also have a revolutionary effect.

That does not mean that Israel needs to lie down and die, to not defend itself, but the defense must be honorable. Every Arab is watching every move here, especially in the Syrian population. I am convinced from my travels, observations, and thousands of conversations that most Arabs want a peace agreement, but only if behaviors are modified. Only then can the tables be turned and they can be challenged to look at their own dishonorable war tactics like supporting suicide bombing. Recall that it was immediately after I publicly humiliated myself as an American by apologizing before the torture victim from Abu Ghraib that the Grand Mufti turned to the three thousand Muslims in attendance, Syrian and Iraqi alike, and rebuked them for not apologizing for their own misdeeds. I have seen few clerics ever challenge their flock this way, especially a very wounded flock. This is the cycle of rapprochement, generosity, and self-criticism, rooted in ancient spiritual principles, that he and I are trying to stimulate across civilizations, and across militant states.

A remarkable development, not directly related to Syria, is that of the voices coming out of Saudi Arabia, the most reactionary bastion of the Middle East. Even here there is a Saudi-induced Arab League proposal on the table that remains unanswered by Israel and the United States. More tellingly, Prince Turki al-Faisal, former ambassador to the United States, has pioneered interfaith relationships in the last few years. He recently stated that it is time for Jews in Israel to normalize their relations in the region, to be considered Arab Jews by the rest of the Middle East, to be visited and to visit everyone.[4]

To Jewish ears this was a very odd statement. But to my mind, as a conflict resolution analyst, this is a brilliant move. Prince Turki is finding a cultural way to welcome Jewish Israel into the Middle East if (a) they accept the peace plan which by definition respects Palestinians as equals and thus reverses the tragedy of 1948, and (b) Jewish Israel sees itself more as part of the culture of the Middle East, the Arab culture. This is an expansive definition of "Arab," beyond race, beyond blood, beyond tribe, to be a cultural and geographic term. This is a remarkable invitation and opening, especially from a royal based in a country that has been accused by almost everyone else of racist leanings.

Jews will expect embrace of their own culture in the Middle East, and that would be part of the process of rapprochement and peace. I would argue that with all the violence and stalemate of 2008 the fact is that we are watching major cultural and political representatives of the Middle East, even in Saudi Arabia, finally arriving at the essential questions of coexistence between Arabs and Jews, between Christians, Muslims, and Jews. This is dovetailed by mainstream politicians such as Ehud Olmert, who began his life as an ardent right-wing Zionist, concluding that Israel cannot go on forever in its relations with Palestinians without become an apartheid country.[5]

When it comes to Syria, it is clear that this bastion of self-styled pan-Arabist devotion cannot abide an Asad who makes a separate peace with Israel at the expense of the Palestinians. It is not a love of Palestinians in Syria that drives this reality, but rather the question of Arab pride and Arab solidarity. What we should work for is therefore a comprehensive peace process that takes steps in the direction of the following: normalization of relationships between Israel and all Arab and Muslim states; normalization of relations between Syria and the United States; the return of the Golan; a viable Palestinian state; a modification of Syria's exclusive embrace of Hamas at the expense of Fatah; a moderation of the relationship with Iran and Hezbollah that moves more toward a political rather than a military relationship; a recognition of borders with Lebanon and its independence; Israel's embrace of responsibility for Palestinian refugees, without their full return to Israel but with some agreed upon return. The costs here are high to everyone, but the benefits are very high too. The more things move in the direction of articulating this vision and taking initial steps the easier it will become for everyone to prepare their political structures to accept these dramatic changes.

These dramatic changes will revolutionize life inside Syria. With normalization of relations with Israel, Jordan, Lebanon, and especially the United States, there will be no further need for political repression at home. This is a well-nown reality that frightens the few and the corrupt, but is eagerly anticipated by everyone else. I suspect that the regime and most of its first family will jump on this bandwagon of normalization of external and internal relations to remain popular, as all governments yearn to do to maintain their power.

But this can occur only if normalization is popular, which requires changes in Israel and the United States. That is why international relations are the key to liberal domestic relations inside Syria in the long run. This is the path that my partners and friends in Syria are anticipating, and there is no downside to experimenting with this path. The worst that can happen is that Syria is at peace with all its neighbors, the economy prospers immensely as a result, there are no more boycotts, but the political situation is still repressive. Over time, this too will change; it is inevitable. The path we are suggesting, one of evolution rather than revolution, is the one that is most likely to save the most lives across the region, bring more prosperity and happiness, and bring about far less suffering and fear than what exists today.

THE BURDEN OF CONSCIENCE

The experience of the last few years in Syria has been fraught with opportunities to effect change in civilizations, and to stand with principle between civilizations as a peacemaker. I never dreamed when I began that this would be possible for me, my friends, or protégés. But these years were also fraught with sadness and danger, mostly danger to others, which plagued my conscience and aged me.

Nothing changes you forever as much as speaking on the phone within the same week with people in Beirut, Damascus, Northern Israel, and the West Bank, all of whom are either suffering immediately the threat of bombs in the middle of a war, or who are housing refugees from the wars in 2006. Nothing changes you more than looking out onto to a sea of homeless Iraqi refugees dutifully bowing in Friday prayers, refugees made homeless by your own country's folly.

There is what is within your control in this life, and what is beyond your control. If you can do what is within your control with some degree of guided conscience then it makes it easier to cope with what is beyond your control. If, however, your interventions are as chaotic and irresponsible as that of the misdeeds of governments then it becomes too much to bear. That makes extensive self-reflection and ethical calculation essential, not only to the decency of what citizen diplomats dare to do, but also to their sanity.

I have felt that in my work in diplomacy there has been precious little guidance for how to make choices in gray areas of human decision where clear ethics are impossible. The wisdom traditions of the earth's cultures, in addition to the classical fields of philosophy, literature, and psychology, have a wealth of insights that are indeed relevant but not easily applied to ever-changing and often unique circumstances. There is the beauty of human moral freedom, and also its essential terror. My interventions have been too chaotic, not guided enough, and that has made it difficult for me to be at peace with my work. In the coming chapters, therefore, I will attempt to address in a systematic way the question of ethical guidance for citizen diplomacy.

NOTES

1. See nationalpost.com/story.html?id=216144.

2. Even the Security Council of the UN has adopted special resolutions now that specifically engage women's networks for peacemaking in conflict zones. See reliefweb.int/rw/rwb.nsf/AllDocsByUNID/550a9d4faa49688e8525698a005d4fb8. On networks of women in Somalia, see *Conflict Resolution, Confidence Building, and Peace Enhancement among Somali Women* (Geneva: International Organization for Migration, 2002).

3. See, for example, Robert A. LeVine, "Women's Schooling, Patterns of Fertility, and Child Survival," *Educational Researcher* 16, no. 9 (1987): 21–27.

4. See Prince Turki's remarkable interview with Reuters at africa.reuters.com/wire/news/usnL2057323.html (accessed February 5, 2008). And see my response, "Jewish Arabs and a New Middle East," at middle-east-online.com/english/opinion/?id=25108 (accessed April 22, 2008).

5. guardian.co.uk/israel/Story/0,,2219485,00.html (accessed February 5, 2008).

Section III

DIPLOMACY WITH A CONSCIENCE: THE SEARCH FOR WISDOM IN GLOBAL ENGAGEMENT

6

Confronting the Ethical Dilemmas
of Citizen Diplomacy

In the next two chapters I will present reflections on the ethical choices that
are regularly made by interveners and actors on the stage of global change.
I will base my insights mostly on experiences described in the previous
chapters, but also on other experiences. In this chapter I will first present
some best ethical practices of intervention that have become clear to me.
I will then present the fundamental problem of ambiguity and dilemma
in intervention, and draw upon the various schools of ethics to attempt to
address or at least clarify those dilemmas and choices. I will then present
some ethical guidelines to deal with those ambiguities, and also outline my
own tentative attempt at an ethic of intervention. In the following chapter
I will wed these insights with wisdom traditions East and West in an effort to propose a more meaningful and complete ethic of intervention and
diplomacy.

BEST PRACTICES: WHAT WORKS AND WHY

Deeds versus Words

There is a unique position in citizen diplomacy for the power of the
deed and the gesture. This derives in general from the power of deeds and
gestures as symbols in the human psyche. Symbolic behavior is at the core
of diplomacy.

In a certain sense, the citizen diplomat embodies symbol. A person
comes from one civilization and enters into another, with everyone fully
aware that this person is crossing over boundaries of tension, distrust, and

conflict. The act of arrival *itself* and the presence in the new civilization becomes a symbolic gesture without a word needing to be said.

Sometimes the gesture in and of itself is transformative, but the words that follow undo the gesture! That is why every word of the diplomat must be examined carefully, and the aphorism, "The gate of wisdom is silence,"[1] is apt. Gestures, like pictures, are worth a thousand words, and tell a thousand tales. They are also open to multiple interpretations that can often *enhance* their effectiveness and appeal to many different people. By contrast, the moment words come they can constrict or destroy the power of the symbol.

I was amazed in my work that the symbol of passing into Gaza years ago as a citizen diplomat team—myself and Bryan Hamlin—and coming to police headquarters for a special dinner presented to us by General Nasser Yousef, in the midst of the violence, was received with such gratitude by so many. Or the act of showing up in Damascus in the last few years was in and of itself sufficient to generate numerous expressions of gratitude and awe-inspired wonder. Why? Why did people say such heartfelt thank you's to me, over and over again? I just showed up! And, despite Woody Allen's brilliant quip that "80 percent of life is showing up," I still could not fathom the gratitude. I pondered this for a very long time.

The reason that most members of civilizations in conflict with another do not cross over the void between them is usually recoil at the *impression* of betraying one's own group. But it is also out of fear of being attacked in some way.

On the receiving end, most people who welcome diplomats from across the divide are painfully aware of the radicals in their midst who may attack you, verbally or otherwise. But when you come anyway your courage becomes a symbol of safety, of peace, and hope. By your presence you are vindicating the position of the moderates; you are expressing solidarity with them, and you are modeling courage before extremism. This generates emotional gratitude that is astonishing.

You are also seen by recipients of your gesture as defying your own group's ban on relations, or your own group's various symbols of demonization of the other. You go to Syria, and you are immediately seen as defying American neoconservative ideology and the desire to violently subjugate Syria. You go as an American or as a Jew and you are perceived by many Syrians as plainly opposed to the killing of Arabs or attacks against the country; this is received with gratitude when a country as powerful as the United States threatens military action. The Syrian's fear of Damascus turning into Baghdad at the hands of American imperialists is palpable. And so your presence becomes a positive symbol of life and solidarity that is beyond description.

I have felt similar feelings, sixty years since the Holocaust, without any immediate threat to me in the present, when a German treats me with warmth. Completely irrationally, the warmth from a German makes me feel safe in an unpredictable world—and somehow vindicated in my identity as a Jew, an identity that was so ruthlessly destroyed by the Nazis.

You do not have to say a word when you cross big boundaries. You do not have to agree politically that America or Israel have violent intentions, although it pays not to be offensive or provocative in a way that would be perceived as rude in Arab culture. Just by coming with respect I was received by others as standing in solidarity with them as they waited nervously to see whether the overwhelming power of the United States and Israel would rain down on their heads. It does not matter that you actually are quite afraid of Syria yourself, or that you do not agree with their assessment of the causes and consequences of the afflictive wars; your feelings or your politics need not be identical to theirs. What matters is that your presence is overwhelming evidence of courage and solidarity.

This effect can be enhanced by what you say if you actively seek out that in the local civilization which can be complimented and encouraged. Thus, deeds and words can work together to create a powerful ethical gesture of solidarity and friendship.

The power of combining word and deed together also has old roots in all cultures and religions. As long as you do not appear physically before your enemies then the old archetypes between one warring civilization and another will dominate human psychology, the perception of the Other as demon. But if you do show up and you combine words and deeds in a powerful way, you may be tapping into unknown *positive* archetypes of the civilization. There are also old positive relations between peoples that are sometimes buried beneath contemporary political/military conflict, and you can tap into those buried relations if you are clever.

I came to understand, for example, that, despite the eternal symbol in Ba'athist Syria of the Zionist enemy to the South, for many people in Syria there is a competing archetype. It is what I would characterize as "the Jew as Neighbor," whose presence affirms the superiority of Arab and Muslim civilizations as tolerant and pluralistic—as opposed to the anti-Jewish legacy of European civilizations. There is a pervasive pride in the presence of Jews in Syria. Most have emigrated now, largely for financial reasons of Syria's declining fortunes during the Cold War, but the average Syrian has a palpable pride in and longing for the lost neighbors of the Jewish faith. This aspect of the culture has been overshadowed since the catastrophe in Arab–Jewish relations in 1948.

The exodus of Jews is embarrassing for the Syrian who prides himself on the presence of the Jew as a mark of a superior and tolerant Arab civilization. This may sound odd to the Western ear but I have found this to be absolutely the case in several Arab civilizations, despite the hatred of Israel. The overarching power of European and Turkish civilization in recent centuries, and the technical achievements of the West in recent centuries, has led to a great sense of loss in the Arab world of prestige and honor. But this same, humiliated Arab world takes great pride that they, unlike the Europeans, are tolerant of other faiths. From their view, they do not create Crusades and they did not create a Holocaust. Believe it or not, at least in Damascus, the fact that I returned and honored them as a Jew seemed to tap into an authentic psychological archetype of ancient pride in the Jewish–Arab, Jewish–Muslim partnership of a thousand years.

Let's take this issue of deeds and gestures one step further. Truth be told, it is hard to go wrong anywhere in the world with deeds of honor and respect. It is not just in the Arab world, but is rather a universal phenomenon. Deeds and gestures tend to tap into the most positive emotions that are buried and waiting to be reignited in all of us. This is why our highly symbolic interfaith discourses in Syria have been received so well, and have been seen as unthreatening by the authorities. It is a natural human response to honor. In addition, the discourse has not focused on argumentation but on basic needs of Syrian civilization, such as aid to the poor, investment, tourism, and new cultural openings.

In this sense, symbolic deeds do not always need to address a future *political* vision. The difficulties politically will undoubtedly surface and cause conflict on your trips, and you must be prepared for this. And it is also the case that political discussion and debate is fundamental to any deep address of structural problems locally or regionally. These discussions and debates will come, and you will aggressively engage these issues in private, and you will prepare the way for more formal negotiations by doing so. But moral deeds, gestures of care and respect, require initially no common political vision. *Moral gestures are not sufficient by themselves to solve political and military conflicts, but they are essential to creating the right atmosphere in which to do so.*

This is what is constantly missing in official diplomacy and interventions. There is a disdain for cultural, moral, and psychological context, for addressing basic human needs and appealing to the most basic emotions of enemies. There is an illusion that diplomacy is about getting a deal, a contract between a few leaders in utter isolation from their people. But politics, East and West, is really about masses of people and their impact directly or indirectly on what is politically possible.

Political peace contracts are therefore about relationships with large numbers of people who commit to something, which means it is also about consensus. Consensus and relationships are about trust and seeing the humanity of the other. This simply cannot be done without the power of the moral deed, as well as the power of the positive word, that can deepen trust between millions of citizens.

Religion has the *potential* to be helpful here, only because deeds matter so much to religious efficacy. The moral deed is valued unconditionally in religious life. There are some things that the best religious people in history just do and do very well, like passionately engaging the poor, or healing the sick. Unfortunately official diplomacy does not yet see the power and value of tapping into this religious potential as an adjunct to their work. They look at religious extremists and politicized religion and run in the opposite direction (except when states are using religious extremists to further national interests!). I sympathize with the desire of the average liberal diplomat to run from religion; I often want to myself. But this is to surrender to the extremist reduction of religion to political ideology.

When my friends in Israel and Palestine were actively working with one another they had a habit of combining word and deed, and of visiting the sick, and praying for the healing of illnesses of everyone they knew on both sides. Simple people, Arab and Jew, would actually seek out the prayers of these religious peacebuilders because they saw them as holy men and women on both sides.

But it was such a small circle of people who knew about this network! I felt as if I were privy to a secret universe of religious Jews and Palestinians who loved and cared for each other, and if I described it to others, to my family and cousins, they simply would think I had gone mad. It is fine for such quiet societies to exist, but if their existence could be a crucial symbol of change then it is a crime for them to be unknown. It deprives the muddled majority of a symbol and a vision of a different future.

If the diplomats and secular peacemakers of the Palestinian–Israeli conflict, on both sides, had been more flexible, creative, tolerant, and less self-centered, they would have seen the symbolic power of the work of my religious friends. They could have highlighted it in the media and included it at their various ceremonies, but they did not. This wisdom will come slowly to them, but it is inevitable.

Some reading this might see such moral deeds as a smokescreen, as a way to avoid the real conflict on issues that must be addressed, like borders, territory, equal citizenship, compensation, security, and so forth. My experience has been the opposite. It is precisely in formal diplomacy, when relationships are *not* deepened, that the most important issues can be evaded. But when moral deeds proceed between people, the tough political questions always follow. There is a tendency of those who focus on moral deeds to do a lot of listening to each other. There is a valuation of each other and a love for each other that always devolves into listening, which in turn usually leads to a common understanding of perceptions and needs on both sides. That is why moral deeds must be considered in the future as the essential step of all diplomacy.

Visions versus Nightmares, Opportunities versus Obstacles

The next lesson we have learned of moral practices that consistently work is the power of visions versus nightmares, or a focus on opportunities versus obstacles. Visions tend to be moral in nature, focused on justice, fairness, happiness, dignity, and nonviolent relations between groups and nations. But visions are rarely delved into deeply in politics, and this is a profound error.

There is a tendency in diplomacy, especially if its methodology is rooted in academia, to focus on problems and problem-solving. This in turn is rooted in the tendency of the scientific method to be reduced in the West today to what I would call the technological method. The great sciences, such as physics, are about vision, whereas technology is about fixing things, fixing problems. Of course, true science must be tested in the real world with the aid of technology, but it is not technology itself and it is not about fixing things. It is about vision. Science and technology are not the same at all. Let me explain.

I remember that one of the reasons I had a hard time with physics in high school was not so much the equations as much as the fact that the equations were a way to capture an artistic act, a way of painting the universe with numbers. I understood biology as pure observation of the body, but I did not understand at the time how much of modern physics is an artistic creation of possible universes. Understanding this provides a clue as to how to wed pragmatism and vision.

Diplomacy at its best should be about the artistic creation of the pragmatically possible in human relations; it should be about the construction of possible human universes. Diplomacy requires a healthy dose of pragmatism that is combined with the fundamentally optimistic human appetite for vision of what is yet to be.

Problem-solving, by contrast, comes out of a technical instinct to fix what is broken. But fixing what is broken has a habit of not fixing but being just fixated on what is broken and nothing more. If you are doing conflict resolution and you become fixated on what is broken, then you are as bad off as the people you are trying to help who are caught up in fixations—fixations on the past, fixations on small differences, fixations on selective perceptions of everything that is evil in their adversaries.

That is why citizen diplomacy needs to help assuage the predilection of formal diplomacy, negotiations, and conflict resolution, to fixate on problems that cannot be solved. That is also why at one point a religious citizen diplomat said to me, when referring to working with a very irrational leader, "the most important path to peace here is to recognize that there is no solution for him. When you stop thinking of the problems and solutions then you will know what to do with him." His answer was an exclusive focus on exalted visions and honor, not on problems. And he got further in trust-building with that irrational leader than anyone else had.

I would argue that when you articulate a vision and suspend problem fixation it tends to release a power in the brain that becomes much more adept at problem-solving later on. It is as if problem-solving requires temporarily ignoring problems for the brain to become more flexible and plastic through vision and imagination.[2] This may be due to the fact that a fixation on problems tends to magnify their significance out of all proportion with reality.

Another reason I have come to question the problem-solving approach is that it is particularly unfriendly to traditional nationalist, cultural, or religious mindsets. Millions of people by middle age have become hardwired to a view of life in which their nation, or their culture, or their religion (or all three, God help us!) can do no wrong. Many in my family feel this way, and it seems hardwired.

It is fine to hope that "cooler heads will prevail," that diplomacy will be carried out by people more willing to compromise than the masses. But this ends up being an elitist notion, a secret hope that we can get away with peacemaking when no one is looking, despite the hopeless bigotry of the masses. But this is to disdain the very people you are trying to help, and it is to disrespect their instincts. If the majority does not trust each other on both sides then perhaps the problem is not only with them but also with our feeble efforts at trust-building. Perhaps we failed to give them evidence of a better future before they got hardwired to disbelief and bigotry. Perhaps their instincts for the scientific method are better than those of the elite: they want evidence of a possible future, not problem-solving. Why is that so unreasonable?

There is a compelling alternative to this stalemate. A positive and compelling vision of the future, well articulated, with evidence through deeds of its possibility, is capable of enticing far more of the masses to buy into the future. At least it may make many more people stop and think whether or not they can admit faults on their own side.

Let us take an example. The differences between the Israeli position and the Syrian position on what is needed to be given back in the Golan were relatively minor in the last decades. Most everything was agreed to.[3] Now I am sure at the time of negotiation that the differences between the Israeli and Syrian positions were significant to both sides at the negotiating table. But that was not the crucial problem that divided the sides and made the deal *politically* impossible. One thing that was clearly lacking was a persuasive *popular* vision of a new relationship and a transformed Middle East that people on both sides could embrace. No one made that articulation an essential part of the process, with evidence that it was already being set in motion. But if the political leaders and third parties had done so it is quite possible that the enthusiasm of people on both sides would have made the differences at the negotiating table seem much smaller.

Someday these differences will seem silly. The Shaaba Farms?[4] A couple of hundred meters at Lake Tiberias?[5] How can any two countries continue to war, continue to sacrifice their children on the battlefield, continue to destroy Lebanon[6] and waste thousands of lives over these small differences? These differences are paramount *only* because the grand vision has not been attractive enough to the masses, and those in charge of peacemaking have not cared. A grand vision of Syria in peace and prosperity with a viable Palestinian state to the south is something that can work together in the popular mindset with a vision of Syria at peace with its neighbors, both Lebanon and Israel.

This is precisely what we have tried to articulate in our work in Syria. We did not attack the past behavior of Syria or focus on problems and crimes on all sides; indeed we could not in the present political atmosphere. But we were free to dream and make those dreams attractive. I come to Syria from two enemy entities, America and the Jewish people, both of whom are perceived to be against Syria and to single-mindedly support whatever Israel does. (Most of the Jewish establishment organizations enthusiastically embrace all Israeli policies, actually being to the right of Israel's center, even when innocent Arab lives are lost.[7]) Indeed the Jewish establishment organizations in America have been at the forefront of pushing sanctions against Syria. So the enemy groups, as far as Syrians are concerned, are clear.

With my identity as an American and a Jew quite clear I then articulated a vision of peace, coexistence, a two-state solution for Israel and Palestine, and wealth for average Syrians through tourism, through trade globally and regionally, and through an investment in their oldest and most venerated cultural treasures, like Old Damascus. In so doing I found that I could immediately create bridges even to proud nationalists. There is nothing like promoting business for Syrians, and it is an inherently respectful and caring gesture. And it will eventually form a bridge to their Israeli neighbors. But it cannot be a bribe to abandon fellow Arabs, such as the Palestinians. It must be in the context of a dignified peace settlement.

Hind Kabawat's website, before I got to know her, seemed to me to be more of a nationalist tour guide to Syria. The pride was palpable, and Hind is one of the proudest Syrians I have ever met—and that includes many Ba'athists I know. In fact, we have arguments about this, or miscommunications, because I tend, in private, not to be very proud of anything, and rather self-critical. For me it is easier to have a discussion of everything that is wrong in Syria, America, and Israel. But that is just me and my psychology, or my disappointment with humanity. But I know now that peace and diplomacy must be able to work equally well for optimists, nationalists, and visionaries, as well as it works for problem-solvers, worriers, self-critics, social critics, and nonnationalists. Most peacemakers that I know, including me, are in the latter category and they tend to monopolize peacemaking. But we must have room through shared positive visions for everyone.

Instinctively I began adjusting my vision to Hind's need for positive vision, aligning a common vision of what Syria, the Middle East, and Arab culture could be, and that was the first and most important bridge to her. I have unconsciously emphasized this possible future in every public appearance on Syrian television. On the whole, people crave pride in their heritage, not in the military prowess or deadly capacities of their security forces. But no one enthusiastically embraces cutting down their own identity. The response to a positive moral vision, by contrast, has been universally enthusiastic and grateful. The American Left needs to learn this as well in their critique of the United States. And President Barack Obama's lightening rise is proof of how much Americans crave a positive and hopeful vision.

In addition, positive visions of the future are far more compelling for the religious and cultural imagination. Religious people tend to reject collective self-criticism, or criticism of their religious culture, despite the much vaunted monotheistic commitment to confession and repentance.

Religious people do love fantasy and vision, however. Especially the Abrahamic family of religions loves fantasies of the future. The problem is what those fantasies are. They can be nightmares or visions; they can be dark or bright, inclusive and generous, or exclusive and violent. It is all up to the attractiveness and persuasiveness of the vision. Thus, when religious people, clerics or otherwise, articulate an inviting, tolerant, and generous vision of the future it taps into many positive cultural and psychological instincts for dreaming and fantasy.

If that fantasy is exclusively materialistic it will only go so far. If it is both materialistic and spiritual it will attract that many more people. That is why we have in the Syria work combined visions of material prosperity with visions of interfaith cooperation, social justice, and tolerance in all of our programs and speeches. And the beauty of these visions is that they do not directly threaten the powers that be in any state, even though the implications ethically in terms of human rights and a new social contract are quite apparent to all who think about it.

We are always insinuating into public events words like civil society, equality, pluralism, and tolerance. We are talking about a new Middle East, but without overt threats to any regimes or political systems. These are dreams based on evolution of a moral spirit rather than revolution of the political order, but their implications politically are obvious. I have learned that subtlety and indirectness of this sort is the only form of intervention in the Middle East that stands even a remote chance of success.

What this implies is a new method of citizen diplomacy and conflict resolution involving what I might term "vision negotiation." It would involve select citizens from all sides of a conflict who have become networked into trusting relationships to start spreading a vision of the future, with a number of carefully conceived elements that attract the broadest possible constituencies to this future.[8]

Engage Religion and the Spiritual Dimension of the Human Being with Enthusiasm—And with Great Caution

There is a strong correlation of our engagement in religion and the use of ethical language and ethical precepts. It is easy to appeal to religion and ethics in the same breath, and it helps justify an appeal to ethics for a broad range of audiences, both religious and secular. This works well in the Middle East.

One of the most difficult balancing acts of my interventions in the last twenty-five years, however, has been forging an independent path of simultaneous engagement with and distance from organized religion. I have tried to highlight to secular academia, policy makers, and diplomats, the missing piece of religious persuasion in the arguments for peace among populations. I have tried, at the same time, to warn them of too close a relationship between religion and state, the invasion of religion by political ideology, and the need to engage only select religious leaders and positive religious messages without disenfranchising vulnerable citizens, such as women and homosexuals, who may be at the mercy of religious establishments.

I have succeeded in being misunderstood therefore by everyone, both religious and secular. There is a rebellious part of me that would get nervous if I were *not* misunderstood. I seem to take delight in even my closest political allies not quite getting what I am doing, especially in the Jewish world. Curiously, I have more colleagues in the Christian and Islamic world who understand this balancing act.

Perhaps it is because Christians and Muslims have centuries of experience in which they both embrace their spirituality and are skeptical of their religious establishments at the same time. The Jewish community has tended, unfortunately in this century, to be either radically pro or anti their religious establishments, with those experimenting with middle positions representing a rather small minority. This is especially the case because Israel became an iconic symbol of survival and permanence for the Jewish establishment, an establishment that was traumatized by the loss of 90 percent of European Jewry and its failure to prevent that loss. The majority of Jews in the twentieth century also lost homelands—or any notion of home—from Poland to Yemen. My family has absolutely no memory or sense of homeland in the Ukraine. It is blotted out, and maybe for good reason, but the result is complicated. Israel, instead of being simply a state, something to be critically evaluated—like Christians and Muslims evaluate their regimes and countries—has become the only religious hope of Jewish survival for millions of people.

History has taught me to worry about states founded on ethnic identity. As far as Israel is concerned, I never wanted my work in Israel and Palestine to place more power in the hands of clerics because I did not see them as forces that would encourage greater human rights, democracy, and historic compromises for peace. On the contrary, I wanted to help religious peace-makers, clerical or lay, to gain more prominence to bypass most clerics who were militant. I hoped they could create a greater constituency for peace and justice. I thought that eventually this could lead to new pluralistic states on both sides of the Green Line[9] of Israel and Palestine, new states that did not coerce anyone religiously. I always believed that this reality would be the greatest gift to the future of the Judaism that I believed in.

The past twenty-five years have proven that the greatest benefactor of an unresolved Palestinian and Israeli reality has been militant, political religion,[10] and their political parties who have capitalized on the fears and miseries of this ongoing war; it has only served to strengthen their militant hold on everyone's lives.

The Jewishness of Israel,[11] furthermore, continues to become more wea-ponized and militarized as a vehicle of excluding Arabs.[12] The concept of a "Jewish state" could, under better circumstances, mean to Jews a benign, nonpolitical renaissance of Jewish culture in the ancient Holy Land; this is if Israel could be seen as a democratic state for all its citizens. If the latter were how most Jews defined a Jewish state there would be far less of a quarrel with the idea of a Jewish state, as long as there was an equal Palestinian state across the Green Line. But this is not the way political religion is being played out on either side of the Green Line. Religion for a significant number of people is justifying theft, racism, and disdain for non-Jewish life on the Jewish side, and suicide and murder on the Muslim side of the Green Line.

This is why I sympathize with Israeli and Palestinian secularists but disagree with their strategy of change that excludes religious people. My engagement with Israeli and Palestinian clerics was always highly selective, engaging those who truly were open to peace and coexistence, and there are many. At the same time, I had to face the reality that most of even the peaceful clerics on both sides were far more conservative than I, and often interested in achieving or maintaining some religious control over people's lives. I engaged them nevertheless because I believed—and still believe—that across the world religion is more benign and less violent when basic human needs for dignity, equality, and safety have been satis-fied, or are at least moving in the direction of satisfaction. That is why it is essential for citizen diplomacy and conflict resolution to help create liberal–conservative coalitions to achieve those ends.

When it comes to Syria we were faced with some similar dilemmas. On the one hand, we have engaged conservative clerics of every persuasion. We have had wonderful programs with their full participation. I have not engaged them in discussions about theocracy, homosexuality, the salvation status of people not of their faith, or any other major theological divides. I have certainly recognized that I have to watch my words when it comes to evolution, for example.

On the other hand, I have not reached out to political religion, religious parties, or members of Hamas and Hezbollah. In part it was because I have a strong antipathy to religious parties in every country, including Israel, that have a violent agenda. In part, it was because engaging these radical groups might cut me off from others. Mostly my intuition led me to focus on clerics and lay people, both liberal and conservative, who have a fundamental respect for the state as an organizing construct for the social contract. But I was very tempted to engage radicals.

It is not easy to understand my own motivations as I made these tough political/moral choices. Self-examination is required constantly to check whether there are legitimate moral arguments that can be made for what you are doing, but also to check whether you have slipped over into prejudices and fears.

I am well aware that Hamas and Hezbollah are major players—and spoilers—in the Arab–Israeli conflict, and that not engaging them may be a mistake. I have worked with diplomats and others who do engage them, and I am all for that. I simply had to draw my own boundaries, and I think that the use of suicide bombing by Hamas, attacks on civilians by Hezbollah, and their stated commitment to creating intolerant theocracies, made it harder for me to be motivated to reach out to them with the kind of citizen diplomacy that I want to do. It may also be that the combination of extreme violence against innocents together with fervent religion is so offensive to me that I doubted whether I could work well with them. I have not worked well with Jewish Israeli radicals who fit this mold either. That does not mean that I think no one should work with them, or that I will not change my approach in the future. Perhaps I have not evolved enough as a peacemaker.

I think that I have concluded that, ethically speaking, I want in my interventions to create the broadest possible coalition for a shared public space in which at least the potential of equal civil rights is present. I fundamentally doubt that any religious political parties or violent religious groups who do not believe in states can get us to that space. It will have to be a coalition of religious and secular people of a variety of religious backgrounds who agree on a common space of society to share.

At the same time, I speak to everyone when spoken to. But I tend to focus my citizen diplomacy, coalition-building, and conflict resolution on nonviolent religious and secular people who want to build a pluralistic egalitarian society together without religious coercion. I am loath to overtly and publicly demonstrate support for religious movements that are inherently coercive. My intuition, therefore, based on experience, history, and observation in many places is that supporting a diverse interfaith collection of religious and secular centrists will cause the least amount of suffering and the greatest amount of happiness for the greatest number of people;

it is they who stand the best chance of building a democratic, egalitarian society. I will address below the foundations of this ethical "consequentialist" position.[13] It is also the case, however, that many of my friends who have engaged radical groups often find more agreement on these issues than one might assume. I have found recent evidence of this in my relations as well.

Recall that we began the book with a distinction between methods aimed at the short term and those aimed at the long term. My sense is that the approach outlined here, which is characterized by an openness to everyone but an aggressive effort to support a shared religious/secular vision of an equal social contract for all, is the best combination of short- and long-term strategies.

ADDRESSING DILEMMAS OF INTERVENTION: FIRST STEP TOWARD A COMMON ETHICAL DISCOURSE

This brings us to our next topic of addressing the dilemmas of intervention. As just mentioned, it is helpful to be at least familiar with the variety of ethical schools of thought to manage some of the choices that one has to face.

We have had a legion of ethical questions in our work, too many to list really. But I will list some of them to share the full challenge of citizen diplomacy, as well as the reason why moral reflection and self-examination are essential for its success. I will frame these as questions:

When are my actions putting my colleagues in these societies at risk for their lives, their careers, their friendships? How do I measure what is an acceptable risk? What if they are willing to risk themselves but I am not? Do I always defer to their judgment? Sometimes? Never? Is it a matter of principle or risk calculation? What is the point at which it is worth risking the future of all the work for some dramatic impact at a critical juncture, such as the choice between one dramatic moment in which to impact global opinion, a media moment that risks the future of the quieter work?

Let us say that by showing respect for government authorities I may be letting them use me for propaganda, but I am using them to open up lines of communication between enemies that would never have taken place. How do I measure how much good comes from cooperating with authorities versus the costs? If I remain pure I cannot effect any positive change. How much do I defer to local human rights activists who want no cooperation with the authorities? Do I defer to them as locals, or do I determine that they are excellent and brave in human rights activity but not necessarily in the kind of diplomacy that will lead to peace? What if their position is contradicted by other locals who support our work and intervention? Who is more right? Do I need minimally to be working with some locals, and if not then my intervention is arrogant interference? What do I do when I sense that authorities have interfered aggressively with a meeting and with my relationships with certain people? Do I protest and ruin the whole intervention?

How much do I put myself at risk in this work? Does it matter that I have young children? Do I have the right to risk my life for this work if I have dependents and loved ones?

How much do I owe my country or my religious group? Do I meet with someone who will take me over some red line beyond which my country or virtually all of my people will consider me a traitor? And all for results that cannot be foreseen or guaranteed? How do you make that kind of calculation?

How much time from my job do I forfeit for this work? How much of the field work can be considered part of my work as a conflict resolution professor and how much is going too far, neglecting students and colleagues back home?

Do I accept funds to get me from one place to the other, or do I continue to take from my own pocket? What if the funds are from the American government, which immediately makes one suspect? Do I continue to impoverish myself because people on the ground will unjustifiably suspect me? And is this a moral question or a question of strategy and prudence? It is both. It is a moral question how much of my own resources I give up, but it is a prudential question about how much risk taking money for travel puts on my mission.

How much do I voluntarily censor my words so as not to offend anyone with what I believe to be true? Is this right, dishonest, prudent, because the goals of the mission—peace and justice—are more important than truth-telling? How far do I take this? Do I lie regularly or do I just not say the whole truth, something that most professionals do every day?

How and when do I surrender competing ethical goals, such as women's equality or gay rights, when I am establishing relationships with conservative people and conservative societies?

What gives me the right to interfere in other people's problems? Do I have an obligation to, not a right? What would be the basis of that obligation; how far does it go; and how can I balance that with obligations to myself? Are mixed motives for doing or not doing a particular act merely a problem for Immanuel Kant, or do mixed motives interfere with legitimate moral intentions and calculations? Specifically, is it bad if some intervention is both good for my career and good for the people I am trying to help? Do I have to have only the purest of motives for an act to be ethical? Is it, on the contrary, actually moral to pursue my own interests as well, a fulfillment of self-care, as in Hume's approach to moral sense theory, or is self-interest illegitimate as a violation of Kant's Categorical Imperative? How then to operationalize *anything* if adhering to Kant's strict standards, which appear to be somewhat superhuman? Or are Kant's strictures simply meant as a good reminder of the need to act, *for the most part*, on universal, altruistic principles?

What about the emotional cost of getting involved with so many people on both sides of a war, such as what I experienced during the latest Lebanon war, or meeting face to face with survivors of Abu Ghraib? I got sick in the summer of 2006 and landed in an emergency room, after listening to people on the phone pleading with me for help, from the West Bank to Northern Israel, to Syria, all in danger or whose families were in danger, all suffering, pleading with me to do something in Washington to stop the madness. I think of those moments now, two years later as I write these lines, and my stomach ties up in knots. The feeling of helplessness and outrage were unbearable for me. How far is it right to take this work of always being in the middle, between enemies, or between aggressors and victims, especially when aggressors include people from my own family, before it all eats away at my soul? If you do the work with the "armor" of good spiritual methods of processing the pain of others, then the answer may veer one way. But what if you do this work without any armor, with no protection of your deeper self? When is it too much to justify?

These are just a few of the questions that have plagued me and aged me. This work gets very real sometimes, with friends getting into trouble with authorities half a world away, and you cannot even talk about it on the phone. The sense of helplessness on such occasions is staggering. The reality is that I get through these situations with intuition, mistakes, and a kind of calculation that is always going on in my head. It is a form of moral consequentialism that I will describe below. But before I go into an effort to define my own method of calculating, I want to frame this in the context of a larger discussion on the problems and possibilities of a global moral discourse. Specifically, is it possible for us to have this transcultural, global conversation today on the rights and wrongs in every question I have raised? Or am I just sharing a peculiar, idiosyncratic approach limited to me?

The Search for a Common Global Ethical Discourse across Civilizations and Religions

One of the problems that we have faced in the United States (but I believe it is true of Western civilization in general) is that the discussion of moral values was co-opted by the conservative right. The progressive democratic experiment of the United States has lost the masses to reactionary, so-called "values-based politics." But the problem is that the divide between left and right in the United States is not over whether values are relevant but about *which* values are relevant. The Left has failed consistently to acknowledge this and therefore lost the mainstream of the country.

In 2008 there was a chance to recover some of those losses because the White House became so extreme, beyond the mainstream of the country. The Left has traditionally seen the mixture of ethics and political discourse as the handmaiden of repressive power structures (the Marxist critique), or a violation of absolute individualist freedom (the liberal and libertarian argument), or as a threat to science and objective inquiry (the intellectual elite's argument).

All of these arguments were misplaced because values underlay every one of those positions. The liberal fixation on freedom is based on a moral conclusion that human freedom is the great guarantor of all other human goods and values, and that sometimes society has to resist legislating other specific moral values precisely because freedom is too easily destroyed by state interference. That is a moral position involving an almost exclusive embrace of the freedom of human beings. Marxism, admitting it or not, has its roots in a commitment to compassion and justice for the poor and underclass. At the same time, communism's surrender of all other virtues to pursue the often violent creation of a classless society has proved disastrous from a moral point of view. Finally, even the so-called objective values-neutral scientist actually values truth and freedom of inquiry above all else; simultaneously he looks at the history of legislating morality and sees only tyranny and torment in its wake and prefers the absolute freedom of inquiry and thought. But that is a moral argument!

Whatever position one takes on these matters, I am arguing that progress toward global community will require a fight for the label of "ethical," a fight to secure values as not just the property of religious fundamentalism. As that fight is engaged it will become clear that politicized or weaponized religion with its claims on virtue and justice will be shown to be morally inadequate. A fundamentalist cry of injustice that intends to enforce a system that dehumanizes homosexuals is not a just system at all. Its repressive expressions will be seen in the long run as hollow. But this will happen only if everyone engages the moral argument, and demonstrates the moral underpinnings of their political positions.

There is no substitute for an effort to create a global conversation on morality. That conversation is essential if the emerging global documents of global community, like the Universal Declaration on Human Rights, are to be buttressed by a global engagement in debate about the *inalienable obligations* we have to each other, as well as the inalienable rights. This is an essential step on the path to global community.

We have been missing, for example, a good global community discussion on terrorism. We could have come to a position of agreeing on the deliberate killing of civilians as an international crime and a moral evil. We could have held states, individuals, and nonstate militias equally accountable. Instead we have allowed disingenuous official representatives of states, rogue states—as well as extremists and common criminals—to obfuscate on this crucial issue, covering up their own crimes, and letting all of us flounder in a world that seems to lack consensus on murder. But in fact the global community was never even given a chance to try.

We need global moral debates and discussions, and my experience suggests that consensus is more possible than states and radical groups want us to think on matters such as "terrorism." If you get rid of the word "terrorism" I suspect that the vast majority of people on the planet agree that the deliberate targeting of civilians is murder, and that the negligent targeting of combatants in such a way that most casualties are civilians is either negligent homicide or a war crime in itself. This condemns most parties to war, but it also opens the way for rules of engagement that are more humane; this in turn opens the door to principles and strategies of de-escalation. Citizen diplomats can pave the way in global discussions on these matters. They are the ultimate connectors, unbeholden to states or extremist groups, who can stimulate a global conversation and debate which will eventually lead to consensus. This is how earlier conventions like the Geneva Conventions were formed. At first they were fantasies of individuals, and then with global conversation they moved closer and closer to consensus.

Considerations of Ethical Guidelines for Intervention

Intervention in citizen diplomacy and conflict resolution requires engagement with a competing set of moral principles and goals. There is no one principle that can handle all circumstances. I want to offer a variety of principles that may be helpful in dealing with the complexity of intervention:

- "Do no harm."[14] In other words, studiously avoid damage while supposedly doing good. It is far better and less arrogant to do no harm than to do what is good in your opinion while doing a great deal of damage.
- Defer to as many of those you are trying to help as possible, and balance their conscience with yours. There is a greater moral authority built into those who are on the ground. But never completely surrender your conscience, especially when it comes to actively doing something that you believe is destructive or wrong.
- Always engage the tough calculations of competing principles and goals even if it is a painfully imperfect human enterprise. It is far better

to attempt to satisfy several principles rather than to adhere slavishly to one. This allows for flexibility, which is one of the most important qualities in dealing with ever-changing circumstances.

- Face moral complexity and ambiguity squarely to increase self-examination and to inculcate humility in intervention; this helps to avoid both secular and religious forms of dogmatism.
- Do not be afraid of or ashamed of a mixture of personal and altruistic motives. There is nothing wrong with pursuing multiple goods at once and nurturing your career, your reputation, or your psyche. There is something very wrong with not acknowledging to yourself and trusted others that you are doing so; you need this practice of acknowledgment to prevent mixed motives from turning into purely self-serving choices. This easily happens as interventions get harder and murkier.
- Know that staying consistently decent and unblemished in indecent situations is unlikely. Therefore be prepared to recover from moral failure if you want to invest for the long term in the people you are trying to help.

Advice Based upon Classical Western Schools of Ethical Thought

The effort to develop universal standards of citizen diplomacy and intervention will not be easy. Here are some overarching ethical schools of thought to consider as part of how you formulate your own ethical guidelines:

- Embrace Kantian approaches that emphasize the identification of universal principles to be applied to every situation, such as the maxim, "Do no harm," discussed above. There are drawbacks in terms of flexibility to circumstances, to unique cultural and cross-cultural situations.
- Embrace consequentialism in evaluating morally all of your actions. Consequentialist approaches emphasize a calculation of all the consequences of one's actions and whether they promote (depending on the theory) more or less happiness in the world. This has drawbacks in terms of the difficulty of calculating and anticipating all the future consequences of one's actions—an impossible task. There are also drawbacks in terms of the needs of minorities who might be harmed for the sake of the greater happiness of the majority.[15]
- Embrace the classical moral senses. Moral sense theory focuses on the essential role of positive emotions in evaluating morally all situations. The positive importance of love, compassion, respect, and honor come to mind, and have sometimes been the most important factor motivating our work and evaluating its efficacy. This has drawbacks in deal-

ing with complex cases where such emotions may not be enough of a
guide to calculate what to do.[16]

- Embrace the long-term objective of strengthening the social contract as
  your principal guide to intervention. This ethical position is founded
  on what I would call the social contract approach to intervention that
  is the unwritten assumption behind the work of many international
  agencies. The emphasis is on stimulating and building the structural
  foundations of the good society, the open society. The drawbacks here
  are that this gives you precious little guidance on the gray areas of specific interventions and the unique moral dilemmas that will ensue. This
  can turn out therefore to be dangerously imperialistic, driven from the
  outside, without a calculation of consequences for people's lives or risk
  to life and limb on the ground in each circumstance. It is long on vision and weak on specific circumscriptions to one's behavior. Indeed,
  as these social contract goals become bureaucratized the danger is that
  bureaucrats will follow through with well-funded programs that are
  clearly doing more harm than good. But no one stops them because
  the intervention does not demand it morally by its nature. It is too
  focused on some distant goal and not on immediate consequences.
  Examples include: women's programs that help women in the short
  term but that create extremist backlash against them; development
  projects that get people killed or that make a few rich and others very
  poor, that increase corruption and thus undermine the foundations
  of the society for whom you are building the roads or the schools;
  projects that destroy the environment and destroy cultural identities
  that are tied to that environment. All of this can be justified in terms
  of building the liberal society and the global social contract, but they
  violate all of the other moral schools: Kantian rules, consequentialist
  calculations, and the moral senses. This is the great danger of the mas-
  sively funded state-based programs of international development that
  fail to carefully monitor the consequences of their interventions.
- Be open to and inclusive of the parallels between secular ethical philosophical approaches and religious covenantal approaches. There needs
  to be an interaction of secular ethical methods of conflict intervention
  and religious categories of ethics and intervention. Some examples:
  There is a parallel of Kantianism and absolute religious moral standards. There are parallels of consequentialism and religious values in
  peacemaking, such as calculating what will lead to the greatest amount
  of lives saved, to fulfill a covenant with God to protect all of creation
  and every human life. There are parallels between the efficacy of love
  and compassion in moral sense theory and foundational principles of
  imitation of God in liberal Christianity and the path to enlightenment
  in Buddhism. Social contract theory has many roots in biblical and

koranic approaches to the centrality of treaty, *brit*, power sharing, consensus of the people, *shura*, division of powers, and systems of checks and balances on human power. There is no reason therefore that your interventions cannot be framed in a way that is as attractive to religious traditionalists as it is to secular progressives.

My Own Ethic of Intervention

Most of what I have done in the last twenty-five years in terms of intervention as a citizen diplomat I have done with an intuitive effort to harmonize all the guidelines just listed with the philosophical schools. Based on the circumstances, I have adjusted my decisions of intervention at various times to emphasize some of the paragraphs over others.

I have had many partners in my citizen diplomacy work over the years, including my dear friends Bryan Hamlin, Joe Montville, Yehezkel Landau, Rabbi Frohman, Eliyahu Mclean, Robert Eisen, and, of course, Hind Kabawat. I think that I have gravitated to people who intuitively understand the balancing act of drawing upon at least a number of the guideposts listed above.

It is a given of having many guideposts that partners will disagree on what path to take, and what nuanced positions to experiment with at any given time. Naturally, conflict resolution with partners is at least as important as the work that you do together on other people's conflicts. But, as Proverbs recorded, "Two are better than one" in terms of discovering the wisest path in any situation.[17] It is also a given that this work is trial and error with many variables that are impossible to predict.

Upon reflection I have been surprised that when the circumstances of some interventions get the darkest and most absurd, the moral senses such as love of enemies, patience, tolerance, and compassion have become central to my response. I have worked on cultivating this in myself and with my partners, only succeeding from time to time. I have the strongest of these intuitions precisely for members of groups that hate me, and the least amount of this capacity for my own communities, be it Americans, Jews, or Abrahamic co-religionists. I find the same trend in fellow peacemakers. We are most outraged and embarrassed by our own group's behaviors, perhaps because we are fighting the same tendencies in ourselves that we see in members of our group, at least in the privacy of our own thoughts and instincts. It is easier for me to remember to care for a dangerous man from another group because his behavior does not reflect on me, nor does it embarrass me. This means that it is vital that as friends we peacemakers from enemy communities work with each other constantly, help each other with our weaknesses and intolerances, and help each other to love our own group, no matter how embarrassed we get by their violence.

I have also come to realize how essential balance and flexibility are, as has been attested to by the great ethicists in history.[18] I remember on my trip in the spring of 2007 to Damascus that I was adhering too much to one principle, and Hind would remind me as we raced through Damascus in taxis, "Remember, flexibility is the key." Then there were times when she was so angry at a gross injustice, and at someone who was so outrageous in his treatment of others, and I would say to her, "Remember, Jesus loved his enemies. And this is the only thing that will ever change that man's heart." It gave her pause, because Jesus is central to her. And so we reminded each other intuitively of the delicate balancing act of all these principles and intuitions.

I have been amazed at how important Kant is in my life when I realize that there are red lines that I cannot cross. I want to immediately withdraw from any aspect of an intervention if I feel that a partner is at risk, even if the partner insists on continuing. I cannot defer to them, and it seems to come from a bedrock principle of doing no indelible harm to the innocent, no matter how much good may come out of our work in the long run.

This is a good example to examine more deeply. This red line is either an emotional moral sense, or it is a principle that if the whole enterprise is about the principle of saving human lives then *a fortiori* I cannot put at risk the most precious lives to me, that is the lives of peacemakers who are already risking everything. But maybe my reaction is simply a determination that I could not live with the guilt if they were harmed! Maybe I just could not take that emotionally. This remains murky.

If this sounds like a messy intuitive combination it is because it is. Practical morality as it inhabits our minds and hearts is far messier than the scholars and philosophers want to admit, with perhaps the exception of Simone de Beauvoir, referred to earlier.

As I seek to reflect more on what I have done, perhaps I "check in" with many schools of ethics listed above, and with wisdom traditions that I will explore in the next chapter, including my own religious wisdom tradition; then I add up the weight of which way to go. I always engage, however, in calculations of all possible effects and consequences. That is why for me scouring the news and analysis every day is an ethical act and a psychological obsession. I need to know as much as possible to prognosticate the effects at any given time of my interventions, of symbols, of emotional appeals, of powerful deeds and words, and of their pragmatic possibilities.

I also stay in touch with policy makers and intelligence people to never stray far from what is real as I calculate very imperfectly the possible effects of our actions. In this sense I have determined that consequentialism is something absolutely essential and pragmatic, even though our calculations of the effects of our actions are at best approximations.

I feel strongly that weighing at any given time what will bring the greatest positive effects[19] to the greatest number of people is the most indispensable principle to adhere to in determining the value of a conflict intervention. The experience of making these calculations is weighty and nerve-wracking. And yet I find it distinctly more realistic and responsible than the naïve application of Kantian principle or moral intuitions to every situation without regard to its effects. Perhaps I should emphasize feminism in every encounter with every conservative because it is right. Perhaps I should "speak truth to power" in every conversation because it is right, point out every flaw in every political and military regime. But if I had done that I literally would never have even made it to the border of Syria, nor had any role in the lives of thousands of people in Syria who now have at least debated so many important issues because of my work with Hind and Nizar and many other wonderful people in Syria. Millions of people saw our broadcasts and reflecting on the Middle East in ways that they had never been exposed to before. None of it would have happened if we had stuck in an uncompromising way to those absolute principles. I will let the reader decide right from wrong here, because there are no easy answers.

Another principle I have operated with is negative consequentialism, namely that which will minimize human suffering, and cause the least amount of harm. Both negative and positive consequentialist thinking seem to me to be the most responsible and realistic approach to ethics; they also are most aligned with strategies of nudging realistic politicians and military people to "to do the right thing." What I mean by this is that anticipating consequences is a very realist thing to do, and it is most apt to garner the respect of policy and military people who—when they are competent—are also trying to assess all possible consequences. It is also most possible to cleverly align what is most prudent and most practical with what is the greatest benefit to most people. Most policy makers are not anxious to destroy a country for its own sake. They too want most people satisfied. That is why I have found that evaluating and anticipating the effects of our actions in citizen diplomacy has been a good bridge to conversations with formal diplomats and policy makers in which we can positively influence them.

But sometimes predictions or calculations are impossible. Sometimes there are so many unknowns that it is impossible to choose. Therefore often on the ground I go back to the moral senses when the consequences of actions are impossible to predict.

Furthermore, most moral senses such as love, honor, compassion, or care are not only moral senses, they also qualify as Kantian categorical imperatives. What I mean by this is that they can be universalized, just like the Golden Rule of doing unto others what you want done to you; everyone wants these things for themselves. In all situations—and this is where neoconservative thinking and action is so fundamentally antimoral—love, care, respect, and compassion have seemed to me to be inherently worthy as the essential guideposts of how to engage in interventions, and also how to impact adversaries on all sides.

I have always found that, as long as these lofty feelings are tempered by some consequentialist calculations, the application of moral senses is always productive. They seem to almost always have a good impact. Foolishly, some think that if you talk to an angry, militant person or to a criminal, and respect them, have compassion on them, that somehow you cannot sanction them, embargo them, imprison them, or prepare defenses against them. This is absurd. There is no contradiction between protecting society from rapists, locking them up for a long time, and treating them with great love and respect, searching always for new ways that would effectively cure their rage while they are serving time.

It is the same with war. There is no contradiction between expressing respect, compassion, care, and even love for your enemies and their cultures, while simultaneously preventing them from harming you when all else fails to transform the relationship. This is the balance that we must instill in our souls, in our interventions, and in our policies.

It is the same in the relationship of groups and nations. You can care for government representatives even as you consider them a danger to society or the world, and it is no different on the international scene. You can conclude that a leader is corrupt and dangerous, that society would be better off eventually removing him from office, and yet still have respect and compassion for him, still show him even love. Not only is this an exercise of positive moral senses it often is the best *practical* course of action that will induce change in his behavior, or at least minimize the total suffering that he inflicts.

I have never seen a rational, intelligent argument for the long-term utility of enemy humiliation under any circumstances. Why it is so prevalent in conflict at the hands of so many actors who consider themselves rational and good has only meant to me that they are not facing their emotional need for revenge.

I also always have in the back of my mind a consideration of social contract approaches to ethics. I look for ways that we can encourage the growth of civil society or a renewed social contract. I was always looking in Israel and Palestine for ways to encourage a fundamentally new social contract between Jews and Arabs. In the Syria work everything has been framed in terms of contributions to the growth of civil society, all of the public debates and discussions.

If, however, the other ethical schools are not consulted then social contract building on a communal or international level becomes imperialistic and even violent. Communists and undisciplined capitalists alike are great builders, but they crush countless innocents underfoot in their grandiose plans.

There is a better way and it involves self-control, self-examination, and a qualification of social change by the venerated and time-tested schools of human ethics and wisdom. That is why our efforts to stimulate civil society have always avoided an adversarial approach to authority. It has been an effort to empower citizens, not disempower authorities.

The appeal of focusing always on consideration of consequences has been that it is the most oriented toward creating a new social contract in the future. Consequentialism as an ethic is future-oriented, and the most focused on contributing to the transformation of society as a whole. It is, therefore, the most messianic.

What I mean by "messianic" is the spiritual and secular drive to create the "city on the hill," the good society, based upon the belief that we can profoundly improve the human condition on this planet. The religious roots of this idea are clear in the Abrahamic religions, but for me, as for many children of the Abrahamic traditions, the messianic idea is not a prediction rooted in the appearance of one person, but the positive faith in human history and human change. It is not far from many intuitions going back thousands of years to prophets like Amos of Tekoa.

The kind of consequentialism that has been most important to me, therefore, has not been hedonistic utilitarianism, the greatest pleasure for the greatest number,[20] perhaps due to the austerity of my religious upbringing. My own version of consequentialism is rooted in influence from Judaism. I think, more than any thought, as I dare to intervene in the world, how can I save the most lives? What are the consequences of each action I take in terms of leading toward or away from saving the most lives possible from bloodshed and the miserable effects of destructive conflicts? The essential thought is: will my actions lead to the greatest amount of life and safety for the greatest number of people?

Sometimes, however, my approach has been more in a Tibetan Buddhist/consequentialist frame of how to create the greatest amount of compassion and reduce the greatest amount of suffering. For the Dalai Lama and others this formula is characteristic of specific prayers and meditations, but also as a guide to action. The advantage of this formulation, as inspired by the Dalai Lama's formulation, is that its central emphasis is on compassion for oneself that is simultaneous with compassion for all sentient life. Indeed, there are no distinctions between self and all sentient life. That realization of interdependence, or what many in Buddhism oddly call "emptiness," is what generates the boundless compassion. Thus, it is quite sustainable as a formula for intervention because it aims at every moment at nurturing oneself as much as nurturing others. This helps avoid anger, depression, and impatience—all my problems.

The calculus of how to save the most lives, however, that has been inspired by Judaism has profoundly helped me in avoiding the petty pitfalls of peace work; the petty arguments of ego with others; the overfocus on success of "my" programs or institutions, which to me are transitory, rather than staying steadily fixated on how to avoid the next war; how to create an environment that makes the choice for war more difficult; how to put the enemy other at every moment into the face and the heart of his enemy. For Judaism, and for those who honestly observe its precepts, the principle of saving lives trumped all other laws and commandments because God wanted nothing more than for Adam and Eve, his dearest creations, to safeguard all life in the Garden of Eden. And also because every human being saved from needless violence and death is an entire world that has been saved in that moment.

This principle has become for me a way to calculate at every moment what to do and what to say in exceedingly complex spaces between inveterate enemy groups. It has been coupled with an instinct, an intuition, even when I have my doubts about organized religion as such, that every human being is sacred.

It is that bedrock intuition, absorbed from my earliest teachings, that guided me as I sat before a man like Arafat in 2000, and looked into his eyes with the greatest of compassion. I embraced him; I gave him a gift for his child; I shared and studied a text of the Talmud with him on the ethics of war, peace, and justice; and I blessed him—at the same time that he was allowing the killing of my fellow Jews to go on, as well as the robbery of his own people. It hurt me; I was conflicted, but I would do it again, and again, and again. Because I learned from my inspired peacemakers that we reached further into his heart than anyone else had, with love, with respect, with vision, and that, at a critical moment, he demanded an end to attack on civilians by his own people *because* of the relationship that my fellow peacemakers had established with him.

I learned from dear Middle Eastern peacemakers, and from the Dalai Lama, that hatred is poison. It helps no one; it protects no one; it saves no lives; it makes no one happy. But love, freely given to civilizations and even to the most dangerous people, can at the very least do no harm, and sometimes can be the key to the most profound changes of the human heart.

This is what Hind Kabawat and I, and Grand Mufti Hassoun, and Sheikh Shehadeh, Jews, Christians, and Muslims have tried to practice in Syria. It has done no harm; it has done some good and generated some minor miracles. It is the only way, I believe, to pursue this noble work in a complicated world that is starving for compassion, respect, apology, embrace, and vision.

The Integration of Ethics and Wisdom, East and West

One of the drawbacks of ethical schools of thought in determining the best course of action is that these schools of thought, at least in my experience, have been heavily centered on the European philosophical tradition.

That is not a fatal flaw. On the contrary, the world owes a great debt to European thinking from Aristotle to Grotius to Kant. But as we seek the foundations of a global community through citizen diplomacy and explore the role of the citizen diplomat and his/her actions, the groundwork for the discussion cannot be limited to only the European philosophical tradition. Therefore I will explore in the next chapter the reservoir of wisdom literature that comes from the world's great cultures and religions that I have personally drawn upon in dealing with the ethics of intervention. It is woefully idiosyncratic and merely a tiny sampling of wisdom literature. I merely want to share my personal journey of how and to what degree this literature has added to or filled out the approaches we have outlined in this chapter.

NOTES

1. *Ethics of the Fathers* (New York: Bloch Publishing Company, 1965), chap. 1, verse 17.

2. I am interested in the possible relationship between suspending a focus on problems and the paradoxical increase in ability to deal with those problems; I have seen this in my own work and that of other spiritual peacemakers but it needs more study and reflection. Possibly the new research on brain plasticity may eventually illuminate this quality. See Norman Doidge, *The Brain That Changes Itself* (New York: Penguin, 2007). See also Jeffrey Schwartz and Sharon Begley, *The Mind and the Brain: Neuroplasticity and the Power of Mental Force* (New York: HarperCollins, 2003).

3. See Akiva Eldar, "Israeli, Syrian Representatives Reach Secret Understanding," *Haaretz*, January 16, 2007, Allenby/hasen/spages/813817.html (accessed April 15, 2008).

4. See Joshua Mitnick, "Behind the Dispute over Shebaa Farms," *The Christian Science Monitor*, August 22, 2006, at csmonitor.com/2006/0822/p10s01-wome.html (accessed April 15, 2008).

5. Eldar, "Israeli, Syrian Representatives."

6. For a deep, impassioned discussion of Syrian and Israeli (and Palestinian, among others) roles in the Lebanese Civil War see, among many other sources, Robert Fisk's epic *Pity the Nation: The Abduction of Lebanon*, 4th ed. (New York: Nation Books, 2002). On Lebanon caught between the Syrians and the Israelis, see Elias Khoury, "Do I See or Do I Remember," *London Review of Books*, August 3, 2006, at lrb.co.uk/v28/n15/khou01_.html (accessed April 8, 2008).

7. See Martin J. Raffel, "American Jewish Public Affairs and Israel: Looking Back, Looking Ahead," Jewish Council for Public Affairs, at jewishpublicaffairs.org/publications/raffel.html (accessed April 18, 2008).

8. Lederach defines moral imagination, as "To imagine responses and initiatives that, while rooted in the challenges of the real world, are by their nature capable of rising above destructive patterns and giving birth to that which does not yet exist." John Paul Lederach, *The Moral Imagination* (New York: Oxford University Press,

2005), 182. This is what Lederach recommends as essential for parties to a conflict and for intervention. I would argue that when it comes to the construction of global community across many lines of culture, ideology, and class, we must bring together and *negotiate* many such visions of the moral imagination to create that which does not exist yet, the global social contract of the future.

9. This is the line of Israel's pre-1967 borders that has become the basis for negotiations over a future Palestinian state.

10. I define "political religion" as the use of religious constituencies and their religious sentiments to gain political and judicial power over the public space. It is also often associated with groups that want to establish a theocracy. It tends to focus on those aspects of religiosity that control other people's lives, especially women and the nonreligious.

11. Since 1917's Balfour Declaration, Israel has been envisioned by Jews as a "Jewish" state, without that ever being clearly defined. One could argue that therein lies the crux of the conflict. How could it mean in 1917 a majority-Jewish state when 90 percent of the population at the time was Arab? Did it imply population transfers, or did it refer primarily to a place of refuge, with special rights of Jews to citizenship? This has never been clarified, and to this day no one has and no one wants to, it seems, clarify just what Jews in Israel mean by "a Jewish state." It could mean a demographic majority; it could mean culturally Jewish; it could mean a place of refuge for persecuted Jews; or it could mean a place where Jews are privileged. This same question is open-ended in how one would define a Muslim state or a Christian state.

12. The results of a poll published in 2008 by *Haaretz*, conducted by Haifa University, reveals that 50 percent of Israeli Jews surveyed do not want to live near Arabs while 54 percent responded negatively when asked if they had Arab friends. See Fadi Eyadat, "Poll: Nearly 50% of Israeli Jews Don't Want to Live Near Arabs," *Haaretz*, at haaretz.com/hasen/spages/963698.html (accessed April 18, 2008).

13. See the discussion below.

14. See the work of Mary Anderson with the Collaborative Learning Projects and the Collaborative for Development Action Inc., at cdainc.org/dnh (accessed April 17, 2008).

15. It is for this reason that there are, among consequentialists, "rule utilitarians" versus "act utilitarians" who evolve rules based on the primal utilitarian calculus, but that then have to be applied to everyone. This is some middle position between a Kantian, rules-based approach, and a purely consequentialist position. In addition, calculating hedonistic happiness, or the pleasure principle, is not the only approach to utilitarianism. Happiness can be defined in other ways, including the higher pleasure of living by virtues that apply to everyone in a decent society. In addition, the approach of utilitarianism that is focused on the greatest happiness for the greatest number is not the only kind of consequentialism. I will argue later that calculating how to achieve the greatest amount of compassion for the greatest number, or the least amount of suffering for everyone, or how to save the most lives as possible in the long run, are all forms of consequentialist ethical thinking. They are all based on focusing less on the virtue of each of one's acts but instead more on calculating their impact. You try to judge each action as to whether it can create the greatest happiness for the most people, for example, or the least amount

of suffering, or whether it can save the most lives. For an overview of these positions, see Joseph Mendola, *Goodness and Justice: A Consequentialist Moral Theory* (Cambridge and New York: Cambridge University Press, 2006); Ward Edwards, ed., *Utility Theories: Measurements and Applications* (Boston: Kluwer Academic Publishers, 1992); and Harry J. Gensler, *Ethics: A Contemporary Introduction* (London and New York: Routledge, 1998). I am arguing that this approach to ethics makes it the most possible for ethics and political strategy to work together, in that calculating the rational interests of parties to a conflict can also be seen as an ethical act of trying to safeguard the interests and lives of most parties to the conflict.

16. This is where a clever interaction between moral sense theory and consequentialism can be most useful. You may begin with the initial intuition of acting based on love, compassion, or respect. But when things get complicated it may not be clear whether an act can be simply an expression of love. For example, it may show respect for someone to honor them, but at the same time it will put their lives at risk due to jealousy or paranoia by regime authorities. One can then turn to consequentialism and try to calculate all the consequences of one's action and determine whether the moral sense of respect, in this case, will actually lead to the desired impact of those intuitions on the world. Or, put another way in terms more friendly to moral sense theory, if the emotional act of offering public respect leads to the endangerment of someone's life then another moral emotion should become paramount over respect, namely care and love for someone else's life.

17. Ecclesiastes 4:9, 12. "Two are better than one, and the three-fold thread is not easily broken."

18. For example, on balance, harmony, and the mean, see both Aristotle's *Nicomachean Ethics*, W. D. Ross, trans. (Oxford: Clarendon Press, 1908), and Confucius, *The Analects*, Arthur Waley, trans. (New York: Knopf, 2000).

19. There are many schools of thought within consequentialism. The hedonistic focuses on calculating the greatest amount of pleasure. For others today it is calculating what satisfies the greatest number of human preferences, which may have interesting parallels to human needs theory in the field of conflict resolution. On human needs theory, see John W. Burton, ed., *Conflict: Human Needs Theory* (Basingstoke: Macmillan, 1990); for an introduction to consequentialism, see Stephen Darwall, ed., *Consequentialism* (Oxford: Blackwell, 2002). On consequentialism as related to the ethics of justice and retribution, see Anthony Duff, *Punishment, Communication, and Community* (Oxford: Oxford University Press, 2001).

20. See Daniel Holbrook, *Qualitative Utilitarianism* (Lanham, MD: University Press of America, 1988); Samuel Richard Freeman, *Justice and the Social Contract: Essays on Rawlsian Political Philosophy* (Oxford and New York: Oxford University Press, 2007).

7

A Global Ethic of Citizen Diplomacy

LONGING FOR EACH OTHERS' WISDOM

The astonishing thing about the world of peacemakers and citizen diplomats is just how much creative interaction is occurring today between many cultures. I find myself inhabiting worlds in which people, both traditional and progressive, are increasingly comfortable with the cross-fertilization of ideas between many cultures at once.

This growing phenomenon is not just because of the frequency of intercultural and interfaith gatherings, and it is not just based on a natural curiosity about the unknown. It is a conscious intellectual and spiritual effort on the part of many people to understand similar patterns of thinking emerging around the world. There are patterns of thinking and especially sources of wisdom that seem to overlap continually. It is as if we are witnessing today a discovery by humanity of itself.

That passion for discovery is rooted in a sense of incompletion, as if we are looking for a more complete sense of ourselves as human beings by discovering many cultures. In my own journey I broke many barriers to move beyond the narrow confines of my religious upbringing, and I moved toward a deeper understanding of the Christian and Muslim cultures, a project that is still underway. But I also knew that the outer bounds of where I was heading was not limited to the Abrahamic traditions of Judaism, Islam, and Christianity. On the contrary, I am a student of Jewish history, a history that is saturated with the remains of Jewish community after community marred by the inveterate and senseless jealousy of these three children of the biblical world. I knew that there had to be more wisdom out there beyond Abraham's progeny, more wisdom that would help the

Western and Abrahamic worlds to repair the damage that they have caused each other over the centuries.

I know very well that for the lion's share of the last two thousand years Jews were on the receiving end of Abrahamic intolerance and imperialism until the recent past of unprecedented Jewish empowerment. On the other hand, as a student of Jewish texts since I was five, I was keenly aware that the legacy of the Hebrew Bible and the Talmud is also not one of universal tolerance. All three biblically rooted religions have a problem with accepting other religions and other people in their basic right to exist as equals. I had to take some responsibility for that as a Jew who received and transmitted to everyone else the biblical stories of Abraham, the slavery in Egypt, the genocidal orders to conquer Canaan and wipe out entire peoples, and so on.

The truth is that we Abrahamic peoples need some added wisdom of humanity to refocus on our best ethical legacies and circumscribe our worst instincts of prejudice, exclusivity, and patriarchy. The more years I worked in the Middle East, the more I felt that this cradle of Abrahamic civilizations needed the added wisdom of all of humanity, ancient and modern. We needed the wisdom emerging out of the Enlightenment, including from its antireligious critics. And we needed the wisdom of the East and the South to curb our imperialist tendencies.

In a word, the world, east and west, north and south, needs all civilizations and their wisdom to complete the march toward global community. In fact, no one can avoid the very human urges of imperialism and patriarchy without correcting each other.

Reaching globally for wisdom traditions is a crucial step in the application of diplomacy and conflict resolution to many indigenous environments in ways that make sense culturally. But it is also the case that there are flaws and trends in civilizations around the world. No civilization or culture is perfect, and there is no sense in romanticizing about it. This suggests that we need each other to move the human experiment in civilization to a higher level of completion, to its last and most complete social contract. If we enthusiastically seek out each other's wisdom we may discover the way to move beyond our own peculiar flaws and the unfortunate levels of oppression that have occurred in every civilization.

One of the people I support the most in this work is Eliyahu Mclean,[1] a deeply religious Jew living in Jerusalem, a tireless interfaith networker for peace among all groups in Israel and Palestine. I had been trying to help him in small ways for years. He, like all the most courageous peacemakers I know, is relatively unsupported by philanthropy. One day, back in the United States, I caught a video of him in the midst of some of the work. To my astonishment, there he was in Israel with an African chief, scantily clad, who was calmly observing the give and take of dialogue between Jews and Arabs at a retreat in the Galilee.

My first reaction was astonishment; my second quite honestly was why would this man from Africa care about my problems? My third was to wonder to myself what he could contribute, and my fourth reaction—all of them in rapid succession—was to be moved and comforted that this African chief was in Israel.

I must admit that as a Jew I still carry in me thousands of years of tough emotional baggage, and one of those bags is that no one gives a damn about Jews or their fate. "They" (non-Jews) only pay attention to "us" when they need us for something, like business or science or medicine, or when a scapegoat is called for. It moved me that someone from Africa, the cradle of human existence on earth, was coming to witness the suffering of senseless wars, and to try to help out, whatever that help was, even if it was just the symbol of his ancient presence as a blessing for our efforts.

I can still see this chief, calm and attentive, and later in the video I saw him engaging in a spiritual dance. I remember from my youth receiving endless *hasbarah*, public relations information, from Israel about how much technology and help Israel was giving to struggling African nations. Those optimistic images are long gone in my mind, and in many others, as the Jewish–Arab wars for the land continue endlessly. I felt comforted that this man was coming instead as a helper to Israel to try to get it right in human relations—someone with no stake, someone not bought and paid for in political office, and not there for guilt over the Holocaust, just an ancient human, who actually gives a damn about our mess. That moved me, and it made me realize how much we need each other on this planet.

Another lesson in our radical interdependence comes from Thich Nhat Han. He is the great Vietnamese Buddhist teacher, and he is as far from the traditional world I grew up in as one can conceive. After all, he is a Buddhist, and so he would be considered either an atheist or a polytheist and might be considered an idolater from the perspective of traditional monotheism, not someone you were supposed to gain wisdom from, at least according to the traditional world of my upbringing.[2] That has turned out to be so wrong.

I remember once listening to Thich Nhat Han tell a story to a large audience. He was recounting how a young man came to visit him, very frustrated that his spiritual growth and practices were not proceeding fast enough, and the young man was speaking fast and analyzing the entire problem in great detail. Thich Nhat Han looked at him and said, "Here, have one of my oranges." And so the man continued analyzing, tore at the orange, and wolfed it down, as he continued talking rapidly about his problems. And so Thich Nhat Han said, "Here, eat another of my oranges." And the man did the same thing all over again. And then Thich Nhat Han stopped telling the story and told the audience, "I feel I wasted my oranges!" The audience erupted in laughter, because he was trying to get the young man to stop analyzing and start seeing, really seeing, the details of the world right before his eyes, to appreciate the immediacy of the orange, to let go of his excessive attachment to his brain, to his impatience, and his own self-centered analysis.

I have grown up with so many people like this young man, so brilliant at analysis, and so completely lost in worlds of science and research that they cannot see the face of the bus driver in front of them, or reflect upon the face of the stranger. I have tried to shed this trait inside of me.

One thing I have always noticed about places of conflict, from Israel, Palestine, and Syria to Northern Ireland, is an inescapably sad narcissism. So many people are experts on what's wrong. In fact this afflicts the whole field of conflict resolution. Everyone knows every last detail in the web of misery and cycles of actions and reactions, so many brilliant analysts! And they need two things from you, one to realize how important all those analytic details are, and two why they make a solution impossible. And they know this narrative in brilliant detail.

The real challenge of conflict, however, is desisting from analysis. The challenge is looking into the face of the enemy "other" without thinking, without analyzing. And it is terrifying. You would then experience the stark reality of the other who you are poised to murder, or have your police torture and murder. You may emerge with a completely different mind and heart if you just sat with the face of the other and just looked.[3] It may lead to a very different kind of encounter of the mind and heart. I certainly have spent many years now, in the Middle East since 1983, just staring in wonder, in amazement. I used to go throughout Israel, and especially the streets of Jerusalem, just watching in wonder.

The first step in healing a troubled mind may be really looking at an orange. But a heart and mind open to the immediacy of the face of the other is a heart and mind ready for the understanding of radical human interdependence and the futility of killing or prejudice. And that is why my friends, such as Yehezkel Landau, from at least the 1980s, were reading Thich Nhat Han, right in Jerusalem, the heart of strict monotheism. It astonished me that right in Israel people were thirsting for Thich Nhat Han and his tales of oranges, of boat people, of napalm, and the experience of not just pursuing peace but being peace.[4]

We plainly need each other. How could I as a Jew live in a world without Thich Nhat Han and the Dalai Lama? In an age that has to make you wonder about the sanity of our species, these precious souls testify to the genius of God's creation.

Another thought: Japanese culture has much to teach the West, and it has much to learn. Is this not the greatest impression one gets of the post–World War II environment? Is there not some fascinating interaction at work between the United States and Japan, not long after one of the worst bloodlettings in human history, between Japan's atrocities and America's unprecedented nuclear killing of hundreds of thousands of human beings in seconds in Hiroshima and Nagasaki? Does not the closeness of Japanese and American cultures today suggest some unconscious way in which we need each other after seeing the horror? We need each other to put to rest the great barbarities of war and see each other as we really are. We need each other's wisdom to flourish in the future, but it would be better if we could be conscious that some special tie binds us, a tie that forces us to look at each other.

Is it not ironic that Chinese Confucian civilization is reaching unprecedented powers of modern success just as the Tibetan Buddhist civilization is reminding it, in the most nonviolent way, that massive China has much to learn from tiny, old-fashioned Tibet? Is it possible that were the master himself alive, Confucius, based on his commitment to balance, ethics, and respect for tradition, would not see the wisdom of a leader like the Dalai Lama? Would Confucius not discover immense respect for a man who courageously and repeatedly reminds the Chinese leaders that they need to have a give-and-take relationship with their subjects; this is just as Confucius himself had taught, a covenant of mutual commitment and ethical obligations between rulers and the governed.

The Dalai Lama believes in such principles of governance because of the Buddhist wisdom principle of "emptiness," which asserts, according to his interpretation,[5] that we are all interconnected and interdependent, and therefore we should exhibit unlimited compassion for each other. The differences in intellectual rationale for this political position do not matter. The fact is that the Dalai Lama comes to the same place as Confucius who insisted on a mutual ethical interdependence of governors and the governed. Someone needs to remind the Chinese leaders of these ancient Confucian ethical values before Tibetan culture and its people are completely eliminated from their ancient homeland. Is it not interesting that one colleague after another of mine in the blood-drenched, Abrahamic Middle East has countless books on his shelf by the Dalai Lama and Thich Nhat Han? That increasingly they practice yoga and meditation? That there is a seamless quality of affection and respect among those who utilize Jewish mysticism, Sufi Islamic mysticism, and the wisdom of the East, as they pursue peace? It is as if there are answers in the Far East that help to mollify the patriarchal and clerical inanities of the Middle East and West. Is it not interesting that tens of thousands of Israeli Jewish kids make a beeline for India and the Himalayas the moment that they are released from the Israel Defense Forces, an army locked in an endless war of attrition with an entire Palestinian population?

The fact is that to rise above our greatest weaknesses we all need each other, as a family of humanity. Our theologians seem to forget this in their zeal to propagate one faith or another. And our academic scholars narrowly and endlessly analyze each miniscule detail of faith, in utter isolation from the search for wisdom. But wisdom only comes from the integrative side of our minds, and the integrative approach to moral decision making.

Something better is happening, though, than these small-minded approaches, and I see it in Sheikh Bukhari, Eliyahu Mclean, and a steady flow of very special people, young and old, who pass through their many meetings in Jerusalem. I see there, in the crevices of the Holy City, at the center of the conflict, Jews and Muslims and Christians relating to each other in ways that are dramatically opposite of what one sees on the news. The few and the special among them are deepening their relationships, and this looks to me immensely powerful in its potential. These are the emerging peacemakers, the future citizen diplomats and networkers, the spiritual seekers, who are combining in their hearts a love of the earth, a love of all of humanity, and a determination to live life in an entirely new way.

Sheikh Bukhari said to me in the winter of 2008 that our task as peacemakers must be to help people believe that peace is possible. I had asked him honestly what he thought was wrong with my approach, as I was suffering from self-doubts when I came back from Syria. He did not say anything was wrong with my approach, but effectively he told me precisely what was wrong with me. I had become too negative, too analytic, too mired in details. I had forgotten that first and foremost people in conflict, people in danger, are looking to me for inspiration, for hope. But I had come with too much negative energy, too much worry, too much analysis, too many nightmares. I was Thich Nhat Han's young student devouring my orange. I had become the angry Jeremiah of the Bible despite my best efforts not to. The war and continuous killings, the stubborn stupidities on all sides, my miserable body, had finally gotten to me. But the people in danger don't need a broken man. They wanted me to help them believe that peace is possible.

This was such a simple recommendation from Sheikh Bukhari, and in a few words he helped me understand what had gone wrong in my recent work in the Middle East. I was failing to inspire; I had become infected with the same despair that I was supposed to come to heal.

So I need the Sheikh, this scion of Arab, Muslim, and Sufi masters who lived in Jerusalem for centuries. I need him just as surely as I need air to breathe. I need to picture him in his very special house on the Temple Mount in the Old City, right on the Via Della Rosa. I need to see the ancient documents of his Sufi ancestors. I need to see him praying for all of humanity, and I need to believe that there is a spirit of love for all of humanity right at the heart of the contested city of Jerusalem.

The more we need each other the more we are witnessing the beginning of our completion as a species. And we need that completion now more than ever, because of the damage we have all done to this earth.

Sheikh Bukhari and so many other idealistic people in Jerusalem are surrounded by hatred, prejudice, and fear on all sides. These are passions which distort the cultures and religions of their fellow citizens. One could look at my peacemaker friends and say that they are so small by comparison to the populations and the forces on all sides. But all the most precious and good things of the earth, like children, for example, begin in infancy.

What remains a challenge to me as a peacemaker is that much of the religious work of peacemaking in the Middle East, sincere efforts to create a religious social contract across enemy lines, goes on independently of secular efforts to do so. The two universes remain alien from each other. But peace will only come with consensus-building on shared public space and realistic political structures. We need the kind of wisdom that moves forward across this divide.

HOW WILL WE FIND THE WISDOM TO COMBINE SACRED AND SECULAR SOCIAL CONTRACTS?

We need to see the global community that we will create as not only tolerant, ethical, and enlightened but also sacred. What I mean by this is that the same constructs of peace and coexistence that will satisfy all the secular security and political requirements of justice and fairness should also appeal to religious people as a sacred achievement. Let me explain why.

The human being craves worship of the sacred. Four hundred years into the Scientific Revolution we can see this as a fact about human nature by virtue of hundreds of millions of people who accept science and technology while still craving regular worship; the search for the sacred is not going to go away.

On the other hand, we can no longer afford blind obedience to clerical structures of *human* authority set up by organized religions that so often become imperialistic and exclusive if they attempt to control the public space. This would just continue the bloodbath of religious history. What we *can* afford is the creation of a global, liberal, social contract that sees the achievement of international tolerance as not only a good secular goal of liberty and democracy, but also as a sacred achievement that will fulfill our deepest religious dreams. But we need to persuade far more people to dream this religious dream. We should provide them with a dignified entry into the global social contract that helps them see the value spiritually of a global, unprecedented experiment in human community.

The great strength of the original founders of the Enlightenment and its democratic-leaning institutions is that they brought to their political creations a kind of spiritual zeal. We have lost that zeal in the West, and we have done so at our peril, and replaced it with zeal for the marketplace.

But democracy and enlightenment are not identical with naked capitalism. Millions of citizens in democracies around the world take their democracy for granted, as an opportunity to engage in endless shopping and consumerism, not as an opportunity to participate in the practice of democracy. At the same time that the great-grandchildren of the Enlightenment are floundering, much of the most zealous traditional religious education, even in the democratic West, provides no basis of commitment to democracy, to the social contract, or to sharing society with nonbelievers. This cannot continue without inviting great violence in the future.

Liberal citizens, secular and religious alike, must stand up and insist upon a complete reform of secular and religious instruction that will be committed to democracy and human rights. This is a long-term advocacy project that will safeguard a democratic and tolerant future for everyone, from conservative to liberal, in the global community.

At the same time, democracy can and should be seen as a sacred privilege, as a fulfillment of sacred dreams, such as the religious embrace of the sacred value of every human being. If we manage to move toward a global social contract it can and should be seen as a spiritual achievement of far greater significance than anything prior in the history of human religions. It is up to us how we frame our future, and we are capable of developing a positive moral and religious construct that embraces the global social contract of mutual commitments.

The sacralization of the good society composed of all of humanity encapsulates the only kind of unification of the sacred and the political that humanity can afford in the future. We will either have a totalitarian religious future or we will have a revolution in religious embrace of democracy and tolerance.

A biblical argument can be made that global community and its inherent pluralism of identities is the only realistic fulfillment of ancient prophetic dreams of a pluralistic earth in which the lamb can lie down with the wolf in safety, where the poor and vulnerable can be honored and feel safe without fear of being devoured by lions.[6] If we will it and develop consensus on this with a wide array of communities then the evolution toward global community can be seen in religious education as the realization of the vision of each person sitting under his own vine and fig tree with no one to fear.[7]

The global social contract needs everyone's support to be fulfilled. It is not enough to support it with merely capitalist dreams or exclusive biblical messianic dreams. It is going to require the support of the world's wisdom traditions to become embedded in the heart of humanity.

The appeal to a cooperative construction of wisdom between the world's religions that I am proposing is not meant to exclude nonreligious or secular people from this future. On the contrary, what is necessary is an enthusiastic sacralization of the global social contract with a free public space, so that hundreds of millions of conservative religious people can *nonviolently* acquiesce to this experiment in inclusivity.

We need in the future world order for religious clerics and hierarchies to give up power over the public space so that they will be respected rather than feared. I have seen repeatedly in my work in the Middle East how resented and despised organized religion is precisely when it tyrannizes the most over public space.

Despite the fact that this sounds like a very radical idea for traditionalists to accept, the fact is that I have heard these same ideas reverberate more and more in the Islamic world at rather high levels. From muftis to high sheikhs, from Shi'ite scholars to Sunni scholars, I am hearing increasingly that an embrace of secular authority will be the healthiest thing for their religion. I certainly have come to that conclusion myself in terms of the future of Judaism and Jewish identity in Israel. Furthermore, if there is ever an enduring Palestinian–Israeli peace then the vast majority of Israeli Jews will prefer a much more benign definition of Jewish identity or the Jewishness of the state.

Clerics of the Islamic world who are advocating for secular states are not insensitive to the pervasive popular rage at secular authorities and wealthy classes that are either selfish or corrupt or both. But there is an increasingly pervasive insight that the vulnerability of the masses to religious fascistic manipulation puts the integrity of religion at grave risk.

No one knows how this will play out on a mass scale, and what degree of balance between religion and state will emerge in the world's religious communities, from Pakistan to Morocco to Indonesia to Texas. But there is learning going on, and the future of conservative religion in its relationship to power is very much up in the air. This is the time for us to conceive of a persuasive set of arguments as to the best course of action that will lead to a tolerant social contract.

In addition to conservative religion giving up coercive power over people's lives in the future, it must do something else that is hard. The only kind of spiritual or religious enthusiasm that has ever been peaceful has been the kind in which ethical impulses and values have been applied to *every* human being, with no border or boundaries. This means that conservative religions in a global social contract will have to limit their more restrictive virtues—virtues limited to those who accept the discipline of a conservative religion—to private instruction to children, and not imposed on the global social contract community.

If, for example, monogamous marriage between a man and a woman is the only acceptable form of sexual engagement, then let that be taught in the privacy of the home or private school, *with* the proviso that it be taught alongside the value of love and acceptance of others regardless of difference.

There are inevitably, even with these recommendations, some difficult places of contact between religious and secular culture that create conflict and will have to be nonviolently contested. How far does each community, religious and secular, enter into each other's space of child rearing? How much do my progressive children need to be bombarded with religious media or advertising, and how much do my conservative children need to be exposed to highly sexualized media in the public space of television? These are borders and boundaries that must be negotiated.

But what must decisively change is that we must agree as a global community to focus on a much greater area of consensus when it comes to common virtues, such as an opposition to gratuitous violence, for example. There is every reason to embrace a bipartisan commitment to education in nonviolence, and to sacralizing that effort, making it religious as well as secular, for it to be a shared moral global commitment in terms of our children and their education.

WHAT WISDOM DOES ABRAHAMIC
CIVILIZATION NEED FROM OTHERS?

In previous books I have laid out in detail some of the strengths that the Abrahamic traditions bring to humanity's collective wisdom. There are extensive Abrahamic traditions about self-examination, confession, apology, forgiveness, and rituals of repentance and change.[8]

Perhaps one of the most significant implications of these traditions is the optimistic idea that the human being can begin again, can be born again, can achieve a new identity, no matter what he or she has done or experienced. It seems to me that nothing better helps human beings recover with resilience from the horrors of war, or from negative identities of enemy systems, than the idea of being a new being, of being born again. I do not refer here to just the Christian sense of being born again, but a faith in human renewal in all three Abrahamic traditions.

I also analyzed in previous books the importance of sacralizing the act of peacemaking itself. This gives added passion and sustainability to the difficult work of peacemaking. I also discussed the added benefit of the sacralization of this undertaking when it is reinforced by a tightly woven religious community.[9]

In addition, the Abrahamic traditions mostly contain approaches to peace that are inseparable from justice. It is the artful combination of peace and justice that is called for in so many Abrahamic texts and traditions, and this is essential to conflict resolution that creates lasting peace.

Finally, there is in the Abrahamic traditions the optimistic and pervasive faith in a future that is transformed, that brings with it a more just social order. This is the messianic possibility that forms the foundation of every optimistic Western notion that led to the institutionalization of democracy and human rights in the West. From Williams to Grotius to Kant to Jefferson there is hardly a liberal visionary who was not profoundly influenced by these optimistic foundations of Abrahamic wisdom literature.

What is missing? How to account for the magnificent failures of Abrahamic civilizations to realize these optimistic dreams, and instead to often create hell on earth rather than heaven on earth? The greatest weaknesses generally emerge from the greatest strengths of systems of human thinking and behavior. The very optimism that leads to hope and enthusiasm for a better future gives rise to an obsession with the future, and a tendency to hasten it at the expense of other people. There is a tendency to stress, anxiety, and impatience, the opposite of calm, patience, balance—indeed, the opposite of sanity. The very thirst for justice often can lead to fury and rage, impatience with reality and with other people, and this gives rise to revolutionary terror.

There is a dark side to the thirst for God and the just order that the Abrahamic God demands. The passionate prophets and priests of these great traditions are all male, and their driven determination to change social orders for the better also seems to generate, or at least support, forceful patriarchal structures that become a source of great injustice rather than a response to it. They set in motion structures of command and control that become oppressive, militant, and built for destructive conflict.

The insistence on radical good, indeed the obsession with righteousness, also seems to generate a search for evil, the demonization of the idolater, the unbeliever, and "the possessed of the devil." The passionate search for the perfectly good seems to generate a passionate witch hunt for the perfectly evil; this has deadly results.

There is a tendency toward monotheistic dissatisfaction with the political order, as if a jealous God is inherently suspicious of human agency and power. This can generate prophetic rage in monotheistic advocates, a need to advocate the violent overthrow of political orders, and the demonization of enemies. But, in fact, such jealousy for God's sake often is a thinly veiled grab for power by monotheistic advocates themselves. This has provided a religious handmaiden for every violent campaign of the Western empires in history, and it is has also disguised the most nefarious desires to steal and pillage from weaker peoples.

This has also been bad news for anyone who can be considered an outsider, an agent of evil, a misunderstood minority who can become the reason for all evil in one's midst. In the words of the Bible, "And you shall burn out the evil from your midst."[10] Bad news for those chosen as definitive outsiders, such as "idolaters," homosexuals, "witches," even dark-skinned people, women, Roma people, infidels, you name it. The creative designation of who is outside the community of the faithful and the saved knows no bounds in the history of monotheism.

Let me be very clear: any sober analysis of religions east and west, north and south, will see many similar patterns of patriarchy, demonization, and the use of religion for warfare against outsiders. These tendencies are not missing from Eastern religions, but everything is a matter of degree and emphasis.

There is a greater Eastern focus on the inner life, in many lifetimes, and less on transformation in this lifetime of the social and political order, at least in classical Buddhism, Hinduism, and Taoism.[11] In addition, Confucianism and Shintoism are highly oriented to state structure, and are therefore focused more on stability and less on violent overthrow of power.

Of course, I can see the hackles of my esteemed friend and work colleague, Richard Rubinstein, being raised.[12] He believes that the intellectual foundations of revolt against unjust authority are critical to human development and the removal of unjust social orders, and therefore the prophetic monotheistic tendency to dissatisfaction with political orders is to be lauded.

I agree with this thinking, but only up to a point. Righteous rage is a dangerous thing, and millions have been murdered in history in the name of creating just or spiritually redeemed social orders, particularly in the name of monotheism. In other words, I agree with embrace of the prophetic social critic but not with the embrace of prophetic rage, messianic impatience, and cursing. The latter have proven to be a more deadly model of Western approaches to struggle and change.

The debate and the political choices here come down to some of the ethical calculus of consequences that I have described in chapter six. Perhaps Richard believes that the militant passion for reform of the social order is vital and creates the best consequences for humanity, but I will not speak for him.

As I demonstrated in the narrative study of our Syrian work, I have come to believe that nonviolent *evolution* of the human spirit and the social order, not revolution, produces the least suffering for the greatest number of people and generates the most positive change in the long run. And it manages to do so in a great variety of political, social, and military orders. A combination of the Abrahamic passion for justice together with a respect for structure, the rule of law, and the virtue of patience, produces an evolution of human spirit and the social order that avoids the horrors of righteous revolutions and holy wars. And that preference for nonviolence, patience, and compassion also subverts self-righteous excuses for imperialism when monotheists find themselves in positions of power over others.

There is implicit in Eastern spiritual wisdom literature a greater patience (patience of many lifetimes) to deal with suffering and an unjust social order. Religion is therefore less prone to be a hammer. Let me be clear. I know well as a scholar of religions that there have been many Buddhist armies, and brutal classist orders based on Hindu caste systems. I am not stating a preference for one system of human wisdom over another as intellectual constructs, but rather examining the impression that they are making on our thinking today. I am arguing that we have much to learn from each other, from our strengths as well as our weaknesses, from our foibles as well as our genius. And devotees of classical monotheism have to do some soul-searching and wisdom-seeking in the light of their history.

At the present time, contemporary Western interpretations of Eastern religions continue to have an interesting impact on Western cultures in this regard. Many Westerners are quite attracted to liberal forms of Eastern religions that emphasize the discovery of calm, contentment, and a stimulation of responsible behavior not through righteous rage but through inner joy. Compassion is discovered through joy and contentment not command and guilt, and this inner discovery then spills over into one's relations to other sentient beings.

What emerges from even a cursory overview of the popular titles in bookstores of the West is a thirst for Eastern wisdom that specifically seems to address or respond to the worst excesses of Abrahamic religions that I have listed. This does not suggest, however, that one religion in its essence is superior to another, because one can find problems in every native religion in its context.

I don't want to be misunderstood. I am not really interested in comparative religion—and even less in competitive religion. From the point of view of citizen diplomacy, peacebuilding, and the effort to create a peaceful social contract in today's globe, I have a pragmatic agenda. I merely want to point out how much we need each other. Organized religions in all places tend to become more and more oppressive over time in their indigenous environment, and that is why distant religions may be more inspiring, easier to pick and choose from, select the good, without baggage and bad memories.

That is why spiritual seekers of all kinds, east and west, north and south, may need each other to move to a new stage of human development. As we explore this new global social contract, we need to be open then to what is new and novel in the culture and religion of "the Other" and how it may complete or correct what has gone wrong in our own culture.

PERSONAL JOURNEYS

Let me explore for a time now a narrative approach to understanding these matters. In my own journey I began to search for answers beyond the Abrahamic religions the more that I became troubled, possessed really, by the tragedy of the wars of Israel and the Palestinians. This began in earnest in 1982 with the Lebanon War, in the midst of me receiving my rabbinical ordination. As I started searching more and more for spiritual answers I became at the same time engaged in pursuing a PhD in Jewish studies during the 1980s. It was a classic "Enlightenment" PhD in the sense that all religious texts were subject to scientific scrutiny in a most antifundamentalist way. Thus, at the same time that I was deconstructing sacred Western texts, removing a naïve view of them, I was seeking out and discovering the icons of contemporary representatives of Eastern religions. For me this was first and foremost Mohandas Gandhi.

I remember that in the winter of 1983, in the Harvard Square Theatre, I watched Attenborough's *Gandhi* for the first time. I would eventually watch it at least twenty times since then. It was an epiphany, and I remember being unable to move after the film finished. For the first time I saw someone in the modern era who had truly acted upon the most idealistic principles that I had loved in prophetic and rabbinic Judaism, principles of reverence for life, for justice, and for peace. I had not been able to find anyone who was putting these into practice today at the political level of the Jewish community in the same way that Gandhi had in his Hindu community. This would be the first but not the last time that the discovery of the sacred outside my own tradition would be a source of discovery and sadness at the same time—an enhancement of human identity and a loss of pristine identity, all at once.

Discovering such deep political truth outside my own community was extremely confusing to me as a young man raised in an atmosphere of intense piety. The pietistic spirit that I had aspired to as a young person did not allow for leaving the sacred Jewish realm. In general, religious piety cannot understand the world outside of itself. It cannot understand a reason to leave the beauty of a particular religious world.

I will never forget the words of my religious study partner, my *havruta*, a deeply pious Brooklyn Jew who had a brilliant mind and was at the same time an unusually humble person. His name was Mel, or Yaacov. Mel knew that even by 1981 I was immersed in the study of non-Jewish philosophy in my search for answers to many questions. He looked up at me one day, with the text of the Talmud open before him and me, clearly troubled. Earnestly and respectfully, he said these simple words, "I understand that there may be many beautiful things in the world, all of them made of beautiful silver. But if you live in a golden palace, why would you want to leave?" He was trying with a pure heart to bring me in completely to the world of Torah study.

Those words penetrated my heart like a knife. I was not insulted, but Mel had just shown me the door. In his effort to keep me in, he had given me an understanding of why I had to leave. In that instant I understood fundamentalist piety and the deeper worlds of the pious in all the Western religions.

The inner palace of ethno-religious identity was indeed golden, but something terrible was happening right outside the palace walls. And the terrible thing happening outside the palace walls was not due to some evil emanating from non-Jews, from "the *goyim*." Maybe that made sense of the world in the era of the Nazis, but not any longer. No, the traumatic discovery for me was that it was something terrible that emanated from within, something that took the palace gold and turned it into a weapon of war, of possession, and of dispossession.

The moment I sought out and discovered just a few Palestinians in 1983, got to know them at the level of the human heart, I knew that "the palace" was over for me. In fact, the more I got to know the Middle East, the more I knew even then that "the palaces" Judaism, Christianity, and Islam had produced something very problematic. But I have never forgotten the lure of "the palace," its beauty, and its simplicity. And I have never gotten over its loss.

Then came Gandhi, like a prophetic epiphany. I saw the possibility of a thoroughly nonviolent sacred reality with profound political implications and demands. At the time I hoped that this would lead to my own rereading of Judaism. Thus, the Eastern religion of this one man played a role in a revolutionary rereading of my own tradition, which was articulated in part in my first two books. He not only set a precedent for the courageous application of spiritual values to dangerous political realities, he risked his life for it, and ultimately surrendered his life to the extremists in his religion.

Gandhi also set a precedent for the twentieth century of the creative evolution of interpretation of religious tradition. Throughout hundreds of books and articles, he articulated a Hinduism—despite its frequent mythic engagements with war in the *Bhagavad Gita* and elsewhere—that was ultimately about the *futility* of external wars, that was really about the war inside the soul and the search for the higher self. In so doing he demonstrated a bold combination of his intellectual, moral, and political positions. Many creative interpreters of traditional religions in the eighteenth and nineteenth centuries had done this. But very few people in human history were like Gandhi, who had captured the imaginations of tens of millions of people beyond his own culture by defying empires and extremists alike, and by inspiring millions of his own people to do the same.

I stayed traditional in many ways, in terms of ritual observance, but Gandhi permanently changed my spiritual politics. I could never again embrace ethnonational politics. Empathy with ethno-nationalist and sacred chauvinists, however, is a given of the bridge-building work that I or any respectable peacemaker does among the Western families of Christianity, Islam, and Judaism. You can't do serious peace work without empathy for ethno-nationalism and chauvinism. These are the bedrock human worldviews and emotions at work in warfare between religious and cultural groups. You have to empathize with the compelling nature of these worldviews, even as you attempt to present possible alternatives.

As I continued to read Gandhi over the years, travel to India, and get to know many Gandhians, I started to have difficulty with Gandhi's approach as a way to deal with the difficult conflicts that I had concentrated on in the Middle East. Gandhi's approach was perfect for a persecuted group not knowing how to stand up for itself, where basically one knew on which side justice lay; in other words, he was perfect for British-occupied India. It got more complicated as a model if that persecuted group was being funded from the outside to commit violence against civilians. And it got even harder to apply his model of nonviolent resistance where there was a great deal of moral failure and violence on all sides of a conflict. I started to find that Gandhians had a tendency to need to decide which of their enemies was the perfect victim; it was precisely because their model of solving conflicts did not easily apply unless there *was* a perfect victim.

In addition, Gandhi's political philosophy had been profoundly influenced by Western, Christian thinking, especially that of Tolstoy. I sensed more and more that his role model was very difficult to follow without it leading to the same ills of Abrahamic messianism that I mentioned earlier, namely impatience, and a need to find perfect victims and perfect devils, even though Gandhi himself resisted this completely. He was not flawed in this regard, but it seemed to me that his model was. Gandhianism was not giving me or others the tools to deal with complex conflict and the havoc it wreaks on the soul as one tries to empathize with multiple enemies who are all deeply troubled and flawed.[13]

It is true that I, among many others, felt strongly that in the Palestinian–Jewish conflict, it would have been better if Arafat had allowed a robust Gandhian nonviolent resistance movement to develop that eschewed violence. Many of us felt strongly that this would have completely changed the political dynamics of the Jewish community as well as the American community. But he specifically disallowed that, in addition to the persecution of Palestinian nonviolence activists that the Israelis consciously and consistently imposed. Nonviolent Palestinian resisters were persecuted and marginalized on all sides in the Middle East.

Arafat's symbol was always the gun together with the olive leaf, and his funding and practices followed exactly that path. But Gandhi completely disallowed that path as being ineffective in helping persecutors to see their own violence. It had to be perfect nonviolent resistance if the persecutor was to face himself. I felt that, based on polls and surveys, a nonviolence movement from the Palestinians would have been joined by thousands of Jews and Israelis, and the entire process of resistance and negotiation would have been different. It would have impacted the American public very differently than suicide bombings against synagogues and hotels.

This really begs the question, though, of Gandhi's tactics in a place like the Middle East. The fact is that we did not have massive nonviolent resistance movements free of bloodshed. Not at all. I am not going to place blame for that on any one group. The fact is that it has not been an available option. Everyone on all sides has preferred military resistance and aggression with some variations between groups and governments as to how barbaric that resistance and aggression becomes.

What then? How to proceed? How does the peacemaker or citizen diplomat act, or even survive? Gandhi's personal model of persistence in citizen diplomacy was inspiring. The engagement he had with Muslims and Pakistanis was compelling. But ultimately it was a depressing model because he was killed for his efforts and seen as a traitor. No one saw him as a traitor when he resisted the British because it was the perfect resistance of the persecuted. But when he stepped over into shuttle diplomacy and peacebuilding with enemies who were more evenly matched, namely Indian Muslims and Indian Hindus, he lost his own people—big time.

Gandhi had stopped his resistance efforts before when even a few British troops were killed.[14] But as a result of an independence movement that he had pioneered over one million people were killed and tens of millions ethnically cleansed from their homes when India and Pakistan were created in 1948. This was a disaster in terms of his spiritual and ethical priorities. That is why I believe he was perfectly ready to die trying to reach out to Pakistan, because the failure of the independence movement at the moral level was so wrenching, so opposite of what he had aspired to and envisioned.

We all operate on very small scales by comparison to the Gandhis of history. But even on my own small scale, I was not interested in supporting approaches to a Palestinian–Jewish settlement that would end up in ethnic cleansing, or in two states at war with each other. That is why I doubted the entire approach to diplomacy that led to the creation of India/Pakistan as well as to Israel/Palestine. I was never a big fan of the Oslo peace process because I did not think it was leading to deeper reconciliations of the peoples, which is indispensable to avoiding bloodshed.

I have come to doubt one thing that makes my politics suspect for all sides of the Arab–Israeli conflicts: I doubt the justice of even liberal democratic national states that are based on the dominance of one ethnic or religious identity. That puts me at odds with Jewish nationalists, Palestinian nationalists, Arab nationalists, as well as Islamists. But I have had less of an interest in pushing my own politics or in assigning blame. I am only interested in the simple question of what can I, or any other relatively powerless person, do that may make a modest difference in the level of hatred, rage, and violence. It is the relatively simple question of the citizen diplomat.

A Change of Mind

As I have noted earlier, and in previous writings, I am coming to see how wrapped up that question is with my own state of mind. It is so easy in this work to become a warrior just like the warriors who fight for one side. A warrior for peace can be just as bitter and hateful as any other warrior. In fact, my hatred can be worse, because the sense of isolation is so much more intense than that experienced by ethno-nationalists who usually embed themselves in very supportive communities. But the warrior state of mind just makes you part of the problem. I did not want to be an angry warrior for peace, like so many on the Left. I was searching for something else, especially because I knew how much anger was a part of my soul.

That is why the writings, teachings, and political model of the Dalai Lama have been such a revelation to me, and they are leading me to a reinvigorated approach to diplomacy and religious life. In very simple form, the Dalai Lama has offered the world a way of being that promotes personal happiness and simultaneously the happiness of others. Its cardinal principles are the discipline, at every hour of every day, of patience and kindness. It is based on a simple motivation to become enlightened for the sake of all other living things by way of compassion and an internalization of the idea of "emptiness."

The Dalai Lama's understanding of emptiness refers to the interdependence of all things. In contemporary terms, it is the simple notion that we all need each other, and therefore we need to value all things as if they are us. We are all connected because we all crave security, respect, and happiness, and therefore it only makes sense to bestow compassion at every opportunity. For me this was a classic Buddhist parallel of the biblical/rabbinic principle of loving others as you would love yourself.[15]

Let me quote here from the Dalai Lama who explains in detail what this approach entails. "The highest form of spiritual practice is the cultivation of altruistic intention . . . to attain enlightenment for the benefit of all sentient beings, known as *bodhichitta*."[16] He goes on to explain that "enlightenment" means the elimination of afflictive thoughts and emotions, thus uncovering the essential nature of mind that is enlightened.[17]

There is a basic optimistic faith in the mind, in its essential nature being one of perfection and enlightenment.[18] The practice of *bodhichitta* is also inseparable from the practice of compassion. "So compassion lies at the root of all the Buddha's teachings, but it is within the *bodhisattva* ideal that we find special emphasis on the concerted development of compassion by means of cultivating *bodhichitta*."[19] The Dalai Lama integrates the internal discipline and enlightenment of the mind with the embrace of compassion in one's attitudes and behaviors toward oneself as well as to the external world in its entirety. These are inseparable for him. The *bodhisattva* ideals referred to include generosity, morality, patience, enthusiasm, concentration, and wisdom.[20] Most importantly, it is a compassion that is as much inner-directed as it is outer-directed. Indeed, the two are inseparable.

Is this a political philosophy? Is this a method of diplomacy and negotiation? Is it a realistic approach to citizen diplomacy? Is it an effective strategy for achieving a global social contract and community? I used to think it was not. But after all of my field work I have come to believe that it is what is missing in all Western and Abrahamic approaches to conflict, approaches that tend to obsess about outcomes, but not the internal condition of any of the parties, especially not the peacemaker herself. It is the only way to explain "peace processes" like Oslo that people seemed to think were working even as millions affected by it were utterly miserable and angry.

Peace processes, it is true, need to be about borders, boundaries, security, economic justice, and so forth. But they also need to be about the inner transformation of human beings and the legitimate human search for happiness. This seems utopian but it is actually *far more* practical than the alternative. Without progress on the front of human misery and human happiness, conflict situations and the people who cause them are bound to deteriorate. The peacemakers in their frustrated misery will also not be up to the task of moving everyone onto a realistic path to peace. Hatred is a poison and misery is a destructive drug. Without working on these poisons and drugs you are not really engaged in peacemaking.

Is the Dalai Lama's approach one that only devout Buddhists can have? I used to think so, but as I have experienced the field work I believe that anyone, religious or secular, can embrace some of the internal disciplines and concentrations of the mind that the Dalai Lama recommends. It can form an important preparation and backdrop for our day-to-day operations in peace work and diplomacy. It is more than anything else a psychological discipline, even though it is plainly a sacred discipline for some. Furthermore, I am convinced that many of my deeply conservative friends who are monotheistic peacemakers intuitively live by the same inner discipline that the Dalai Lama recommends. I marvel, for example, at their capacity for joy in the midst of war, and I know that they share with the Dalai Lama a commitment to the same *bodhisattva* virtues and inner disciplines.

Even more compellingly, a fundamental principle that informs all Abrahamic faiths is the principle of *imitatio dei*, namely the virtue of imitating God's positive character traits. No monotheist will deny the principle that God is compassionate, and therefore so should we be. The problem comes in countervailing laws, myths, and rituals that compel an anticompassionate posture.

For example, there may be a monotheistic principle of compassion, but there are so many statements in monotheistic traditions that will demonize an enemy, despite Jesus' pronouncements in The Beatitudes. Thus the compassion is cancelled. But in volume after volume, the Dalai Lama records a trend of thinking and practice that leads him to *gratitude* to his persecutors, the Chinese, for teaching him patience—this at the same time that he continually reaches out to them in a conciliatory spirit. This suggests an activation of the abstract spiritual principles of patience and kindness right at the core of his way of coping with very real persecutors of his people right now.

This is controversial but straightforward and consistent. It is controversial because many in the Abrahamic traditions sense that it suggests a capitulation in terms of injustice. But it does not. It merely recognizes a deeper truth underlying all of human reality, a deeper level of interdependence that connects us to even our worst enemies, the worst leaders, and the worst governments, which just consist of people like us.

Explaining this principle of kindness and patience with enemies is where I have had the hardest time before audiences from every culture. And I have been attacked for it many times. I would say that there are countless people in my own community who will never forgive me for reaching out to Yasser Arafat. I can try to explain that Yasser Arafat is to Jews what every Israeli prime minister has been to Palestinians—a source of great suffering and the death of many innocents; yet they expect Arab conciliatory approaches to such prime ministers.

It is to no avail with many people. Logic has no place where wounds define a personality. The need to demonize is so overwhelming in human nature, and the need to externalize evil in someone else is ubiquitous. I have been amazed at how much this is consistent across audiences of enemies in the family of Abraham. It seems to be the only way to cope with a world that is supposed to be ultimately just in the Abrahamic story—but plainly is not! So it must be some human being's fault, not God's. The drive in a few Arab audiences that I have spoken before to blame everything, all of history, on Zionists, on the West, and sometimes on Christians, is awe-inspiring. The aching desire of some right-wing Jews today to place all human ills onto Arabs and Islam is visceral, palpable, and very close to uncontrolled rage.

On one level, I completely empathize with these feelings. If I were subject to television images and stories for thirty years of Arabs beaten by Jewish soldiers my rage would be right at the surface. If I had watched Jewish children blown to bits on television one decade after another in the name of Arab nationalism or Islam I would be apoplectic with rage. What astonishes me is that this enraged approach to the world admits of no exceptions, no good news, no alternative possibilities. It is as if a threat to this enraged view would throw the person or group into a chaotic stupor, into loss of faith in a just God, perhaps.

After all of my years of practice, I cannot adequately explain where Eliyahu Mclean, Sheikh Bukhari, and the Dalai Lama come from, and why it seems to be another planet by contrast to the enraged crowds that I have sometimes confronted. I know two things. One is that there are many saints here, extraordinary people in the Abrahamic family whose spirituality guides them to embrace love over hatred, compassion over jealousy and anger, patience over temper. Two is that despite their paradigms I am having a hard time with the Abrahamic family, and I seem to crave wisdom from the outside to help this family.

I am finding that the Dalai Lama's reading of Buddhist insights and practices is giving me a better way to cope with the enraged reality of the Abrahamic family, and a better way to be a vehicle of compassion myself, rather than an angry prophet or a broken peacemaker. He offers happiness, which everyone needs. It is a path of happiness not through personal indulgence but through kindness, patience, and meditation on becoming enlightened for everyone's sake.

My analytic brain tells me that the Dalai Lama would fare just as badly before the angry crowds as I have. But then I remember how disciplined his inner life is, how many hours he works on it every day, and I remember how I have performed in public sometimes. I realize that I have so much farther to go in personal discipline as I confront rage, especially if it is directed against me. Perhaps he too would be disappointed in such crowds, but then perhaps his discipline would kick in, and he would approach them with kindness, patience, and humility. This is something I have managed to do only occasionally. Mostly I have avoided these crowds, like most liberals, and that is why a polarized environment persists. The bridge is too far for our impatient hearts.

A "Lamaist" Moral Consequentialism?

The Dalai Lama's approach implies a pathbreaking version of moral consequentialism. In the previous chapter I referred to the classic form of utilitarian consequentialism as "the greatest happiness for the greatest number." I would add to this an emphasis on suffering. Perhaps a "Lamaist" consequentialism—to coin a phrase—would entail acting in such a way as to bring about the lessening of as much suffering for the greatest number of people as possible.

First and foremost, the Dalai Lama's contribution is to the *style* of interaction that one brings to diplomacy, peacemaking, and teaching, and the personal discipline that this requires. But pursuant to the concerns of the last chapter about ethical calculus, the meditative state of attempting to become enlightened for the sake of all beings, and the meditative practice of cherishing oneself and all others simultaneously with each breath, implies an approach to ethical calculation of what is right to do in each situation of conflict.

Perhaps it could be rephrased philosophically in the following way: I should act in such a way as to bring about the lessening of suffering for the most number of people with every one of my thoughts and actions. This would imply several things. It implies that not only what I do but also *how I do it* will either cause more or less suffering. It also implies that I cannot consider the effect of my actions, behaviors, or decisions *only* on the people right in front of me. If I want to please a crowd in front of me that wants me to join them in their various hatreds, it may lessen their suffering if I hate in solidarity with them. But I will create *more* suffering overall in the world because I will alienate so many others, and I will also fail to be a vehicle of kindness in giving into their hatreds. I can sympathize with their rage, but if I join it I will fail to lessen suffering for the greatest number of people in the world. This is the major problem with left/right divides in politics.

Finally, this approach also implies that my own happiness or suffering cannot be left out of the calculation. I cannot lessen the suffering of others while dramatically increasing my own. I also cannot dramatically increase the happiness of businessmen and politicians in a peace process while dramatically increasing the suffering of poor mothers. We are all interconnected and interdependent, and the calculus of peace requires that we intervene accordingly.

TAOISM AND DIPLOMACY

I want to add some reflections on the wisdom of another Asian pattern of thought that is embodied in Lao Tzu's *Tao Te Ching*, a pattern of inner thinking that has had a profound effect on my experiments with intervention in the last decades. This small book, which is a sacred book for millions of people, has been critical as a backdrop of how I have made decisions and what goals I have set for my citizen diplomacy. Essentially this book reverses the normal human conception of power.

> A man is supple and weak when living, but hard and stiff when dead. Grass and trees are pliant and fragile when living, but dried and shriveled when dead. Thus the hard and the strong are the comrades of death; the supple and the weak are the comrades of life. Therefore a weapon that is strong will not vanquish; a tree that is strong will suffer the axe. The strong and big takes the lower position, the supple and the weak takes a higher position.[21]

The *Tao Te Ching* is all about the attainment of power, but it questions the typical ways in which men seek power. It argues that what appears weak is actually strong and what appears strong is actually quite weak, that attaining the power of leadership often entails being invisible rather than grabbing attention and commanding everyone, that victory over enemies is often attained indirectly, not through direct confrontation. Water looks weak but over millennia it cuts a path through mountains. Rocks appear very strong. They do break heads, but they also break and disintegrate themselves relatively quickly. You can put your hand through water in a stream and it appears to give way. But then it simply moves resolutely in its own direction, in the direction it was already going before.

This has affected my practice on several levels. First of all it has made me an optimist, despite the fact that my realist analysis of military and political realities can often be quite sobering. The fact is, however, that Lao Tze is absolutely right. Nothing appears more invincible and strong than military superiority. Nothing appeared more invincible in the history of mankind than the Nazi Third Reich. But instead of it being a thousand-year Reich as promised, it hardly lasted a decade before the world crushed it. Why? Because its overwhelming use of brute force came back on its head. And thus brute force seemed very strong but it turned out to be very weak because it always invites a counter-response that is equally strong.

By contrast, the "pen" does appear to be mightier than the sword. The idea of democracy, for example, appearing in countless visionary writings in the last few hundred years, seems incredibly weak. Democracy seems to weaken the power of leaders to make streamlined tough decisions against enemies, for example. But it turns out that democracy has practically an hypnotic effect on the human spirit. Everyone wants it, and this is its great staying power in history. Without armies it seems on the march across the globe today, not overtly but rather inside the minds of hundreds of millions of people's dreams for themselves and their children.

This has affected my work in that as I build relationships with enemies on all sides, I try to help them attain *true* power, mastery over their own fates. Mastery is the key to optimism and the enemy of despair, frustration, anger, and self-destructive violence. Everyone wants power in conflict, because they are either afraid or angry. The more as a diplomat and third party that you suggest indirect forms of power, quiet ways to get what you want, and the more convincing the evidence that this path can succeed, the more that you can shift real conflicts and legitimate grievances into the nonviolent realm.

It is not only sports that can be a channel for violent competition between adversaries. Even more compelling is nonviolent competition in the search for power, not to mention competition in public relations, a positive public image; all of these require subtle nonviolent strategies. This is the line I take very often, for example, with both Israelis and Syrians in my public talks and private dialogues. I emphasize to both sides the virtues of public relations competition, public relations coups (as opposed to neoconservative coups) because it shifts the grievances and struggles to a subtle nonviolent realm. It thus generates a competition among enemies that is inherently less destructive and may even be very productive in terms of peace moves.

Lao Tsu also appeals to me in the context of dealing with the difficulties of dialogue. The experience of enemy meetings is fraught with false under- standings of power and success. People seem to think that if you outshout someone, or if you show that you are cleverer than someone else, somehow you have won the argument.

Humiliation and defeat in debate appears to be effective, and appears to be stronger. But it is not. In fact, making someone else feel humiliated is weak and foolish because it always invites vengeance. Making them feel that they have won, however, and that you have heard them, is often the best way to attain respect and understanding from an adversary.

Lao Tsu teaches essentially that "nothing is as at seems"; true strength and true weakness do not meet the eye, which turns upside down traditional notions of defeat and victory. This adds a dynamism to nonviolent forms of struggle and diplomacy that propels it forward, even for those with a skeptical eye to the possibility of peace.

This has figured prominently in how I want to operate as a third party to conflicts, how I want to handle my own position as part of an adversary group, and also the advice I want to bring to both sides of a conflict. I man- age to live by its wisdom occasionally.

What I have explored in this chapter is just a small sample of what we can learn and glean from the great wisdom traditions. It is not meant to be exhaustive in any way but as an enticement for the reader to study the wisdom of the world and glean from it a greater variety of truths that will be necessary to weave together a global community and social contract. Our future as a species depends on this effort.

I want to conclude with a few observations. First, I want to emphasize that my embrace of the Dalai Lama's approach does not imply that all Eastern approaches are bereft of prophetic anger, demonization, or othering. I have seen examples of Buddhist approaches that do not live up to the Dalai Lama's example. Just as importantly, I find a great deal of kinship between the Dalai Lama's approach and some of the Abrahamic peacemakers I have described earlier.[22] What this adds up to is not an embrace of Buddhism or the East, but rather an embrace of the potential there is to learn from wisdom traditions the world over, and that we need each other to recover the most essential teachings that will help us all survive the massive changes afoot on the planet.

A LIFE-CENTERED CONSEQUENTIALISM

As I analyze my deepest thoughts and reactions in the field and go over all my memories, I have come to realize that there is yet another overarching influence on my moral intuitions. It is an influence that drives me to a radical kind of pragmatism when I make ethical and strategic calculations in the field. It should be obvious to the reader how much Western ethics have influenced my practice, as well as how much major figures such as Gandhi and the Dalai Lama have influenced me.

I cannot ignore, however, the most essential teachings of Judaism, or the prism through which I have received them. Despite all my problems with Abrahamic faiths, I am influenced by the most essential teachings that meant the most to me. Judaism was always presented to me by teachers and preeminent classical texts as focused first and foremost on the sacredness of every human life. Saving a life (*pikuah nefesh*) is supposed to trump all other desirable goals, be they religious or secular.[23]

This principle has consequences as you try to apply it to the complexities of conflict resolution and diplomacy. It has driven me to seek out partners who were pragmatic and very flexible, such as Hind Kabawat, among others. It is pragmatism and flexibility that stand the best chance of steering us toward life-affirming paths. The key arbiter of consequentialism for me is not happiness (utilitarianism) but the saving of as many lives as possible, and the prevention of bloodshed. Happiness, it seems to me, is a luxury that anyone can work on once their life is secured, but I owe it to my fellow human being first and foremost to nurture and guard her life so that she even stands a chance of pursuing happiness.[24]

This priority, the worry about every human life, does get you back to the angst of desired outcomes, anticipating them, and being disappointed (even driven a bit mad) when wars do begin that you dreamed of preventing, and countless lives are lost. It also involves having nightmares, anticipating the bad that is coming, what violence is about to come because human beings are on a clear collision course. This definitely brings you very close to prophetic angst and rage that is endemic to the biblical legacy, as mentioned earlier.

But I cannot see being an ethical consequentialist without facing nightmares. I cannot see how to protect people from themselves when they are driving off a cliff, or when two or three cultures are driving off a cliff together and you can just see it coming. I want to embrace the optimistic mindset that Martin Seligman has recommended for success, as referred to earlier. I want to anticipate and expect the positive outcomes. But it is Panglossian and morally irresponsible to not also anticipate the possibly bad, as well as envision the possibly good.[25]

This kind of consequentialism and its difficult embrace of conflict anticipation is precisely why I have introduced so extensively the wisdom of the Fourteenth Dalai Lama. I would argue that if we as a global community are to work energetically on conflict prevention and diplomacy in the context of terrible wars, then we need the Dalai Lama's day-to-day recommendations of psychological discipline for patience, kindness, and the attainment of happiness. We need to achieve a level of concentration on patience, compassion, contentment, and enthusiasm that can overcome the dark dangers of a worried mind.

There is danger in a mind that is brooding over the possible outcomes of dangerous conflicts and the danger into which they place people and the earth. Seligman argues that rumination and brooding are at the core of pessimism and depression. Yet how else can you intelligently enter into violent conflict, empathize with the devastating effects of war on people's heart, and also see the next wars on the horizon? How can you not see all that if compassion is an essential tool of your diplomacy and peacemaking?

The answer is that we must see and anticipate the darkness; and yet we also must find a way to be a source of hope not a burden of despair. This is where the Dalai Lama's approach, the Tonglen exercises referred to earlier,[26] and the daily concentrations on kindness, patience, and enlightenment for the sake of all sentient life can become the foundations of emotional and spiritual strength for others.

We are called upon today, to meet the challenges of healing the earth and building global community, by combining the analyst with the healer, the dark visionary with the beacon of hope, the dissatisfied social critic with the centered and content counselor, at peace with himself and others. This is a tall order, but in many ways it is a more generous approach to human nature, one that offers happiness to the messenger as well as the recipient of the message. Indeed, perhaps what has been missing from the Abrahamic prophetic message of peace and justice all this time has not been the message, but a messenger at peace with himself, patient with all sentient life, and with only kind intentions. Perhaps this is the only kind of message that can ever be heard.

One of the most profound prophetic stories of the Bible is the tale of Jonah. He was a man whose task was to foretell catastrophe, and, worst of all, to persuade the king of Assyria, the sworn enemies of the Jewish people, to repent before catastrophe comes. Not only did Jonah not want such a dark mission, but he was also terrified, and so he ran. But the deep pathos of the prophetic story comes when the Assyrian king does repent together with his people, which sends Jonah into a suicidal depression! Jonah had the right message but his inner life was a hell of rage and selfish resentment. And he is rebuked by God for not having any compassion for his enemies, the people of Assyria who had repented. He was just interested in his own pain and his own problems. An exclusive obsession with your own pain and your own problems is the kiss of death for a peacemaker, or for anyone who wants a life of happiness.

Perhaps the most precious legacy of ancient Jewish literature is the capacity for self-criticism, and this small prophetic book encapsulates everything that is right and wrong with the biblically inspired social criticism of the last two thousand years of Western history. Its message of social justice is right on target, but its delivery leaves a lot to be desired. It is not patient, it is not kind, it is not happy, and it is not loving. And it leaves the messenger miserable while the message itself cannot be heard. That is why we need wisdom from all places today to prod the world into a new global social contract, one based on the best prophetic values of social justice and equity. But it would be better if it is a message that is kind and patient with all human beings despite their outrageous imperfections, a message of unconditional love, a message that can be heard by all regimes and all people.

I want to emphasize to the reader that in these pages I am principally describing my own journey of integration of East and West as I confront the ethical dilemmas and challenges of diplomacy. The world is increasingly multipolar, with centers of power emerging all over the planet, from China to Europe, from South America to India.[27] Diplomacy in this new world, and the hope of creating the consensus for a peaceful global community, will require the greater integration of wisdom from all over the earth's many cultures. What I have described here is merely my own experiments with integration.

I submit that thousands of citizen diplomats should consider pursuing this journey, each with their own experiments in integration, so that the sum of all these efforts leads us closer to a global communal consciousness. This is the only way that we can handle the overwhelming effects on all of us of development, globalization, competition, militarization, stale-mated wars, and environmental assault.

We need a consensus on wisdom that can guide the wild engine of human transformation that is sweeping the planet. This is no longer a question of domination and leadership by one culture or another, one religion or another. That is anachronistic. It is about a new integration of wisdom into the ethical choices we make concerning conflict anticipation, conflict management, citizen diplomacy, and our steady march toward something awesome and sacred in its unprecedented reality, a new global community.

NOTES

1. jerusalempeacemakers.org/eliyahu/index.html.

2. In book-based monotheism, "truth" depends on who is doing the interpreting and what kind of mood they are in, historically speaking. The Bible itself has many literary "moods" regarding idolaters, and so does the Talmud. On the one hand, the Bible is a book filled with obligations to expel idolaters or kill them. On the other hand, it recounts numerous stories of the Hebrew patriarchs who made treaties with idolaters and developed real alliances and friendships. More radical still, there are

hints in various biblical texts that suggest an acceptance of henotheism, not monotheism, namely a commitment to Jews following their God, who is the greatest god, but a kind of acceptance that each nation has its own god. See Micah 4:5. In addition, there are various Talmudic statements indicating learning ethical practices from non-Jewish idolaters. On respect for parents among pagans, see *Talmud Bavli* Kiddushin 31a; *Deuteronomy Rabbah* 1:14.

3. On the classic parallel to this approach in phenomenological ethics, see Emmanuel Levinas, *Totality and Infinity: An Essay on Exteriority*, trans. A. Lingis (Pittsburgh: Duquesne University Press, 1969).

4. Thich Nhat Han, *Being Peace* (Berkeley, CA: Parallax Press, 1996).

5.

All events and incidents in life are so intimately linked with the fate of others that a single person on his or her own cannot even begin to act. Many ordinary human activities, both positive and negative, cannot even be conceived of apart from the existence of other people. Even the committing of harmful actions depends on the existence of others. . . . Thus interdependence is a fundamental law of nature.

The Dalai Lama, *The Compassionate Life* (Somerville, MA: Wisdom Publications, 2003), 6.

Nowadays I always meditate on emptiness in the morning and bring that experience into the day's activities. . . . A consciousness that conceives of inherent existence does not have a valid foundation. A wise consciousness, grounded in reality, understands that living beings and other phenomena—minds, bodies, buildings, and so forth—do not inherently exist. This is the wisdom of emptiness. Understanding reality exactly opposite to the misconception of inherent existence, wisdom gradually overcomes ignorance. Remove the ignorance that misconceives phenomena to inherently exist and you prevent the generation of afflictive emotions like lust and hatred. Thus, in turn, suffering can also be removed. In addition, the wisdom of emptiness must be accompanied by a motivation of deep concern for others (and by the compassionate deeds it inspires) before it can remove the obstructions to omniscience, which are the predispositions for the false appearance of phenomena—even to sense consciousness—as if they inherently exist.

The Dalai Lama, katinkahesselink.net/tibet/dalai2.html (accessed May 20, 2008).

6. "The wolf and the lamb shall eat together, and the lion shall eat straw like the ox; and dust shall be the serpent's food. They will not hurt nor destroy in all My holy mountain, saith the LORD." Isaiah 65:25.

7. "Each man shall sit under his own vine and his own fig tree, with none to make him afraid," Micah 4:4. See also Isaiah 66:12. Of course, I am using Abrahamic metaphors here, with the assumption that interfaith communities would discover parallel visions in other world religions.

8. See G. Muller-Fahrenholtz, *The Art of Forgiveness: Theological Reflections on Healing and Reconciliation* (Switzerland: WCC Publications, 1997). And see an extensive bibliography on forgiveness at brandonhamber.com/resources-forgiveness. htm. On a critical examination of Western approaches to forgiveness, see my *Holy War, Holy Peace*, 108ff.

9. See generally my *Between Eden and Armageddon*.

10. Deuteronomy 19:19; 24:7.

11. A Taoist exception would be the famous Yellow Scarves Rebellion of CE 184.

12. See his excellent *Thus Saith the Lord: The Revolutionary Moral Vision of Isaiah and Jeremiah* (New York: Harcourt, 2006).

13. To be honest, I think this requires further study. The subtle ways in which Gandhi managed conflicts between ethnic groups, classes, and castes was quite remarkable and requires further analysis. Rajmohan Gandhi's brilliant and exhaustive *Gandhi: The Man, His People, and the Empire* (Berkeley: University of California Press, 2008) shows in great detail the subtleties of Gandhi's methods of intervention and conflict management.

14. On the Chauri Chaura violence and the halted campaign, see Rajmohan Gandhi, *The Good Boatman: A Portrait of Gandhi* (New Delhi: Viking, 1995), 109.

15. Leviticus 19:18.

16. Dalai Lama, *Transforming the Mind: Teachings on Generating Compassion* (London: Thorsons, 2000), 52.

17. Dalai Lama, *Transforming the Mind*, 53.

18. There are interesting parallels here between, on the one hand, the Dalai Lama's faith in the mind of the human being as the enlightened mind of the Buddha that simply needs to be uncovered or recovered, and, on the other hand, the monotheistic faith in the pure human soul that is a spark or image of God, and that merely needs to be uncovered and released from imperfections or sins that invariably arise through temporal existence.

19. Dalai Lama, *Transforming the Mind*, 111.

20. Dalai Lama, *Transforming the Mind*, 110.

21. Lao Tzu, *Tao Te Ching*, trans. D. C. Lau (New York: Penguin, 1963), 138.

22. There is a fascinating parallel between the Dalai Lama's de-emphasis on theology in favor of simple compassion and that of a very traditional Jewish philosopher whom I wrote about in *Holy War, Holy Peace*, previously cited. Samuel David Luzzatto in nineteenth-century Italy independently developed his own traditional reading of Judaism that was centered on compassion. Furthermore, at certain junctures he had the audacity as a monotheist to suggest that faith in one God is not the overriding goal of God's teachings or the Torah, but rather it is the practice of compassion.

23. See *Talmud Bavli* Yoma 85b; *Shulhan Arukh*, Orah Hayyim 328:2.

24. This has different implications than pacifism. Pacifism is a nonpragmatic ideal. The life-centered consequentialism that I am proposing may also insert itself into military choices of how to minimize the loss of life, or how to shorten the course of war. This is notoriously treacherous moral territory because it involves trust in military and political authorities for information that may be faulty or directly misleading. I do not take these matters lightly. But the reality is that we are surrounded by regimes the world over that think mostly or only in terms of military solutions. How do you get *them* to minimize the loss of life, or in Buddhist terms, the amount of human suffering. To leave them to their own designs is to surrender moral complexity to the main actors on the battlefield, with no advice at all. I cannot do this. At the same time, I am constantly stepping back from military and political mindsets and asking myself, "Wait a minute, why are they only thinking of military solutions? Are they deluding themselves? If so, exactly how, and how could I propose a practical alternative?"

25. Seligman even admits in one telling section that pessimism or depression may be functional up to a point, in terms of the human psyche, especially because

since the Ice Age we as humans have had to anticipate as adults innumerable dangers of rapidly changing environments. This also tends to hardwire children as optimists because it is more functional for them to feel safe growing up, whereas adults are supposed to worry more, as it were. Our trouble today, he claims, is that we tend to go overboard with our instincts for worry and stress. See Martin Seligman, *Learned Optimism* (New York: Vintage, 2006), 107–12. I fully agree with his assessment of adults in our society.

26. See Sogyal Rinpoche, *The Tibetan Book of Living and Dying* (New York: HarperOne, 1994) 191–213.

27. See Parag Khanna, "Waving Goodbye to Hegemony," *New York Times Magazine*, January 27, 2008.

Section IV

CONCLUSIONS ABOUT OUR FUTURE

8

The Future in Our Hands: Citizens Building a Social Contract across Civilizations

CONCLUSION

We began this book with an overview of the current state of religion, conflict, and peacebuilding, as well as a definition of terms relevant to this field. I made the case that in view of the rise of religious militancy globally it is necessary to strategize in terms of short-term and long-term approaches to peacemaking. In the short term it is necessary to work with the most conservative elements of all cultures. But in the long run it will be important to develop a global social contract based upon principles and values that a majority of mainstream secular and religious people can agree upon.

I suggested that the best approach to both short-term and long-term strategies of conflict resolution consists of an engagement with social networks. Considering the diversity of political regimes around the world and the relative lack of freedom in many places, I also argue that we need to explore the special place of citizen diplomacy as a way to bridge barriers between enemy groups, countries, and civilizations. Social networks are best engaged by energetic individuals, citizen diplomats, who can span many disparate networks that cut across the boundaries of religious groups, ethnic groups, and warring nations.

Furthermore, I argue that our approach to evaluation of peacebuilding, both as it is done by NGOs as well as by individual practitioners or citizen diplomats, needs to be completely reworked. Responsibility for success, for failure, and for replication must be distributed among a much wider range of actors, rather than placing the burden exclusively on the activists on the ground. The march toward global community must rest on the shoulders of a much larger array of actors who share the responsibility for social change.

Finally, I explore the ethics of intervention as a critical ingredient of social change and the evolution of global community.

CRITICAL REFLECTIONS ON THE SYRIA WORK

The central case study of this book is my work in Syria with colleagues that began in 2003 and continues as of 2009. What amazes me about the work is how far we have come. We faced enormous obstacles and we had many setbacks. The obstacles we faced were the entrenched positions of the major enemies of the region: the Palestinians, the governments of Israel, Syria, and Lebanon, including outside actors supporting nonstate groups such as Hezbollah and Hamas.

During the years that we have been active we also faced one of the most extreme American governments in recent memory that had determined, unbeknownst to us at the time, to pursue regime change, a violent coup, in Syria. We faced a stream of refugees flowing from Iraq due to an American-led war. We faced a war in Lebanon, in addition to an assassination of a Sunni prime minister blamed upon Syria, a proxy conflict between Saudi Arabia and Syria, a humiliating withdrawal of Syria from Lebanon, and a humiliating defeat for Israel in Lebanon. We faced a Damascus Spring, the hoped-for political reform in Syria of 2000 that rapidly deteriorated in the ensuing years due to all the above developments. In the midst of all of this violence and positioning of enemies, we stepped in with the outrageous message for Washington and Jerusalem that there was someone to talk to in Syria, that there was an address for peace, or at least an address for discussions about peace.

My work was met with incredulity in Washington and in Jerusalem, and our work in Syria was difficult to say the least. I was treated honorably at all times, but my status as an American and as a Jew made our work suspect in the context of the wars swirling around us, from Lebanon to Palestine. In the region, we were accused of coddling the Syrian regime, and inside Syria there was always concern about our motives.

We persisted with public events, endless private consultations, and the conveying of messages between communities and civilizations. To my amazement, with each passing year, more and more seasoned observers, from Israel to Washington to Syria, began to agree with our observations about the possibility of a realignment of relationships in the region. What was seen before as hardened positions of enemies was increasingly seen as tactics and bargaining positions.

More and more members of intelligence communities agreed with our assessments. More policy makers quietly visited Damascus, and I was gaining an audience at higher levels in Washington and Israel. At the same time the position of the White House was seen increasingly as unnecessarily violent, a failure in Iraq, and out of touch with the realities. More and more Israeli defense officials and then policy makers became aghast that the White House would want to prevent them from establishing relations with a formidable enemy with some leverage over Hezbollah and Hamas.

To our amazement we eventually discovered that, from the beginning, our public events in Damascus unleashed strong and good debate in the State Department about the wisdom of their prevailing Syrian policy. Serious NGOs started developing contacts we had established with senior figures and were able to bring significant former American policy makers to Damascus. I myself established contacts between Syrians and American policy makers, and enabled a very conservative congressional delegation to visit Syria precisely when it was most crucial to undermine other forces in Washington that wanted only a violent approach to Syria.

The credibility of our citizen diplomacy work, and especially our focus on something as benign as interfaith tolerance, made it much easier for us to be believed in the halls of power. After several years of being avoided in Jerusalem I was amazed by an avalanche of Israeli interest in Syria. Our work in Syria was featured in Israeli newspapers and TV. Jewish newspapers began covering my work in Syria. An Israeli–Syrian Friendship Association was established in Israel by some very prominent citizens with high government positions, several of whom I had introduced to Syrian contacts.

Then came the breakthrough of Syrian–Israel indirect talks in Turkey in 2008. This is much to the credit of Turkey, but it was part of a constellation of third-country efforts over several years, including certain countries that had also provided us with crucial help in our work inside Syria.

None of this can be spoken of explicitly at this time, but here is the most important point as we assess our own work. We have been told quite clearly by third parties active in the region that the public venues and symbols of dialogue that we initiated in 2003 and persisted in for four years had a direct impact on leadership of all parties and on the opening of dialogue between Israel and Syria.

We played a quiet, definitive role in this process of de-escalation and thawing of relations. This confirmed for me my thesis that the most important contribution of citizen diplomacy, social networking, and friendship among enemies that leads to partnership is a critical early stage of social change between enemy states and enemy communities that only private citizens can pursue.

It must be understood how delicate and risky all of this was. This was taking place at the same time that Israel made a decision to attack a secret facility inside Syria in 2007, an attack that the Syrians chose not to respond to. Additionally and more ominously, Israel's bombing campaign in Lebanon in 2006 that left so many refugees fleeing for their lives to Syria, so many dead, could have actually led to all-out war with Syria. It did not. We have been told in fact that there were forces at the highest levels in Washington insisting that Israel bomb Syria as well, which is precisely why Prime Minister Olmert repeated many times, between 2006 and 2008, that he had no intention of bombing Syria.[1] The world came very close to a major regional war, at U.S. prodding.

What one hopes for at such times is that the evidence of nonviolent alternatives that you have put before policy makers and military leaders makes it harder for them to bomb, and easier to see the benefits of restraint. Israel, in my opinion, should never have reacted so harshly to Hezbollah provocations in the Lebanon War of 2006. At the same time it is easy to see why military and policy makers in Israel saw no downside, and saw no reason for restraint against an enemy such as Hezbollah. No one has succeeded in creating any back channels between Hezbollah and Israel that would encourage or induce any restraint by either party, as a matter of fact.

By contrast, Israel at least had enough information about Syria and its leadership as to give them pause, and even resist the prodding of an extreme American White House in terms of widening the war to Syria. Widening the Lebanon War in 2006 to include Syria would have been disastrous for Israel, for Syria, and for the region. We now know how poorly Israel's ground troops were doing in Lebanon.[2] Stretching resources to include a second front would have been a catastrophe.

The little that peacemakers can do in the heat of war is lay the groundwork in advance for caution against escalation. The critical work of citizen diplomats is not only to open up new possibilities of relations but also to make it harder, in the heat of war, to engage in reckless behavior. We make it easier for the key decision makers to see someone on the other side who they may realistically consider building a bridge to at some later time, and this often encourages restraint.

This is what we had hoped to accomplish with our Syria work, and to our surprise many felt that this is precisely what we did. This was the result of a focus and fixation on relationships, on networks, on long-term commitments, and a studied attempt to engage the principles of intervention that I outlined in chapters 6 and 7. We also developed a capacity for maximum freedom and flexibility that allowed us to engage partners and include people who may otherwise be excluded from this kind of work. Our work continues and will require still a maximum level of flexibility and patience with all sides.

I would like now to conclude the book with a few general observations that move beyond the Syrian case study.

"GOD BLESS THE SECULAR STATE":
A NEW APPROACH TO RELIGIOUS AND CULTURAL RENEWAL

It is time in global history to embrace the basic premise that secular democratic power and secular states are good for the average person, good for minorities, and good for the integrity of organized religions. The basic premise of the secular, liberal state, furthermore, is that no one is completely trusted. The state is designed to be of minimal interference in the life of the individual, only there for the sake of preserving the peace and pursuing some goals of the common good. This can mainly be reduced to safety, broadly defined, as it expresses itself through police, courts, healthcare, economic security, a rational approach to poverty prevention and alleviation that is for the good of all, good roads, and a good foreign policy that minimizes the number of enemies and maximizes friends.

This is not an antireligious position at all. On the contrary, from the earliest prophets there was recognition that too much power in the hands of priests (i.e., men with the power to designate anyone as pure, impure, good, or evil) was a dangerous and corrupting affair.[3] In a crowded world where every one of our societies is multireligious, as well as filled with agnostics, atheists, and syncretists, we simply cannot afford the hegemony of anyone over anyone. Those days are over as a rational construct of life. Such systems are now vestigial and manifestly destructive, especially to women, girls, and minorities all over the world, and they must transform over the long term.

This book has demonstrated some of the efforts at engagement with all kinds of religious people. We must engage all of our skills of conflict management and peacebuilding to build a greater and greater circle of human beings who can embrace a shared model of the state. I think that there is beginning to be evidence of this coming, from young evangelicals coming to embrace Jesus' more universal dreams for a transformed earth that is based on love, not hate, to muftis and sheikhs who, at risk to their own lives, are standing openly for a vision of Islam that is utterly noncoercive with no state power.

Some will argue that surrender of the state to secularism is a surrender of the messianic dreams of Judaism and Christianity. I disagree. At the heart of those dreams is a vision of utterly transformed human relations, an embrace of everyone from the richest to the poorest as equal, and a vision of everyone worshipping together in some way. But there is only one way this can happen in this world, and it is staring us in the face: it is through a deep embrace of pluralism with an overarching state structure that is minimal in its coercive powers, that is strictly for the common good, and that is secular. The secular state is the only way to remove the curse of coercion from human history and its bloody stain on the human religious impulse or its abuse by ethnic tribalism.

I am suggesting this only in the context, however, of the sacralization of the secular, liberal state. The state will be revisioned by millions of spiritual people as a path to the fulfillment of religious dreams of equality, the valuation of all human beings, and care for the earth, as if it were a precious Garden of Eden. This will take the building of a common vision of the future, secular and religious simultaneously. Spiritual peacemakers will play a key role in the weaving together of that common vision.

THE UNIQUE PLACE OF OUR BEST SPIRITUAL PEACEMAKERS IN BUILDING GLOBAL COMMUNITY

As we conclude this chapter I would like to return to the title of this book. Making the earth whole will require an integration of short-term coalition building and long-term visions of covenant and social contract. It will require a coordinated evolution of secular and religious thinking and behavior. It will require a critical mass, a tipping point, of religious and secular citizens who envision together the contours of global community, and the courage to begin the practice of its construction.

Spiritual peacemakers may hold the key to "making the earth whole," or establishing a peaceful global civilization, and that is why we must study them as we would study a healthy heart to see why it pumps so efficiently and persistently. Just as the medical industry needs to spend less time studying diseased hearts and start studying healthy ones for what works, so must we.

The best of the peacemakers recognize our common humanity and they harmonize this with their spirituality, making them true heirs of the future. They are spiritual but not coercive; they live with their eyes on the sacred in such a benevolent way that nothing noble in secular visions of human rights or democracy is alien to them. On the contrary, they welcome those who also value the sacredness of life that human rights embody.

They know how to weave peace and justice together without violence in a unique way that enters into the hearts of average people of faith. They have taken the best of religious inspiration and wedded it to nonviolence. They are trained in radical empathy, trained in visualizing the whole. As such they seem to be perfect partners to build together an enlightened global civilization that represents something meaningful and transcendent, beyond the endlessly driven and wasteful consumerism of capitalism.

They can help build something that is attractive to the millions who are not satisfied by a stale vision of capitalist Shangri-La. Those in the Middle East, for example, who—out of spiritual conviction or poverty—cannot participate in a Dubai culture that supports indoor ski slopes in the midst of global warming, can still find meaning, inspiration, and a peaceful approach to justice and social change through these spiritual peacemakers alone. Religious peacemakers and progressives can combine the ideals of enlightenment together with respect for religion that need not be coercive.

Some may be thinking that the extraordinary peacemakers in each of these cultures and religions are like drops in the ocean, insignificant due to the fact that they are far and few between. But we do not say this when it comes to medical cures, rare plants that contain the ingredients that can save millions of lives. We do not say that because most plants are inedible and have no medicinal value that it is useless to pursue, cultivate, preserve, and cherish the rare plants that contain within them medical miracles. We do not scoff at the Amazon Basin that contains these miracles. On the contrary, we have become keenly aware of rare gifts all around us in the natural world.

It is the same with people. Some people are rare gifts to the world. I think the extraordinary spiritual peacemakers number in the millions, at least, but are still a rarity. They are the wise men and women of our species who celebrate the lives of people on all sides of war, who touch hearts wherever they speak and work, and who weep for the wounded, the tortured, and the dead, on all sides. We cherish rare plants that hold the cure for diseases. What are we doing to cherish these people as the keys to the future survival of the earth and its inhabitants?

BORN AGAIN INDIVIDUALS
BUILDING BORN AGAIN CIVILIZATIONS

Working toward an utterly new global social contract requires looking anew at human potential. Spiritual peacemakers are one crucial element of human renewal and new potential. But there is also something that has potential within every one of us. I was quite taken with Friar Ivo Marcovic's framing of his peace work in terms of being born anew.[4] I have sensed in my own life that at critical junctures in which my community and my understanding of community changed, that something was dying inside of me, but something was being born as well. This is the kind of struggle of renewal that we all must face as citizens of a revitalized human civilization.

The classic religious notions of repentance, including confession of past mistakes, remorse, apologies, penance, a commitment to a new future, often result in or even require a sense of a new identity. This is an essentially optimistic understanding of the human capacity for not just change but radical change.

The fatalistic and deterministic scientific thinking of the past few hundred years has been mistaken. It is true that some of what is inside us is hard-wired, but it is also true that much of how we think and what we do is not hard-wired.[5] Our capacity to build or destroy this planet—or ourselves—lies largely within our brain's control. It lies largely within the construction of our nightmares and dreams, how we choose to cognitively construct our role in the world and our attitude toward each other.

The religious position on renewal also has its parallel in new thinking about how the world changes, and how we humans make it change. I am referring to the power of the associative thinker, the person who is constantly making connections between disparate subjects and fields, integrating them in his or her mind.[6] This is at the heart of human genius and creativity which has always propelled our progress as a species.

This is true not only of the networking of ideas that goes on in the brain but also to the social networking which we analyzed earlier, the kind that gives rise to the great connector who stimulates endlessly new human relations and therefore new ways of thinking. Such a person constitutes the ideal citizen diplomat who stimulates change.

I am proposing then that there is a parallel between four phenomena: (1) classical religious notions of renewal, (2) the healthy brain that is constantly making new connections, building itself anew, (3) the healthy social networker who is constantly making connections between and among others, and (4) a new and networked construct of liberal states that constitute a global civilization. These are all evolutionary developments that will be necessary to create a peaceful global community out of great complexity and diversity.

There is an additional phenomenon that constitutes a difficult challenge. Overstimulation of the brain, especially as it appears in some illnesses, increasingly affects all of us to some degree who suffer from information and contact overload in the contemporary world. Stress is increasingly the number one cause of our illnesses and our dysfunctions. We don't know how to handle the amount of information coming at us and the amount of people coming at us in this overcrowded earth. Some of us are adapting to this better than others, in terms of coping skills, mind training, and so forth.

I want to suggest that we need to rise to this challenge in a paradoxical way, by consciously embracing it. We need to embrace what is happening to us, this unprecedented and overwhelming networking of difference and disparity. This is the only way to forestall ethno-national and fundamentalist backlash. The latter always holds out the fantasy of simplicity, of simplifying the world, of making most people evil and the few good. This is a regressive way of coping with complexity.

We need to embrace instead the changes that a new vision of global community requires for our brains and for our interaction with others. We need to embrace the secular, liberal state as a path to restoring the integrity of the religious impulse. But we also must embrace the human being as global citizen, to help him and her to become emotionally and cognitively prepared to engage the world in all its diversity and infinite complexity. This can be done if we will it cognitively to be done, if we recognize the challenge and prepare our minds for a stretch of its immense capacity, perhaps one of the biggest stretches in human history. We can educate for this as parents and teachers, but only if we will ourselves to do so.

Here is the crucial condition, however. That stretch of the mind needs to be an embrace of infinite diversity *at the same time* that the root of our emotional and spiritual lives has something simple and essential at its core. That is where I think that the Dalai Lama's simplification of the spiritual impulse, its reduction to enlightenment for the sake of all living things, its focus on mind training for patience and kindness, is of great value. Especially helpful is the psychological construct of the self as achieving happiness and enlightenment *through* compassion to others. This in turn is due to the cognitive construct of the mind that says we are all related and connected. Parallels to the Dalai Lama's wisdom on this subject can be found in all the major religious traditions, although this should constitute a separate study.

The spiritual constructs of the mind that I have just outlined are very simple notions, but profoundly meaningful at the emotional and spiritual level. They can be embraced to create a relatively simple inner life. They are necessary as a bulwark, as a rock of certainty, even as we must face the pain and the cognitive complexity of a world filled with an immense number of people, all different in certain ways, many often in struggle. This complexity and pain is the battleground of diplomacy and peacebuilding. But, (1) the simplicity of the inner spiritual discipline of universal compassion, and (2) the disciplined discovery of compassion for oneself, can constitute an antidote to the dizzying complexity of the coming global experiment.

OUR DISCOVERY OF TRUE POWER

Another way to look at this is through the human relationship to power. The more overwhelming that life becomes in all its complexity the more that we crave mastery over it. All of us crave some mastery over our lives, over our fates.[7] We also crave power to feel some mastery over complexity and uncertainty. But we do not need to crave destructive power or the power to lord over others.

There is nothing wrong with the benign power that we humans crave. On the contrary, we exalt and value the human acquisition of power. We even weep at the first acquisitions of human power when we watch children, or accident victims, take their first unassisted step, their first word uttered, their first word read. What a beautiful image! It is the most beautiful of human images, and yet it involves mastery and power. Power in the sense of self-mastery is beautiful. Power in the sense of subjugating others is the bane of humankind.

This is the essential choice that every person, every country, and every religion faces: do we need beautiful, benign forms of mastery and true empowerment, the kind that Lao Tze envisioned, or do we need to have coercive power over others; do we need to torture, kill, possess to feel power? What kind of power do we need? This is where the Eastern wisdom of Taoist writings has relevance, as we have studied. True power is not violent or coercive.

The power of peacemaking and citizen diplomacy that we have shown in this book is nonviolent, noncoercive, but immensely empowering. It is hardly passive.[8] The power of this diplomacy is to enable its practitioners to participate in the building of a new world, a world that is sustainable and peaceful. It enables its practitioners to work together in a connected and integrated way for the benefit of all living things.

Peacebuilding and citizen diplomacy is an immensely difficult task, however, as we have shown. But I believe that with the right renewal of our minds and the right renewal of our hearts millions of us will be up to this task. Our new networks and relations will transform human history as we build the foundation for global community.

NOTES

1. See Jim Lobe, "Neo-Cons Wanted Israel to Attack Syria," InterPress Service, December 19, 2006, at commondreams.org/headlines06/1219-04.htm, and ynet.co.il/english/articles/0,7340,L-3528049,00.html.

2. On the Winograd Commission report, see haaretz.com/hasen/spages/854051.html.

3. Isaiah 1:15, for example, attacks sacrifices offered "with hands full of blood." It is a taunt of the sacrificial system but primarily aimed at the priests who may do the rituals but are guilty of a murderous neglect of the poor and oppressed. This is a repeating prophetic theme. In other words, Isaiah is attacking the choice of organized religion to fixate on rituals at the expense of its moral foundations.

4. David Little, ed., *Peacemakers in Action: Profiles of Religion in Conflict Resolution* (Cambridge: Cambridge University Press, 2007), 116.

5. On brain plasticity, see wired.com/medtech/health/news/2002/10/55779.

6. For a good overview, see Hans Jurgen Eysenck, *Genius: The Natural History of Creativity* (Cambridge: Cambridge University Press, 1995).

7. Seligman cites the amazing research on senior citizens who live in convalescent homes who are healthier and live longer on average when they are even given the most basic mastery over food and personal habits, by having to or being allowed to choose which dessert for which day of their week! See Martin Seligman, *Learned Optimism*, 169.

8. I am moved by the creation of a new group of elders who consist of many former world leaders who have some degree of moral authority. See theelders.org. It strikes me that the enormous extension of life that we are witnessing due to modern medicine suggests an untapped resource for global citizen diplomacy. The elders of all our civilizations upon retirement could gear themselves up physically to engage the world. Millions of them already go on endless tours around the world. Why not tours with a purpose, tours that bind the world together through citizen diplomacy? There is nothing more empowering and that extends the quality of life more than being useful, being indispensable. This should not be limited to the famous like Nelson Mandela. We have millions of people who should be visiting the world with the kind of message that wise elders should be giving. There are many people of great talent, who, with a few thousand dollars, could develop friendships across civilizations and form the foundations of millions of interconnecting and cross-cutting ties that would make war harder and peace and global community more of a living reality. I have been in senior circles long enough to realize that those in senior diplomacy and political leadership run the gamut of capabilities from talented to ingenious to abysmal. It is the same with nonfamous people. With some decent training, I believe millions of people could make a major difference in contributing each in their own way to the foundations of a global community.

Bibliography

Abd al-Rahim, Moddathir, Harold Coward, Robert E. Florida, Peter J. Haas (authors), and William H. Brackney (series editor). *Human Rights and the World's Major Religions*. Westport, CT: Praeger, 2005.

Abdul Rauf, Faisal. *Islam: A Search for Meaning*. Costa Mesa, CA: Mazda, 1996.

———. *Islam: A Sacred Law*. Watsonville, CA: Threshold, 1999.

———. *What's Right with Islam: A New Vision for Muslims and the West*. New York: HarperOne, 2004.

Abu Nimer, Mohammed. *Non-violence and Peacebuilding in Islam: Theory and Practice*. Gainesville: University Press of Florida, 2003.

———. "The Miracles of Transformation through Interfaith Dialogue." In *Interfaith Dialogue and Peacebuilding*, 2nd printing, edited by David R. Smock, 21–26. Washington, DC: USIP, 2007.

Ahmed Hassoun (Mufti). drhassoun.com (accessed January 18, 2008).

An-Na'im, Abdullahi Ahmed. *Toward an Islamic Reformation: Civil Liberties, Human Rights, and International Law*. Syracuse: Syracuse University Press, 1990.

Annan, Kofi. *Prevention of Armed Conflict*. New York: United Nations Publications, March 2002.

Appleby, Scott. *The Ambivalence of the Sacred: Religion, Violence and Reconciliation*. Lanham, MD: Rowman & Littlefield, 2000.

Aristotle. *Nicomachean Ethics*, translated by W. D. Ross. Oxford: Clarendon Press, 1908.

Asma Society, Islamic Culture and Arts. "Daisy Khan," at asmasociety.org/about/b_dkhan.html (accessed January 18, 2008).

Azar, Edward, and Renee Marlin. "The Costs of Protracted Social Conflicts in the Middle East: The Case of Lebanon." In *Conflict Management in the Middle East*, edited by Gabriel Ben-Dor and David B. Dewitt, 29–44. Lexington, KY: Lexington Books, 1987.

Azmeh, Aziz. *Islams and Modernities*. London and New York: Verso, 1993.

BBC. "Rabbi Denounced as War Criminal," at news.bbc.co.uk/2/hi/world/monitoring/media_reports/1272343.stm (accessed January 18, 2008).

———. "Timeline: Syria," at news.bbc.co.uk/2/hi/middle_east/country_profiles/ 827580.stm (accessed October 1, 2008).

Boxer, L. J. "Using Positioning Theory to Make Change Happen." In *Proceedings of the 5th International and 8th National Conference on Quality and Innovation Management*, edited by M. Terziovski. Melbourne: University of Melbourne, Faculty of Economics and Finance, February 2001.

Boys, Mary C., and Barbara Veale Smith. *A Select, Annotated Bibliography on Jewish-Christian Relations*. Institute for Christian & Jewish Studies, at icjs.org/info/bibliog.html (accessed January 18, 2008).

Buber, Martin. "The Question to the Single One." In *Between Man and Man*, translated by Robert Gregor Smith, 48ff. New York: Routledge, 2002.

———. *A Land of Two Peoples: Martin Buber on Jews and Arabs*. Chicago: University of Chicago Press, 2005.

Burton, John W., ed. *Conflict: Human Needs Theory*. Basingstoke: Macmillan, 1990.

Bush, Kenneth, and Robert Opp. *Peace and Conflict Impact Assessment*, at idrc.ca/en/ ev-27981-201-1-DO_TOPIC.html (accessed May 15, 2008).

Castels, Manuel. *The Rise of the Network Society*. Oxford: Blackwell, 1996.

Center for Islam and Science. "Mustafa Abu Sway," at cis-ca.org/bios/mustaf~1.htm (accessed January 18, 2008).

Chacour, Elias. *Blood Brothers*. Grand Rapids, MI: Chosen Books, 1984.

Chacour, Elias, with Mary Jansen. *We Belong to the Land: A Story of a Palestinian Israeli Who Lives for Peace and Reconciliation*. Notre Dame, IN: University of Notre Dame Press, 2001.

Chaitani, Youssef. *Post-Colonial Syria and Lebanon: The Decline of Arab Nationalism and the Rise of the State*. New York: Palgrave McMillan, 2007.

Cheldelin, Sandra I., Wallace Warfield, with January Makamba. "Reflections on Reflective Practice." In *Research Frontiers in Conflict Analysis and Resolution*. Fairfax: The Institute for Conflict Analysis and Resolution, 64–78. George Mason University, 2004.

Chödrön, Pema. *The Practice of Tonglen*, at shambhala.org/teachers/pema/tonglen1. php (accessed May 27, 2008).

Chomsky, Noam, Gilbert Ashcar, and Stephan Shalom. *Perilous Power: The Middle East and U.S. Foreign Policy*. Boulder, CO: Paradigm Publishers, 2007.

Church, Chayenne, and Mark Rogers. *Designing for Results: Integrating, Monitoring and Evaluation in Conflict Transformation Programs*. Washington, DC: Search for Common Ground, 2006, at sfcg.org/programmes/ilr/ilt_manualpage.html.

Circles of Light. "Dalai Lama's Meditation for Millennium Practice," at circlesoflight.com/articles/dalai-practice.shtml (accessed December 15, 2007).

Coalition for Citizen Diplomacy. coalitionforcitizendiplomacy.org.

Cobb, Sara. "A Narrative Perspective on Mediation: Towards the Materialization of the 'Storytelling' Metaphor." In *New Directions in Mediation: Communication Research and Perspectives*, edited by J. Folger and T. Jones, 48–66. Newbury Park, CA: Sage, 1994.

Collaborative Learning Projects. *Reflecting on Peace Practice Project*. Cambridge, MA: CDA, 2004. cdainc.com/publications/cda_books.php.

———. Do No Harm Project. cdainc.com/cdawww/project_profile.php?pid=DNH& pname=Do%20No%20Harm.

Collins, Francis. *The Language of God: A Scientist Presents Evidence for Belief.* New York: Free Press, 2006.

Collison, Robert. "The Road to Reinvention." *National Post,* at nationalpost.com/ story.html?id=216144 (accessed May 25, 2008).

A Common Word. *A Common Word between You and Us,* at acommonword.com (accessed April 10, 2008).

Confucius. *The Analects,* translated by Arthur Waley. New York: Knopf, 2000.

The Cordoba Initiative. cordobainitiative.org/ (accessed January 18, 2008).

Crow, Ralph, Phillip Grant, and Saad E. Ibrahim, eds. *Arab Nonviolent Political Struggle in the Middle East.* Boulder, CO: L. Rienner Publishers, 1990.

Cummings, Bruce, Ervand Abrahamian, and Moshe Ma'oz. *Inventing the Axis of Evil: The Truth about North Korea, Iran, and Syria.* New York: New Press, 2004.

Dartmouth College. *Heschel Selected Photos.* www.dartmouth.edu/~religion/faculty/ heschel-photos.html (accessed May 27, 2008).

Darwall, Stephen, ed. *Consequentialism.* Oxford: Blackwell, 2002.

Dawkins, Richard. *The God Delusion.* Boston: Houghton Mifflin, 2006.

De Beauvior, Simone. *The Ethics of Ambiguity.* Secaucus, NJ: Citadel Press, 1948.

Deeb, Marius. *Syria's Terrorist War on Lebanon and the Peace Process.* New York: Palgrave Macmillan, 2003.

DeFronzo, James. *Revolutions and Revolutionary Movements.* Boulder, CO: Westview Press, 1996.

Delio, Michelle. "A Word for Brainy People: Plastic." *Wired,* October 15, 2002, at wired.com/medtech/health/news/2002/10/55779 (accessed March 13, 2008).

Demers, David, and K. Viswanath, eds. *Mass Media, Social Control, and Social Change: A Macrosocial Perspective.* Ames: Iowa State University Press, 1999.

Diani, Mario, and Doug McAdam, eds. *Social Movements and Network: Relational Approaches to Collective Action.* Oxford: Oxford University Press, 2003.

Doidge, Norman. *The Brain That Changes Itself.* New York: Penguin, 2007.

Donohue, John, and John Esposito. *Islam in Transition: Muslim Perspectives.* New York: Oxford University Press, 2007.

Duff, Anthony. *Punishment, Communication, and Community.* Oxford: Oxford University Press, 2001.

Dura-Europos. "Pompeii of the Syrian Desert," at le.ac.uk/archaeology/stj/dura.htm (accessed January 18, 2008).

Dyson, Freeman. "Our Biotech Future." *New York Review of Books* 54:12, July 19, 2007, 6.

Edwards, Ward, ed. *Utility Theories: Measurements and Applications.* Boston: Kluwer Academic Publishers, 1992.

Eldar, Akiva. "Israeli, Syrian Representatives Reach Secret Understanding." *Haaretz,* January 16, 2007, at haaretz.com/hasen/spages/813817.html (accessed April 15, 2008).

The Elders. theelders.org (accessed February 12, 2008).

El-Nasser, Haya, and Paul Overberg. "Minorities Majority in More Areas." *USA Today.* Nation, September 30, 2004. www.usatoday.com/news/nation/2004-09-30-census_x.htm (accessed January 20, 2008).

Ethics of the Fathers. New York: Bloch Publishing Company, 1965.

Everett, Flynt L. *Inherting Syria: Bashar's Trial by Fire*. Washington, DC: Brookings Institution Press, 2005.

Eyadat, Fadi. "Poll: Nearly 50% of Israeli Jews Don't Want to Live Near Arabs." *Haaretz*, March 14, 2008, at haaretz.com/hasen/spages/963698.html (accessed April 18, 2008).

Eysenck, Hans Jurgen. *Genius: The Natural History of Creativity*. Cambridge: Cambridge University Press, 1995.

Feldman, Noah. *Divided by God: America's Church–State Problem—What We Should Do About It*. New York: Farrar, Straus & Giroux, 2005.

Fes Festival of World Sacred Music. fesfestival.com/en07/index.htm (accessed November 27, 2007).

Fisk, Robert. *Pity the Nation: The Abduction of Lebanon*. New York: Maxwell Macmillan International, 1990.

———. *Pity the Nation: The Abduction of Lebanon*. 4th ed. New York: Nation Books, 2002.

Fletcher, Joseph. *Situation Ethics: The New Morality*. Philadelphia: Westminster Press, 1966.

Freeman, Samuel Richard. *Justice and the Social Contract: Essays on Rawlsian Political Philosophy*. Oxford and New York: Oxford University Press, 2007.

Friedman, Menahem. "Haredi Violence in Contemporary Israeli Society." In *Studies in Contemporary Jewry*, edited by P. Medding, 18 (2002): 186–97.

Galtung, Johan. "Twenty-Five Years of Peace Research: Ten Challenges and Some Responses." *Journal of Peace Research* 22, no. 2 (1985): 146–47.

Gandhi, Rajmohan. *The Good Boatman: A Portrait of Gandhi*. New Delhi: Viking, 1995.

Gensler, Harry J. *Ethics: A Contemporary Introduction*. London and New York: Routledge, 1998.

Gladwell, Malcolm. *The Tipping Point: How Little Things Can Make a Big Difference*. Boston: Little, Brown, 2000.

———. *The Tipping Point: How Little Things Can Make a Big Difference*. Online excerpt at gladwell.com/tippingpoint/tp_excerpt2.html (accessed January 18, 2008).

Goodarzi, Jubin M. *Syria and Iran: Diplomatic Alliance and Power Politics in the Middle East*. New York: Tauris Academic Studies, 2006.

Gopin, Marc. "The Religious Ethics of Samuel David Luzzatto." PhD diss., Brandeis University, 1993.

———. *Between Eden and Armageddon: The Future of World Religions, Violence, and Peacemaking*. New York: Oxford University Press, 2000.

———. *Holy War, Holy Peace: How Religion Can Bring Peace to the Middle East*. New York: Oxford University Press, 2002.

———. "Jewish Arabs and a New Middle East." *Middle East Online*, March 29, 2008, at middle-east-online.com/english/opinion/?id=25108 (accessed April 22, 2008).

———. "Israelis are Talking to Hamas." *Middle East Online*, at metimes.com/Opinion/2008/05/16/israelis_are_talking_to_hamas/3606 (accessed May 16, 2008).

Granovetter, Mark. "The Strength of Weak Ties." *The American Journal of Sociology* 78, no. 6 (1973): 1360–80.

——. *Getting a Job: A Study of Contacts and Careers*. Cambridge, MA: Harvard University Press, 1974.

——. "The Strength of Weak Ties: A Network Theory Revisited." *Sociological Theory* 1 (1983): 201–33.

Gurr, Ted Robert. "Why Minorities Rebel: A Global Analysis of Communal Mobilization and Conflict since 1945." *International Political Science Review* 14, no. 2 (April 1993): 161–01.

Haaretz. "The Main Findings of the Winograd Partial Report on the Second Lebanon War." *Haaretz.com*, May 1, 2007, at haaretz.com/hasen/spages/854051.html (accessed March 14, 2008).

Halpern, David. *Social Capital*. Cambridge, UK: Polity Press, 2005.

Hamber, Brandon. "Forgiveness Bibliography." December 2002, at brandonhamber.com/resources-forgiveness.htm.

Han, Thich Nhat. *Being Peace*. Berkeley, CA: Parallax Press, 1996.

Harre, Rom, and Luk van Langenhove, eds. *Positioning Theory: Moral Context and Intentional Action*. Oxford and Malden, MA: Blackwell, 1999.

Harris, Sam. *The End of Faith: Religion, Terror, and the Future of Reason*. New York: W.W. Norton, 2004.

Harrison, Victoria S. *Religion and Modern Thought*. London: SCM Press, 2007.

Hinnebusch, Raymond A. *Party and Peasant in Syria: Rural Politics and Social Change under the Ba'ath*. Cairo: American University Press, 1979.

——. *Authoritarian Power and State Formation in Ba'thist Syria: Army, Party, and Peasant*. Boulder, CO: Westview Press, 1990.

——. *Syria: Revolution from Above*. New York: Routledge, 2001.

Hiro, Dilip. *Lebanon, Fire, and Ambers: A History of the Lebanese Civil War*. New York: St. Martin's Press, 1993.

Holbrook, Daniel. *Qualitative Utilitarianism*. Lanham, MD: University Press of America, 1988.

Hopkins, Clark. *The Discovery of Dura-Europos*. New Haven, CT: Yale University Press, 1979.

Human Rights Watch. "IV. Honor Crimes under Jordanian Law." *Annual Report 2004, Jordan*, at hrw.org/reports/2004/jordan0404/4.htm (accessed April 13, 2008).

Ibrahim, Saad Eddin. *Egypt, Islam, and Democracy: Critical Essays, with a New Postscript*. Cairo and New York: American University in Cairo Press, 2002.

——. *Dr. Saad Eddin's Articles*, Ibn Khaldoun Center for Development Studies. eicds.org/english/publications/saadarticles/drsaadarticles.htm (accessed January 18, 2008).

The Idan Raichel Project. idanraichelproject.com/en/index.php (accessed November 27, 2007).

Interfaith Encounter Association. *Projects*, at interfaith-encounter.org/projects.htm (accessed January 10, 2008).

Interfaith Youth Core. ifyc.org.

International Campaign against Honor Killings. stophonorkillings.com (accessed March 13, 2008).

International Center for Religion and Diplomacy. icrd.org/projects.html#kashmir (accessed November 27, 2007).

International Organization for Migration. *Conflict Resolution, Confidence Building, and Peace Enhancement among Somali Women.* Geneva: International Organization for Migration, 2002.

Islamica Magazine. "Open Letter to His Holiness Pope Benedict XVI," at islamica-magazine.com/Online-Analysis/Open-Letter-to-His-Holiness-Pope-Benedict-XVI. html (accessed January 18, 2008).

Jabbour, Elias. *Sulha: Palestinian Traditional Peacemaking Process.* Montreat, NC: House of Hope, 1996.

Jerusalem Peacemakers. jerusalempeacemakers.org (accessed January 18, 2008).

———. *Eliyahu Mclean.* jerusalempeacemakers.org/eliyahu/index.html (accessed January 12, 2008).

Jerusalem's Photostream. flickr.com/photos/jerusalem_peacemakers/sets (accessed May 16, 2008).

Johnson, Steven. *The Ghost Map: The Story of London's Most Terrifying Epidemic, and How It Changed Science, Cities, and the Modern World.* New York: Riverhead, 2006.

Johnston, Douglas, ed. *Faith-Based Diplomacy: Trumping Realpolitik.* New York: Oxford University Press, 2003.

Johnston, Douglas, and Cynthia Sampson, eds. *Religion: The Missing Dimension of Statecraft.* New York: Oxford University Press, 1994.

Kadayifci, Ayse. "Living Walls: Among Muslims Peace Building Takes on its Own Forms." *Harvard Divinity School Bulletin* 35, no. 4 (Autumn 2007): 22–29.

Khanna, Parag. "Waving Goodbye to Hegemony." *New York Times Magazine*, January 27, 2008.

Khoury, Elias. "Do I See or Do I Remember." *London Review of Books*, August 3, 2006, at lrb.co.uk/v28/n15/khou01_.html (accessed April 8, 2008).

Krebs, Valdis, and June Holley. "Building Smart Communities through Network Weaving," at orgnet.com/BuildingNetworks.pdf (accessed January 18, 2008).

Lama, Dalai. "Emptiness and Existence," at katinkahesselink.net/tibet/dalai2.html. (n. d.).

———. *Transforming the Mind: Teachings on Generating Compassion.* London: Thorsons: 2000.

———. *The Compassionate Life.* Somerville, MA: Wisdom Publications, 2003.

Lama, Dalai, with Victor Chan. *The Wisdom of Forgiveness.* New York: Riverhead Trade, 2005.

Landis, Joshua. *Syria Comment.* syriacomment.com.

Lang, Sharon D. *Sharaf Politics: Honor and Peacemaking in Israeli–Palestinian Society.* New York: Routledge, 2005.

Latif, Amir. "Honor Killings Plague Pakistan." *Islam Online,* at islamonline.net/servlet/Satellite?c=Article_C&cid=1168265536796&pagename=Zone-English-News/ NWELayout (accessed March 15, 2008).

Laue, James, and Gerald Cormick. "The Ethics of Intervention in Community Disputes." In *The Ethics of Social Intervention: Goals, Values and Consequences*, edited by Gordon Bermant, Herbert C. Kelman, and Donald P. Warwick, 202–32. Washington, DC, and London: Hemisphere Publishing Corporation, 1978.

Lederach, John Paul. *Building Peace: Sustainable Reconciliation in Divided Societies.* 6th printing. Washington, DC: USIP, 2004.

———. *The Moral Imagination.* New York: Oxford University Press, 2005.

Lesch, David. *The New Lion of Damascus: Bashar Al-Asad and Modern Syria*. New Haven, CT: Yale University Press, 2005.

Levinas Emmanuel. *Totality and Infinity: An Essay on Exteriority*, translated by A. Lingis. Pittsburgh: Duquesne University Press, 1969.

LeVine, Robert A. "Women's Schooling, Patterns of Fertility, and Child Survival." *Educational Researcher* 16, no. 9 (1987): 21–27.

Levitt, Steven D., and Steven J. Dunbar. *Freakonomics: A Rogue Economist Explores the Hidden Side of Everything*. New York: Harper Collins, 2005.

Liebes, Yehuda. *Studies in the Zohar*. New York: SUNY, 1993.

Little, David, ed. *Peacemakers in Action: Profiles of Religion in Conflict Resolution*. Cambridge: Cambridge University Press, 2007.

Lobe, Jim. "Neo-Cons wanted Israel to Attack Syria." *InterPress Service*, December 19, 2006 at commondreams.org/headlines06/1219-04.htm (accessed November 15, 2007).

Markovic, Friar Ivo. "Would You Shoot Me, You Idiot?" In *Peacemakers in Action: Profiles of Religion in Conflict Resolution*, edited by David Little, 97–122. Cambridge: Cambridge University Press, 2007.

McCarthy, Rory. "Israel Risks Apartheid-like Struggle if Two-State Solution Fails, Says Olmert." *Guardian*, November 30, 2007, at guardian.co.uk/world/2007/nov/30/israel (accessed February 5, 2008).

McCrummen, Stephanie. "U.S. Evangelist, a Critic of Islam, Reaches Out to Sudan's President." *Washington Post*, February 14, 2007, at washingtonpost.com/wp-dyn/content/article/2007/02/13/AR2007021301255.html (accessed May 16, 2008).

Mclean Eliyahu. "Recent Activities," at jerusalempeacemakers.org/eliyahu/writings-recent-0412.html (accessed April 13, 2008).

Mendo a, Joseph. *Goodness and Justice: A Consequentialist Moral Theory*. Cambridge and New York: Cambridge University Press, 2006.

Mernissi, Fatima. *The Harem Within*. New York: Doubleday, 1994.

Mitnick, Joshua. "Behind the Dispute over Shebaa Farms." *Christian Science Monitor*, August 22, 2006, at csmonitor.com/2006/0822/p10s01-wome.html (accessed April 15, 2008).

Moltmann, Jurgen. *God for a Secular Society: The Public Relevance of Theology*. Minneapolis: Fortress Press, 1999.

Morgerthau, Hans J. *Politics among Nations: The Struggle for Power and Peace*. 5th rev. ed. New York: Alfred A. Knopf, 1978. Online excerpt at mtholyoke.edu/acad/intrel/morg6.htm.

Moubayad, Sami. *Mid East Views*, at mideastviews.com.

Muller-Fahrenholtz, G. *The Art of Forgiveness: Theological Reflections on Healing and Reconciliation*. Geneva, Switzerland: WCC Publications, 1997.

Nan, Susan Allen. "Conflict Resolution in a Network Society." *Negotiation Journal* 13 (2008): 111–31.

National Association of Evangelicals. "Environment and Ecology 1971," at nae.net/index.cfm?FUSEACTION=editor.page&pageID=199&IDCategory=9 (accessed November 27, 2007).

National Council of Churches. "Jewish and Christian Dialogue Shows Signs of Maturity," at ncccusa.org/news/050525christianjewishdialogue.html (accessed January, 18, 2008).

Nichols, Bruce. "Religious Conciliation between the Sandinistas and the East Coast In-
     dians in Nicaragua." In *Religion: The Missing Dimension of Statecraft,* edited by Douglas
     Johnston and Cynthia Sampson, 73–74. New York: Oxford University Press, 1994.
Noakes, Greg. "Egyptian Religious Leaders Stress Interfaith Tolerance." *Washington
     Report on Middle East Affairs,* at wrmea.com/backissues/0395/9503049.htm (ac-
     cessed January 18, 2008).
Nye, Joseph. *Soft Power: The Means to Success in Global Diplomacy.* New York: Public
     Affairs, 2004.
O'Brien, Connie. "Integrated Community Development/Conflict Resolution Strate-
     gies as 'Peace Building Potential' in South Africa and Northern Ireland." *Commu-
     nity Development Journal* 42, no. 1 (2007): 114–30.
Orgnet. "Social Network Analysis: A Brief Introduction," at orgnet.com/sna.html
     (accessed January 20, 2008).
Patel, Eboo. *Acts of Faith: The Story of an American Muslim, the Struggle for the Soul of
     a Generation.* Boston: Beacon Press, 2007.
Peace Center. *Dalai Lama's 5 Most Important Questions,* at salsa.net/peace/article22.
     html (accessed May 27, 2008).
Plastino, Goffredo, ed. *Mediterranean Mosaic: Popular Music and Global Sounds.* New
     York and London: Routledge, 2003.
Presbyterian Church (USA). "PC(USA), Jewish Leaders Reach Accord on 'New Sea-
     son of Dialogue and Understanding,' Pledge to Work Together on Middle East
     Peace, Domestic Social Concerns," at pcusa.org/pcnews/2006/06644.htm (ac-
     cessed January 18, 2008).
Pruitt, Dean G., and Sung Hee Kim. *Social Conflict: Escalation, Stalemate, and Settle-
     ment.* New York: McGraw-Hill, 2004.
Putnam, Robert. *Bowling Alone: The Collapse and Revival of American Community.* New
     York: Simon & Schuster, 2000.
Rabil, Ribert G. *Embattled Neighbors: Syria, Israel, and Lebanon.* Boulder, CO: Lynne
     Rienner Publishers, 2003.
———. *Syria, the United States, and the War on Terror in the Middle East.* Westport, CT:
     Praeger Security International, 2006.
Raffel, Martin J. "American Jewish Public Affairs and Israel: Looking Back, Looking
     Ahead." *Jewish Council for Public Affairs,* at jewishpublicaffairs.org/publications/
     raffel.html (accessed April 18, 2008).
Raichel, Idan. idanraichelproject.com/en/index.php.
Ramsbotham, Oliver, Tom Woodhouse, and Hugh Miall. *Contemporary Conflict
     Resolution.* 2nd ed. Cambridge, UK, and Malden, MA: Polity Press, 2006.
Rawls, John. *A Theory of Justice.* Cambridge, MA: Belknap, 1971.
Relief Web. "Security Council, Unanimously Adopting Resolution 1325
     (2000), Calls for Broad Participation of Women in Peace-building, Post-
     conflict Reconstruction," at reliefweb.int/rw/rwb.nsf/AllDocsByUNID/
     550a9d4faa49688e8525698a005d4fb8 (accessed May 27, 2008).
Religions for Peace USA. "Interfaith Organizations," at rfpusa.org/links/other.cfm
     (accessed October 20, 2007).
Religious Action Center of Reform Judaism. "Reform Jewish Leader Denounces
     Rabbi Yosef's Remarks," at rac.org/Articles/index.cfm?id=2507 (accessed January
     18, 2008).

Rinpoche, Sogyal. *The Tibetan Book of Living and Dying*. New York: HarperOne, 1994.

Rostovtzeff, Michael Ivanovitch. *Dura-Europos and Its Art*. Oxford: Clarendon Press, 1938.

Rouner, Leroy S. *Human Rights and the World's Religions*. South Bend, IN: The University of Notre Dame Press, 1988.

Royal Aal Al-Bayt Institute for Islamic Thought. "True Islam and Its Role in Modern Society." Statement Issued by the International Islamic Conference, Amman, Jordan, July 4–June 2005, at aalalbayt.org/en/conferencesandsymposia.html (accessed January 18, 2008).

Rubenstein, Richard. *Thus Saith the Lord: The Revolutionary Moral Vision of Isaiah and Jeremiah*. New York: Harcourt, 2006.

Ruby, Walter. "Imams, Rabbis Deplore Calls to Eliminate Israel." *Jerusalem Post*, March 23, 2006, at jpost.com/servlet/Satellite?cid=1139395659456&pagename=JPost%2FJPArticle%2FShowFull (accessed January 18, 2008).

Sachedina, Abdulaziz A. "Is There a Tradition of Pacifism and Nonviolence in Islam?" Paper presented at USIP workshop on *Religious Perspectives on Pacifism and Nonviolence*. Washington, DC, July 28, 1993.

———. *Islamic Roots of Democratic Pluralism*. New York: Oxford University Press, 2001.

Sadowski, Yahya. "The Evolution of Political Identity in Syria." In *Identity and Politics in the Middle East*, edited by Shibley Telhami and Michael Barnett. Ithaca: Cornell University Press, 2002.

Salame, Ghassan. *Democracy without Democrats: The Renewal of Politics in the Muslim World*. London and New York: IB Tauris, 1994.

Salem, Paul, ed. *Conflict Resolution in the Arab World: Selected Essays*. New York: American University of Beirut, 1997.

Schmitt, Eric, and Thom Shanker. "U.S. Adapts Cold-War Idea to Fight Terrorists." *New York Times*, March 18, 2008.

Schon, David A. *The Reflective Practitioner: How Professionals Think in Action*. New York: Basic Books, 1983.

Schulweis, Harold M. "Two Prophets, One Soul: Rev. Martin Luther King Jr. and Rabbi Abraham Joshua Heschel." Shalom Center, at shalomctr.org/node/122 (accessed May 24, 2008).

Schwartz, Jeffrey, and Sharon Begley. *The Mind and the Brain: Neuroplasticity and the Power of Mental Force*. New York: HarperCollins, 2003.

Seale, Patrick. *Asad of Syria: The Struggle for the Middle East*. Berkeley: University of California Press, 1989.

Seiple, Chris. "From the President: Engaging Conservative Islam." *Institute for Global Engagement*, at globalengage.org/media/article.aspx?id=6276 (accessed January 18, 2008).

Seligman, Martin. *Learned Optimism*. New York: Vintage, 2006.

Sharp, Paul. "Making Sense of Citizen Diplomats: The People of Duluth, Minnesota, as International Actors." *International Studies Perspectives* 2, no. 2 (2001): 131–50.

Sloan, Richard. *Blind Faith: The Unholy Alliance of Religion and Medicine*. New York: St. Martin's Press, 2006.

Smith, Adam. *The Theory of Moral Sentiments.* Reprint. New York: A.M. Kelley, 1966 [1759].

———. *The Wealth of Nations.* Reprint. New York: American Home Library Co., 1902 [1776].

Smith, Christian, ed. *Disruptive Religion.* New York: Routledge, 1996.

Sorenson, David S. *An Introdcution to the Modern Middle East: History, Religion, Political Economy, Politics.* Boulder, CO; Westeview, 2008.

Soros, George. "Toward a Global Open Society," at project-syndicate.org/commentary/sor4 (accessed January 18, 2008).

Spirit of Fes. spiritoffes.com (accessed January 18, 2008).

Spiritual Care Program International. *Three Tonglen Practices,* at spcare.org/practices/tonglen-practices.html (accessed May 27, 2008).

Stenger, Mary Ann. "Gadamer's Hermeneutics as a Model for Cross-Cultural Understanding and Truth in Religion." In *Religious Pluralism and Truth: Essays on Cross-Cultural Philosophy of Religion,* edited by Thomas Dean. Albany: State University of New York Press, 1995.

Stern, Jessica. *Terror in the Mind of God.* New York: HarperCollins, 2004.

Stobbe, Stephanie. "Using Narrative to Understand Conflict and Conflict Resolution among Laotian Refugees." Paper presented at the annual meeting of the International Studies Association, Hilton Hawaiian Village, Honolulu, Hawaii, March 5, 2005, at allacademic.com/meta/p71806_index.html (accessed May 5, 2008).

Sulha Peace Project. sulha.com/ (accessed November 27, 2007).

Tanenbaum Center for Interreligious Understanding. tanenbaum.org/conflict_resolution.html (accessed November 27, 2007).

Taylor, Paul. "Senior Saudi Prince Offers Israel Peace Vision." *Reuters Africa,* January 20, 2008, at africa.reuter.com/wire/news/usnl.2057323.html (accessed February 5, 2008).

Thompson, Henry O. *World Religions in War and Peace.* Jefferson, NC: McFarland, 1988.

Tilly, Charles. *Identities, Boundaries, and Social Ties.* Boulder, CO: Paradigm Publishers, 2005.

Tze, Lao. *Tao Te Ching,* translated by Stephen Mitchell. New York: Harper, 1988.

Tze, Sun. *The Art of War,* translated by Samuel B. Griffith. Oxford: Oxford University Press, 1963.

United Nations Security Council. *Resolution 1325 (2000),* at un.org/events/res_1325e.pdf (accessed January 25, 2008).

U.S. Center for Citizen Diplomacy. uscenterforcitizendiplomacy.org.

Uvin, Peter. "The Development/Peacebuilding Nexus: A Typology and History of Changing Paradigms." *Journal of Peacebuilding & Development* 1, no. 1 (2002): 5–24.

Volkan, Vamik. *Bloodlines: From Ethnic Pride to Ethnic Terrorism.* New York: Farrar, Straus and Giroux, 1997.

———. *Blind Trust: Large Groups and Their Leaders in Times of Crisis and Terror.* Charlottesville, VA: Pitchstone Publishing, 2004.

———. *Killing in the Name of Identity: A Study of Bloody Conflicts.* Charlottesville, VA: Pitchstone Publishing, 2006.

Voltaire. *Candide, ou l'Optimisme,* translated by Burton Raffel. New Haven, CT: Yale University Press, 2005.

Warfield, Wallace. "Is This the Right Thing to Do? A Practical Framework for Ethical Decisions." In *A Handbook of International Peacebuilding: Into the Eye of the Storm*, edited by John Paul Lederach and Janice Moomaw Jenner, 213–23. San Francisco: Jossey-Bass Publishers, 2002.

Wellman, Barry. "Network Analysis: Some Basic Principles." *Sociological Theory* 1 (1983): 155–200.

Wickham, Carrie Rosefsky. *Mobilizing Islam: Religion, Activism, and Political Change in Egypt*. New York: Columbia University Press, 2002.

Williams, Paul. "The Competent Boundary Spanner." *Public Administration* 80, no. 1 (2002): 103–24.

Winsdale, John, and Gerald Monk. *Narrative Mediation: A New Approach to Conflict Resolution*. San Francisco: Jossey Bass, 2000.

World Congress on Imams and Rabbis for Peace. imamsrabbis.org (accessed January 18, 2008).

Yacoubian, Mona, and Scott Lasensky. *Dealing with Damascus: Seeking Greater Return on U.S.–Syria Relations*. New York: Council on Foreign Relations No. 33, 2008.

Ynet. "Olmert Reassures Syria: Home Front Drill Not a Threat." *Ynet.com*, at ynet.co.il/english/articles/0,7340,L-3528049,00.html (accessed May 6, 2008).

Zartman, William. "Ripeness: The Hurting Stalemate and Beyond." In *Conflict Resolution after the Cold War*, edited by P. C. Stern and Daniel Druckman, 225–50. Washington, DC: National Academy Press, 2000.

Ziser, Eyal. *Asad's Legacy: Syria in Transition*. New York: New York University Press, 2001.

———. *Commanding Syria: Bashar Al-Asad and the First Years of Power*. London: Tauris, 2007.

Ziser, Eyal, and Paul Rivlin. *Syria: Domestic Political Stress and Globalization*. Tel Aviv: Moshe Dayan Center for Middle East and African Studies, 1999.

Zogby, James. *What Arabs Think: Values, Beliefs, and Concerns*. Washington, DC: Zogby International, 2002.

Index

Abbas, Mahmoud, 128
Abdel Rauf, Feisal, 27n22
Abrahamic family: and Abraham, 143;
    and Dalai Lama, 212; and faiths,
    religions, traditions, civilizations 4,
    21, 35, 46, 50, 57, 60n13, 64, 89
    n20, 128, 147, 180, 184, 189–90,
    198–201, 207–9, 212–14, 216n7;
    and future, 169; and military
    and political gain, 128; and
    peacemakers, 212
Abu Ghraib, xii, 140–46, 156, 175
Abunimer, Mohammed, xvin2, 23n10,
    25n15, 31n40
Afghanistan, xvin2, 14, 23n10, 127
African Americans, 75
Africans (including Africa, African), 35,
    48, 190–91
Aleppo, xi, 135, 140–42, 144, 146–47.
    See also Syria
Allenby Bridge, 107–10, 111, 130, 152
Al-Qaeda, 14
apology, xi, xvin2, 70, 185; and
    Abrahamic traditions, 198; public,
    146
Appleby, Scott, xviin4, 29n31, 37, 59n6
Arab, xi, 13, 14, 29–30n34, 82, 98, 101,
    103, 105, 109–10, 11; and equality

with Jews, 84; and Muslim Sufism,
    97, 193, 194; and -Israeli conflict,
    xiv, 79–80, 94; and nationalists,
    xiii; and press, 17; and *sulha*
    (reconciliation), 20
Arafat, Yasser, 185, 204, 208
Armageddon, 14
Asad, Bashar, 116, 118–19, 123–24,
    128–30, 146 154–55, 157
Asad Library, 106, 118
Axis of Evil, xiv, 126
Azar, Edward, 86n3; and protracted
    social conflicts, 86n3

Ba'ath Party, 136; and Aflaq, Michel,
    Bitar, Salah al-Din, xiii; and
    ideology in Syria, xiii; and Iraq, xiv
Balfour Declaration, 187n11
Barve, Sushoba, 23n10
The Beatitudes, 207
Benedict XVI, pope, 32n46
bodhichitta, 206
boundary spanners. *See* social network
    theory
brain plasticity, 113, 186n2
Buber, Martin, 83–85, 101
Buddhism, 133n6, 179, 184, 200, 212;
    and Tibet, 133n6

About the Author

Marc Gopin is the James H. Laue Professor of Religion, Diplomacy and Conflict Resolution, and the director of the Center on Religion, Diplomacy and Conflict Resolution (CRDC) at George Mason University's Institute for Conflict Analysis and Resolution (ICAR). He has lectured on conflict resolution in Switzerland, Ireland, India, Italy, and Israel, as well as at Harvard, Yale, Columbia, Princeton, and numerous other academic institutions. He has trained thousands of people worldwide in peacemaking strategies for complex conflicts in which religion and culture play a role, and conducts research on values dilemmas as they apply to international problems of globalization, clash of cultures, development, social justice and conflict.

He has engaged in back channel diplomacy with religious, political and military figures on both sides of conflicts, especially in the Arab/Israeli conflict. He has appeared on numerous media outlets, including CNN, CNN International, Court TV, *The Jim Lehrer News Hour*, Israel Radio, National Public Radio, The Connection, Voice of America, and the national public radios of Sweden, Ireland, and Northern Ireland, and has been published in the *International Herald Tribune*, the *Boston Globe*, the *Christian Science Monitor*, and his work has been featured in news stories of the *Times* of London, the *Times* of India, Associated Press, and Newhouse News Service, regarding issues of conflict resolution, religion and violence.

His research can be found in numerous book chapters and journal articles, and he is the author of *Between Eden and Armageddon: The Future of World Religions, Violence and Peacemaking* (Oxford University Press, 2000), *Holy War, Holy Peace: How Religion Can Bring Peace to the Middle East* (Oxford University Press, 2002), a study on what was missing from the Oslo

Process, and what will be necessary culturally for a successful Arab/Israeli peace process, and *Healing the Heart of Conflict* (Rodale Press, 2004).

Dr. Gopin was ordained as a rabbi in 1983 and received a PhD in religious ethics from Brandeis University in 1993. He is now working in partnership with the Fetzer Foundation to create a web-based video series and book on enemies who become friends and close partners. Filming began in the summer of 2008. He is creator and principal author of www.marcgopin. com, a weblog dedicated to addressing the transformation of conflicts facing humanity.

Hind Kabawat, The Grand Mufti of Syria, Sheikh Ahmed Hassoun, and Marc Gopin, Aleppo 2007. Courtesy of the author.